P9-DUX-803

High Cotton

ALSO BY GERARD HELFERICH

Humboldt's Cosmos:
Alexander von Humboldt and the Latin American
Journey That Changed the Way We See the World

High Cotton

Four Seasons in the Mississippi Delta

GERARD HELFERICH

COUNTERPOINT
A MEMBER OF THE PERSEUS BOOKS GROUP
NEW YORK

Books published by Counterpoint are available at special discounts
for bulk purchases in the United States by corporations, institutions,
and other organizations. For more information, please contact
the Special Markets Department at the Perseus Books Group,
11 Cambridge Center, Cambridge, MA 02142, or call (617) 252-5298
or (800) 255-1514, or e-mail special.markets@perseusbooks.com.

Designed by Trish Wilkinson
Set in 10.5-point Goudy by the Perseus Books Group

Library of Congress Cataloging-in-Publication Data

Helferich, Gerard.
    High cotton : four seasons in the Mississippi Delta / Gerard
Helferich.
        p.   cm.
    Includes bibliographical references and index.   "/o7
    ISBN-13: 978-1-58243-353-0
    ISBN-10: 1-58243-353-4   3224 0557
    1. Delta (Miss. : Region)—History. 2. Delta (Miss. : Region)—
Biography. 3. Cotton farmers—Mississippi—Delta (Region)—
Biography. 4. Cotton growing—Mississippi—Delta (Region) 5. Farm
life—Mississippi—Delta (Region) 6. Seasons—Mississippi—Delta
(Region) 7. Delta (Miss. : Region)—Social life and customs. 8. Delta
(Miss. : Region)—Description and travel. I. Title.
F347.Y3H45 2006
976.2'4—dc22   2006035951

10 9 8 7 6 5 4 3 2 1

In memory of my parents—
William H. Helferich Jr.,
who gave me a love for words,
and
Marion Helferich Rehn,
who gave me the confidence to set down my own.

To understand the world, you have to understand a place like Mississippi.

—WILLIAM FAULKNER

Contents

Prologue:
"The Most Southern Place on Earth"

In the northwest corner of Mississippi, bounded on one side by the baroque coils of its namesake river and on the other by the equally tortuous Yazoo and Tallahatchie, lies the extraordinary diamond of land known simply as the Delta. Beginning roughly at the Tennessee border, the region extends up to seventy miles across and nearly two hundred miles end to end, from Memphis in the north to Vicksburg in the south. Long a land of cultivated fields and muddy sloughs, antebellum mansions and sharecropper shacks, courtly manners and human depravity, the Delta has served as the emblem of an entire region, "the most southern place on earth."

Graced (or cursed) with an overwhelming sense of place, the Delta has exerted an influence on the nation out of all proportion to its 7,000 square miles. Its flatness and fertility alone would have ensured its uniqueness. But as cradle of the blues and home to myriad writers, the Delta has stamped not just our culture but that of the world. Even more significant has been the region's long association with cotton. Once the nation's greatest producer of the fiber, today Mississippi is second only to the much larger state of Texas. And 80 percent of Mississippi's crop is still grown in the rich soil of the Delta, blanketing nearly a million acres and producing fiber valued at almost a billion dollars annually. Though cotton has been raised for thousands of years, from India to Arizona, it is identified with no other region as strongly as here.

So central is the story of the plant to the story of the place that it is impossible to tell one without telling the other. Cotton is the starting point from which the rest of the Delta's narrative flows— the reason the land was settled, the reason it was peopled with slaves, even why so many African Americans later fled to northern cities such as Chicago and Detroit. The Delta was mostly wilderness in antebellum times, but it was in the area's settled tracts that plantation agriculture, and the system of chattel slavery that supported it, attained its perfect, terrible expression. And for a long century following Emancipation, it was in the Delta that white landowners battled most ferociously to maintain the prerogatives of an earlier, racially unambiguous era, as though the levees built to control the rivers could also hold back waves of social and political change.

Not only did cotton determine the history of the Delta and the South, it shaped the story of the nation. In the antebellum era, the United States was the world's greatest exporter of the fiber—and so it is today, claiming 40 percent of the world market. It was cotton that paid the early Republic's bills and cotton that fueled America's first factories. Without cotton, slavery would not have taken root so deeply in the South, loosing the economic and sectarian tensions that led to civil war. Without cotton, in all likelihood there would have been no Republican Party, no Reconstruction, no battle to reclaim civil rights that had not been "self-evident" to the Founding Fathers. Absent this single crop, the past two hundred years of American life would have been unimaginably different. Today's racial landscape would be unrecognizable as well, for the enduring rift between black and white is also part of the legacy of cotton.

Even more than the story of an exceptional plant and a singular region that have shaped the history of our country, this book is a chronicle of the people who still risk everything to raise this ancient and essential crop. Zack Killebrew is a small-time operator who, except for a youthful stint on Mississippi riverboats, has lived and farmed in the Delta all his life, as his parents and grandparents did before him. For thirty years, Zack has struggled to raise cotton, sometimes with only his prodigious know-how and Rebel stubbornness to sustain him. The enterprise has altered dramatically, and as we follow Zack through his annual cycle from planting to harvest, we will see that the challenges he faces are very different from those of his forebears. The perennial threat of rising water in the Delta has been all but eliminated by a historic flood-control initiative. With a blizzard of farm programs, the federal government now assumes some of the risk inherent in growing cotton. Sophisticated machinery and potent chemicals perform work once done by human hands. Even the cotton plant itself has been genetically altered to resist insects and herbicides. But perhaps more impressive than all these changes is how little cotton growing has altered in its fundamentals. Government and technology have not eliminated the essential precariousness of the farmer's life, which still hinges, as always, on the unreliable weather.

In addition, fierce new economic and political pressures now threaten to accomplish what droughts and floods and weevils could not—to drive small farmers like Zack off the land. Every year has become a make-or-break season, and a single bad harvest could be enough to put him out of business, as it already has done many of his neighbors. Every year, more than anything, Zack is fighting for the privilege of starting again the following spring.

But even if the Delta is due for a change of tenants, that doesn't mean the immutable landscape will alter fundamentally. Thunderstorms will still rumble across the yawning flatness. Plants will still be sown each spring and harvested each fall. There will still be a huge divide between the Delta's rich and poor. As I have witnessed over the course of three decades, the Delta is a place that abides change but slowly. Even tomorrow, and next year, and the year after that, it will remain "the most southern place on earth." And all the while, its signature crop will continue to exert its influence not only on the course of the region but on the fortunes of the nation, as it has for the past two centuries.

PART I

Spring

ONE

The Land

Driving north on U.S. 49, you enter Yazoo City atop a high bluff. To your left, at the end of a precipitous hill, lies the city's old business district. But the real commercial life has long since moved out here to the highway. Straight ahead, down another long descent, there is an untidy strip with car repair shops, a discount drug store, and half a dozen fast-food franchises. Then beyond the stoplight at Fifteenth Street, the land levels out and the businesses give way. In another couple of miles, at a railroad crossing, you pass the fertilizer plant and the catfish farm. Out here, the landscape suddenly opens up, revealing an abrupt flatness that seems more sky than earth. On this gray February morning, the sun is invisible beyond the loess hills to the right, while far to the west, gray-green smudges delineate bands of woods. In the foreground are long stretches of furrowed earth. That's when you realize you've entered the Mississippi Delta.

In truth the region misrepresents itself. The great swath of flat-land is not a delta at all, since the mouth of the Mississippi lies some 250 miles southeast of Vicksburg in the bayous below New Orleans. The area is instead a vast floodplain. Over millennia, the Mississippi and its tributaries incised deep valleys as they snaked toward the Gulf of Mexico. Then, 15,000 years ago, as the glaciers melted after the last Ice Age, the sea level rose and the rivers slowed, flooding the valleys and filling them with rich silt. Each spring after that, seasonal rains and melting snows would swell the rivers and force them over their banks. The result was a topsoil as much as 350 feet deep, the most fertile soil in the South and some of the richest land on earth.

The source of this alluvial abundance, the Mississippi, is the essential river of North America and one of the great waterways of the planet. The name is said to come from the words *missi sipi*, or "Great River" in the Ojibwa language. Rising in Lake Itasca in northwest Minnesota, it flows 3,800 circuitous miles to the Gulf of Mexico, making it the third longest river in the world, after the Nile and the Amazon. Over this twisting route, the Mississippi drains more than 1.2 million square miles, greater than 40 percent of the continental U.S., including all or part of thirty-one states, from New York to New Mexico. Counting among its tributaries such major rivers as the Ohio, Wisconsin, Illinois, Missouri, Red, and Arkansas, the system boasts 15,000 navigable miles.

Passing through some of the flattest land on earth, the river de-scends an average of only three inches per mile, and has changed course countless times. Over a mile wide in places, it can be more than one hundred feet deep. The main current typically runs a few miles an hour, carrying half a million cubic feet of water and five tons of silt into the Gulf of Mexico *per second*. But during flood stages the current can reach nine miles an hour and its volume more than 3 million cubic feet.

For generations, Delta residents could never forget that the river that had created their land might return to claim it. As memoirist and poet William Alexander Percy wrote, every aspect of life was determined by "the great river, the shifting unopposable god of the country, feared and loved, the Mississippi." William Faulkner suggested that during these deluges, "the River was now doing what it liked to do, had waited patiently the ten years in order to do, as a mule will work for you ten years for the privilege of kicking you once."

After the devastating flood of 1927, Congress voted its largest single appropriation to date, for a massive reengineering of the river's lower course. Now, though constricted with channels and levees and augmented by spillways to contain the high water, the Mississippi is ineluctably changing course again, in a process that will one day shift its principal outlet to the steeper, swifter Atchafalaya River. Joining the larger waterway near its southwestern tip and tracing a slightly more westward course to the Gulf of Mexico, the Atchafalaya is destined to become the main channel of the river itself.

For thousands of years, the Delta was home to Native Americans who hunted its tangled woods and fished its muddy rivers. White men, deterred by the difficult terrain, were slow to take advantage of the region's fertility. The first Europeans to come upon the Mississippi and the Delta, in 1541, were led by Hernando de Soto as he explored the American Southeast for Spain. The party ventured as far inland as present-day Oklahoma searching for gold and other treasure, but found only hardship and hostility. When de Soto died of a fever during the expedition, his men placed his body in a hollow log and sank it in the river to conceal it from the Indians, then retreated to Mexico. After that unpropitious start, Spain made no further attempt to colonize the wild and forbidding Delta.

Over the next century and a half, exploration of the Mississippi was left to Frenchmen—Jacques Marquette and Louis Jolliet; René-Robert Cavelier, Sieur de La Salle; Pierre Le Moyne d'Iberville—who sailed from Canada hoping to find, improbably enough, a water route to China. Though they were no more successful in that ambition than the Spanish had been in theirs, these explorers did secure a huge territory for France, which La Salle, on discovering the mouth of the Mississippi in 1682, christened Louisiana in honor of his sovereign, Louis XIV. New Orleans was founded on the banks of the great river in 1718, African slaves were imported from Guinea, and plantations of sugar, cotton, tobacco, and rice were established.

In 1763, after its victory in the Seven Years War, Great Britain acquired from France the portion of Louisiana east of the Mississippi, and from Spain it received the huge tract known as Florida, which included parts of the current states of Florida, Louisiana, Mississippi, Georgia, and Alabama. English settlers brought more slaves to the region, and Governor George Johnstone echoed the common sentiment when he declared that without captive labor, it would prove "impossible to raise the colony to any eminence."

By 1774, a quarter of the local population was black; by 1780, a third. After the Mississippi Territory was created in 1798, settlers rushed in from neighboring states and even from the Northeast, eager to take advantage of the booming market for cotton. With them came more slaves to work the new plantations.

<hr />

As you drive north into the Delta from Yazoo City, you skirt the village of Eden (population 126), supposedly named by railroad employees who found the residents so enthusiastic about the new right-of-way that the workers thought they had stumbled into paradise. Here the road takes a wide turn to the left, and as you leave the shadow of the bluffs, the eastern limit of the Delta, you penetrate farther into the all-encompassing flatness. Everywhere the hand of man is evident in the tilled rows stretching toward the vanishing point. But it is a desolate landscape, with abandoned sharecropper shacks, rusting cotton gins, little traffic, and plain white country churches glimpsed over vast distances. It's early on a Sunday morning, but the vacant quality isn't just a function of the time of day or day of the week. The Delta has been losing population for nearly a century, and the pace only quickened after the Second World War, when mechanization and chemicals drastically reduced the need for workers in the fields. Industry never caught on here, put off by the rural setting and the poorly educated workforce. So now, when a farmer can grow a thousand acres of cotton with just a couple of hired hands, there's not a lot of work for those who remain in the Delta.

Beyond Eden is tiny Thornton, really just a crossroads with a dilapidated country store. We have entered Holmes County, which straddles the Delta and the hills. Of the 21,000 people in Holmes, 79 percent are black. Forty percent of adults never completed high school, and only 11 percent have graduated from a four-year college. The official unemployment rate is three times the national average, the unofficial one undoubtedly higher still. With per capita income at $10,683, 41 percent of the population falls below the federal poverty line. Educational attainment and earnings are low even for Mississippi, which itself ranks near the bottom of the fifty states.

Twenty minutes beyond Thornton is the town of Tchula (population 2,254), which announces itself with an explosion of shacks and trailers across the road from a bilious cypress swamp. The first white settlers arrived here in 1826, and a few years later, after the Treaty of Dancing Rabbit Creek cleared the way for further immigration, the town began to grow. According to local legend, *tchula* is a Native American word meaning "Red Fox," the name of a Choctaw maiden who had the misfortune to fall in love with a Cherokee brave. When her father, the chief, objected to the match, the lovers sought to elope in a canoe across the nearby oxbow. But the chief discovered their plans and gained the shore in time to shoot an arrow through the lover's heart. Seeing her betrothed fall dead, the story goes, the grief-stricken maiden leapt overboard and drowned herself in the lake, which, like the town, now bears her name.

Taking advantage of its location near the Yazoo River, Tchula expanded into a trading center and port. Like the rest of the

Delta, it suffered crop losses, property confiscations, and slave de-
sertions during the Civil War. Then during Reconstruction (according to *The History of Tchula*, published in 1954 by the Tchula
Business and Professional Women's Club), organizations such as
the Red Shirts were founded to spread "terror among the erring.
It was not until this group took over the election boxes and patrolled the voting places that the white citizens were once again
in a position to deal with the corruption that had overtaken our
County and State." By the early 1880s, when the railroad came,
Tchula was reportedly a rough place, with widespread drunken-
ness and frequent shootings.

Turning off the highway, you come to Tchula's ramshackle
business district. Rebuilt after a fire that leveled the town some
125 years ago, the buildings have a Wild West look, with false
fronts and flat roofs sheltering the sidewalk. BankPlus has erected
a solid brick outpost here, but most of the stores on Main Street
are vacant. Tchula Hardware, located on a prominent corner, is
one of the few merchants still open for business, a battered Kel-
vinator sign swinging over the front door as it must have done for
decades. If you are a middle-aged white man and stop at the hot
tamale stand beside the railroad tracks, the old black men chatting with the proprietor will call you "sir" as they step out of your
way. But Tchula is still said to be a rough place, especially on
weekend nights.

A dozen miles east on Highway 12 lies Lexington, the county
seat. The city was incorporated in 1833, when a diamond-shaped
tract of 769 square miles was excised from neighboring Yazoo
County to create Holmes. The new county's seat was to be located

within three miles of its geographical center, and since no existing town met that requirement, one was founded and named after Lexington, Massachusetts. Plantations were established nearby, with names like Big Egypt, Pinchback, and Silent Shade. By 1838, there were 294 whites and 120 slaves.

Lexington's current population of just under 2,000 makes it a little smaller than Tchula, but there is a feeling of relative affluence here. Per capita income is twice that of its neighbor, and the city is built around a classic southern courthouse square ringed by restaurants, shops, and offices. Just about every denomination of church and even a synagogue can be found in town, and there are some fine old houses. Perhaps Lexington's grandest residence is a new brick chateau set on a manicured rise, built by a local lawyer who made a fortune representing Mississippi in its $3 billion-plus settlement with American tobacco companies in 1998.

On a street of modest but well-kept homes, I turn into the driveway of a 1950s brick ranch. There's a white pickup parked outside. In the back of the truck, Duke, the arthritic golden retriever, struggles to his feet to welcome me. Then Zack Killebrew comes out of the house and wraps his meaty, calloused hand around mine. Zack is first cousin of my wife, Teresa. Although we've known each other for nearly thirty years, we haven't spent much time together. Five-foot-eight and stocky, with the physical power of someone who has worked hard all his life, Zack is in his early fifties, his shaggy dark hair and clipped beard streaked with gray. His pale-blue eyes are surrounded by laugh lines.

He ushers me through the garage and into the expansive, just-finished family room, topped with a cathedral ceiling and paneled with cypress boards salvaged from an old cotton gin. Zack's wife, Pam, has filled the rest of the house with oak antiques and swag curtains, but Zack designed this room to reflect his own taste, down to the overstuffed chocolate-colored sofa, the burgundy leather recliners, the big-screen TV showing a *Leave It to Beaver* rerun, and the brand-new aquarium that he hasn't gotten around to stocking with fish.

Proud as he is of the new family room, Zack would rather be outside. "I'm half outlaw," he brags, and after church on Sunday he likes to go hunting in the woods. Or in the summer he and some buddies will wade into Horseshoe Lake, diving into the murky water without a mask and snaring catfish with their bare hands. "I grab it right chere, behind the neck," he says, demonstrating his technique. But deer season ended in January, and it will be six months before the catfish are nesting. Because of the wet weather, Zack hasn't been able to ready the fields for planting. He likes to keep busy (he calls it his "nervous twitch") and it's been hard, having so much time on his hands indoors. But Zack is only half outlaw. When he shows me the remodeled kitchen, he admits that the stainless steel, six-burner Viking range was his idea, not Pam's. That's where he cooks the game he kills, deer steaks in gravy and quail breasts sautéed in a delicate red wine sauce.

Pam is manager of the BankPlus in Tchula. She's also Zack's business partner, keeping his books and holding him on financial track. Today she's having Sunday brunch with some friends, Zack explains as he leads me into the breakfast room. One wall of the narrow space is filled with family photos, and he lingers in front of each. There's a wedding picture of him and Pam; a black-and-white portrait of his parents, Ethel and Chester; and a photo of his favorite uncle, Lawrence, the twin of my wife's mother, Florence. But most of the space is dedicated to Zack's three children, identical twins Heath and Keath and their older sister, Heather. One snapshot shows the boys at age four, with striped T-shirts and '80s shags, standing in their daddy's cotton field. Directly beneath, they're handsome young men, posing in front of their own first stand of cotton. Their hair is now cropped short and the T-shirts have been replaced by oxford cloth, but they've unconsciously arranged themselves in exactly the same stance as twenty years before. A little farther down, Heather is smiling in a blue cap and gown on the day of her graduation from dentistry school. Next to that is her wedding portrait, her veil pushed back over her blond hair to reveal her pretty features. The remainder of the space is filled with Heather's two children, Hayden and his sister, Lindsey, who in their most recent pictures are seen as a confident, tow-headed five-year-old and a laughing, blue-eyed infant. As Zack takes me through the photos, he tells me more than once how proud he is of his family, and how Pam "raised them right."

We sit down at the oval oak table, and Zack begins to talk. I know from other conversations that he loves a good joke or a cockeyed story. Warming to a subject, he can expound at length on his hunting and fishing exploits, the difficulty of finding good farm help, or how to repair a chain drive. "That don't make walkin'-around sense," he's told me more than once, and many a brainless fellow has been dismissed as a "sapsucker." Talking is as natural to Zack as farming. "I love people," he confesses. "I love talkin' to people. If I didn't have anybody to talk to, I'd go crazy with that. Some say that's my weakness," he adds sheepishly. When he's not working, Zack likes to head down the road to the Rib Depot, staying for a couple of hours, nursing an iced tea and chatting with the other customers. A cousin works there, and several of Zack's hunting trophies hang from the plain plank walls, just a few of the more than two hundred deer he estimates he's shot in his lifetime.

Zack grew up in this part of the world, and he inhabits it utterly. Until it burned down a dozen years ago, he and Pam lived outside Tchula in a tiny house built on land so flat you could hear the wind rush by. It was Zack's parents' old place. His mother grew up in the Mississippi hills, the daughter of sharecroppers. His father was a cotton farmer here in the Delta. After they were married, they started out renting the land they worked. Then, with the help of a government loan, they bought fifty acres along with the house and barn.

Before Zack, his parents had three girls: Renadell, Ruth, and Linda. He was christened after Zachary Taylor, hero of the Mexican War, twelfth president of the United States, and opponent of slavery. His parents saw a movie about Taylor just before Zack was born, and they liked the sound of the name. It's popular enough now, but when he was growing up he never knew anybody else called Zachary.

People raised on a farm can go one of two ways, Zack explains. Sometimes they escape, move to the city, and become doctors or lawyers. And they might be "a little bit smarter than the ones that stick around," he allows. But he decided from an early age that he wanted to carry on the family business. "I don't know why," he says. "I just liked it. It was in my blood, I guess. The way Dale Earnhardt wanted to be a race car driver like his daddy."

Zack's father died when Zack was nine, his mother six years later. At age fifteen, he wasn't ready to take on the responsibilities of farming. His sisters were already married by then, and he could have lived with one of them. But when a neighbor suggested that he go work on Mississippi riverboats, Zack quit school and took the counsel, which he still considers the best advice he's ever had. He was a scrawny kid of 130 pounds when he started as a deckhand on the run between New Orleans and St. Paul, barely able to wield the huge ratchets used to fasten the rafts of barges. But within six months he'd put on forty pounds of muscle. Part of him has always regretted dropping out of school, but on the riverboats, he says, he got a different kind of education: That's where he learned to work.

Zack would crew on the boats for a month straight—"thirty days of nothing but men's faces"—then get two weeks off. In his free time, he'd go back to Tchula and help his uncle Buster, who was working the family farm. After a couple of years on the river, Zack met a girl on one of his trips home and decided to stay. He purchased his sisters' shares in his parents' house and land, then rented some more from a neighbor he knew as Aunt Bea, making a modest spread of one hundred acres. He needed about $20,000 for equipment and supplies to get started, but the land wasn't worth that much and without other collateral he couldn't qualify for a loan. So he worked for a short while on a plantation in Vicksburg, then started as a mechanic at the John Deere concession in Lexington. There, besides his weekly paycheck, he got invaluable practice on the guts of tractors and planters and the other pieces of machinery in the farmer's armamentarium.

Zack saved what he could, and in 1975, at the age of twenty-five, he started working his own land, planting a few acres at a time as money became available. He also scraped together the cash to buy stock in Holmes Gin, the local company founded that year to process its shareholders' cotton. Zack and the girl broke up, but he never went back to the river. Working all day at John Deere, he would tend his farm in the early morning and in the evening, cultivating and spraying by himself and hiring part-time workers for the "chopping," or hoeing, which was still done by hand in those days. Zack showed his acumen right from the start. In only his second year of farming, he surprised his more experienced neighbors—and himself—by picking as much cotton per acre as anyone in his part of the Delta.

A few years later, Zack was offered a job managing an operation of 1,200 acres. Though not large by today's standards, at the time it was enough to qualify as a plantation. As Mississippi writer David Cohn explained, "The Delta owner of extensive lands lived, not on a farm, but on a Plantation. He was known, not as a farmer, but as a planter. 'Farmer' then connoted among us a cautious, small landowner, with a bit of the overalled, goateed hick about him." The planter, in contrast, was a link to "the antebellum past, reminiscent of the dream, if not always the reality, of what had been. It conjured up a certain lordliness of living and a touch of the romantic. . . . The planter occasionally died in a duel; the farmer of lockjaw got by stepping on a rusty nail."

The owner was having some financial problems, and Zack helped bring the plantation back to health, all the while maintaining his own, decidedly more modest operation. Despite their difference in class and outlook, the two men got on well. The planter was "the nicest fellow I ever worked for in my life," Zack remembers, "a real nice fellow." But after eleven years, Zack was ready to be his own boss. So he went to work full-time on his farm, which by then had grown to 250 acres, including some rented land. He signed new leases as other parcels became available, gradually increasing his holdings to their current 1,700 acres. Still a farmer, not a planter, Zack's lifestyle today is decidedly middle-class, leaning toward pickup trucks and deer camp rather than sports cars and country clubs.

Last season, Zack had 1,000 acres in cotton. The weather, he says, was "just like you ordered it from a Sears, Roebuck catalog," with a warm spring, cool summer, and perfectly timed dry spell when the bolls were open. Even in the fertile Delta, a yield of two bales per acre is considered average, but last year Zack got three bales, or 1,250 pounds. And due to a crop failure in China, prices jumped just as he was selling his cotton. "That year relaxed me," he says.

Zack needed a good season, because the two previous ones had been calamitous. The year before last, he also picked three bales an acre, but heavy rains had matted the fiber and turned it strange shades of yellow and gray. As a result, it had been graded very low—perhaps suitable only for stuffing upholstered furniture—and Zack's year ended disastrously. The season before had been even worse, with heavy rains savaging both quantity and quality, and Zack, like every other grower in the area, had barely harvested a crop at all.

In fact if last year hadn't been so good, Zack might have been forced out of business, as happened to plenty of other farmers nearby. He used to have several neighbors who would get together to fry the catfish they caught in Horseshoe Lake or share a cup of coffee in the Rib Depot before heading out to work. But those friends are gone now, closed down by the weather and the banks. Younger men, ranging from their late twenties to their early forties, have moved in to take their place, and Zack seems a bit perplexed to find himself the local sage, his advice sought on everything from crop selection to cotton futures. "There's hardly anybody my age still farmin'," he says.

There are also fewer operations of Zack's size. Not long ago, he estimates, the typical Delta farm had about 2,000 acres. Now he figures the average is twice that, and to be considered a good-size player, he says you need to have at least 7,000; some planters have as many as 40,000 acres under cultivation. It hasn't been just greed driving this growth but survival. To stay in business, small farmers have had to expand.

A major factor is the poor price for cotton. The two great historic variables in farming used to be the market and the weather. Now the federal government has assumed much of the risk of falling prices by guaranteeing planters a per-pound minimum for their crop regardless of the market rate. The problem is that prices for cotton are lower than they were twenty-five years ago—even including the government subsidy. With farmers getting less per pound, they've had to plant more acres to increase the size of their harvest.

But even as the price of cotton has dropped, the cost of growing it has continued to rise. Diesel fuel and fertilizer are much higher than they used to be, and land rents are averaging a hundred dollars an acre. Though sharecropping has died an unlamented death in the Delta, the overwhelming majority of farmers here still don't own the ground they work but lease it, often from several different landlords. Most of Zack's fields are on three-year contracts, some on shorter terms. Land rent accounts for a major part of his annual expenses, and it's due in full every winter, before he puts a seed in the ground.

If a planter is already working efficiently, there's not much he can do to save on diesel or fertilizer or land rent. And increasing the size of the operation won't offer any economies on these items because they'll just increase proportionately. But that's not true with fixed overhead, and it's here that farmers can benefit by expanding. Insurance premiums, for instance, don't increase as quickly as acreage. And a cotton picker costs the same $300,000 whether it's used to harvest one acre or ten thousand. By leveraging such costs over more land and a bigger crop, growers are able to increase their profit margins.

The government may guarantee a minimum market price, but it can't guarantee the grower's other great variable, the weather. Droughts can often be irrigated into submission, but storms can still savage the harvest, as Zack saw just a couple of years ago. And although there is a federal crop disaster program to help planters cover weather losses, it isn't nearly as generous as the one that rewards them for an abundant, high-quality harvest. So if Zack's cotton comes up short in quantity or grade, he can end the year hundreds of thousands of dollars in debt. No matter how diligent he is, no matter how skillfully he applies what he's learned over three decades, in the end his financial success or failure is largely subject to impersonal meteorological forces—just as it's been since the first settlers began planting cotton in the Delta.

It's also not clear how long the federal largess will continue. Cotton farmers now receive $4 billion per year from the government, far more than any other agricultural sector. But farm subsidies have their share of domestic opponents, and Congress is now facing historic budget deficits. The programs have also been a sore point in international trade talks for years, with less-developed countries arguing that the payments depress market prices and make it possible for rich nations to undersell them. Brazil has appealed to the World Trade Organization to force an end to supports on a variety of crops, especially export subsidies, which in effect pay farmers to dump their goods on the world market. For the rich countries, it's a matter of sustaining a traditional way of life and supporting an industry important to the local and national economies. For the poorer nations, it's an issue of economic justice. For Zack and his neighbors, it's a question of survival. Already struggling even with the subsidies, they can't imagine getting by without them.

In order to offset some of this risk, Zack diversifies his portfolio by growing more than cotton. Rice and corn are widely planted in the region, but the most common crop is soybeans, which are easier and cheaper than cotton to grow but also fetch a lower price. So how much acreage Zack decides to put into each crop is in part a measure of his optimism. If he believes the weather and the market will be favorable, he'll plant more cotton; if he's feeling conservative, more beans or corn. Last year, after those two disastrous seasons, Zack put seven hundred acres into beans, more than he'd ever planted before. And despite the strong cotton crop, it turned out well for him. The same weather that was good for cotton was good for beans, and Zack had a first-class yield. Moreover, poor weather in other bean-growing regions, such as Brazil and the American Midwest, pushed up the price, which meant that Zack was able to sell his record crop into an elevated market.

Another way Zack manages risk is to speculate in commodities. If he can get a favorable price, he'll sell futures—contracts to deliver a certain quantity of his cotton on a specified date at an agreed-on price—in order to lock in a guaranteed return for part of the crop. But later in the season, if the market is rising and Zack feels he sold prematurely, he may buy options on other farmers' cotton. Unlike futures, options aren't firm contracts to buy but only the right to do so within a certain period at a given price. So if cotton doesn't go up after all, Zack forfeits only the relatively small amount paid to secure the option. If the market does rise above the option price, he will exercise his right to buy, then resell the cotton at a profit. All this makes Zack a speculator as well as a producer. He looks at such transactions as just another form of crop insurance, but some years these extracurricular activities account for the majority of his earnings.

Knowing the difficulties, Zack discouraged his sons Heath and Keath from farming. Although both had some college, they never really wanted to do anything else. "I just couldn't run 'em off,"

Zack says. He's never considered another way of life either. One day I ask him what attracts him to a pursuit with so much uncertainty. His answer surprises me. It's the challenge, he says right away; the very fact that it's so hard makes him want to do it. Also, he savors the daily routine of working the land, the smell of the earth, the sight of grass being plowed under and rows being created to receive the seed, the feeling when he leaves at night that he has accomplished something tangible. After planting each spring, he goes out to the fields every day, brooding over the germinating seeds like an expectant father. "It's just like a baby bein' born," he tells me in his deep southern timbre. "You have the due date, and you're just waitin'." And when the seeds sprout, covering the earth with pale-green fuzz, it fills him with hope. "That looks good to you," he smiles.

Zack has taken up playing poker a couple of nights a week with some of his younger neighbors, and the game seems an apt metaphor for the Delta farmer's way of life. After all, "I'm a bettin' man out in the cotton field," he says. Even if the worst happens, even if a disastrous year wipes him out, he takes comfort in the fact that he won't be any worse off than he was in the beginning. "I'm not like these big shots," he explains. "When I started out I had nothin'." And if he ends up with nothing, he still won't regret the life he's chosen. After his two bad years, Zack saw his bank account plummet from several hundred thousand dollars to the point where he had to borrow money to pay the light bill. Should he have taken his winnings off the table a few years ago and retired? If he ever has that much money in the bank again, will he be tempted to quit? No, he answers immediately. "People may say, 'That's the biggest fool who ever walked in a pair of shoes,' but I ain't about to give up. I want to do somethin'. I don't want to be a deadbeat sittin' up in the house without a job. If you make a lot of money you'll just have to pay it all to the government anyway, so you might as well keep rollin' the dice." Still, the stakes are higher now, and the odds are increasingly stacked against small players like Zack.

Zack hasn't decided how he'll place his bets this year, how much acreage he'll devote to each crop. If you ask him what he does for a living, he'll tell you he's a cotton farmer. It's not just that he has more land planted in cotton than anything else. Soybeans, corn, and rice are all important in the Delta. But cotton is where the place's heart and history lie. No one here wears a cap or T-shirt bearing a stylized soybean or affixes a corn cob license plate to the front of his car. No one calls either of those crops "the vegetable of our lives." The Delta is still the land of cotton, and you only need to stand in a field of it to feel its peculiar pull. Cotton is among the very few crops—grapes and wheat are others—whose historical and cultural resonance is so compelling that the growing plants themselves inspire a kind of reverence. Besides the challenge, it's this profound sense of tradition, and the fierce pride it engenders, that makes Zack want to keep planting cotton.

The object of Zack's obsession is native to every continent except Antarctica. Flourishing in the tropical and subtropical regions of the earth, cotton is one of the angiosperms, the so-called flowering plants that make up the great majority of botanical species. It is also a perennial, meaning that each shrubby plant, if left to its own devices, would survive for multiple growing seasons. A member of the genus *Gossypium*, cotton is the economic overachiever of the large mallow family, which also includes jute and okra as well as the hibiscus.

There is no evidence that cotton's lint is of any use to the plant itself. However, it is of enormous value to human beings. Outselling all synthetic competitors combined, cotton is the most widely used fiber on earth. Every year, about 50 billion pounds of cotton are grown around the world, and its products find their way into every room of the Western household. In the bedroom and bath, it is ubiquitous in sheets, towels, and clothing; even the dollar bill forgotten in a pants pocket is three-quarters cotton (the rest is linen). In the kitchen, cottonseed oil is found in salad dressings and packaged foods, and elsewhere in cosmetics, soap, rubber, and the paint that coats the very walls. The hulls and meal left after the oil is extracted go into high-protein animal food. Nothing is wasted.

Though other plants such as flax are woven into fabric, none is as abundant, economical, comfortable, or naturally white. The flat, hollow cotton filament, more than a thousand times longer than it is wide, is unique in the plant kingdom, consisting of a single cell of 91 percent pure cellulose, the carbohydrate that is the chief component of plant cell walls. The fibers, 90 million of them per pound, grow in oblong pods called bolls. After pollination, the lint first stretches out to its full length, then swells until it forces the boll to open. Though cotton fibers are shorter than those of flax or wool, they naturally twist as they dry, which makes them easy to spin. A pound of cotton lint yields more than 150 miles of thread, stronger than iron wire of comparable thickness.

No one knows exactly when cotton was first cultivated. In ancient China, it was grown as a garden plant for its handsome foliage and showy blossoms, and men presented their lovers with bouquets of the short-lived, five-petaled flowers. The oldest cotton fiber yet discovered, in a cave in the Tehuacan Valley in southeastern Mexico, has been carbon-dated to 5,000 years before Christ, but it is thought that cotton was loomed even earlier in Pakistan and India.

Arabs introduced cotton to the Middle East, and by at least 3,000 B.C. the fabric was being sewn into clothing in Egypt (though linen was the predominant fiber there). Clothes in ancient Greece were made primarily from wool, in ancient Rome mainly from wool and linen. About 500 B.C., the Greek historian Herodotus made the first surviving European reference to cotton, which he called "tree wool." About six hundred years later, the Roman historian Pliny gave us our first description of the plant: "The upper part of Egypt . . . grows a bush which some people call cotton. . . . It is a small shrub, and from it hangs a fruit resembling a bearded nut, with an inner silk fiber from the down of which thread is spun. No kinds of thread are more brilliantly white or make a smoother fabric than this."

Also around the first century, strong, supple calicos (named after the Indian seaport Calicut) and muslins (their name deriving from Mosul, a city in present-day Iraq) arrived in Europe via

Arab traders from India. So incredibly fine was this muslin that seventy-two hours of labor were needed to spin a single ounce of yarn, leading one admirer to suppose that the luxurious cloth "might be thought the work of fairies or of insects, rather than of men." By the eighth century, cotton cultivation was introduced to Spain via the Moors, who gave us our English term for both the plant and the fabric, from the Arabic word *qutun*. Barcelona became known for its cotton weaving, and its products included the sails for the great voyages of discovery that would soon be launched. During the Renaissance, first Venice and then Lisbon became the center of the expanding cotton market, and Europeans began raising it on islands in the Atlantic, including the Canaries and the Azores.

In the New World, cotton was woven by indigenous peoples not only in present-day Mexico but also in what is now the southwestern United States (though the plant is not native to the continental U.S.). When Columbus landed in the Bahamas in 1492, he found the inhabitants cultivating cotton, and he took some of the cloth back to Europe to prove that he had reached India. Whereas Asia and Europe considered silk the fabric of royalty, the Aztecs awarded that honor to cotton. Among the gifts that the emperor Montezuma II presented to conquistador Hernán Cortés on his landing in Mexico in 1519 was a luxurious robe woven of cotton and decorated with gold. In North America, European colonists started cultivating the plant soon after they arrived. Spanish settlers in Florida harvested a crop in 1556, and by 1616 the English were growing it along the James River in Virginia.

Today cotton is raised in seventeen states along a broad southerly arc from Virginia to Kansas to California. Though classified as a perennial, the plant is grown as an annual to minimize damage from diseases and insects; that is, the stalks are cut down each year after harvest, and new seed is planted each spring. Of the forty-nine species in the easily hybridized genus *Gossypium*, only four are grown commercially, and each produces lint with slightly different characteristics. The longer the cotton's fiber, the easier it is to spin and the silkier the resulting fabric. Most luxurious is the extralong *Gossypium barbadense*, with fibers that range from about 1 to 2.5 inches in length. Although this species is native to South America, it is now grown in Egypt, the Carolinas (where it is called Sea Island), and the Southwest (where it is known as pima, after the Pima Indians, who cultivated cotton). The rest of the United States is dominated by a native of Mesoamerica called *Gossypium hirsutum*, or upland cotton, which has shorter, coarser fibers (ranging from 0.5 to 1.3 inches) but grows better in areas of high humidity. Africa and Asia have their own native species, *Gossypium herbaceum* and *Gossypium arboretum*, respectively, which have even shorter fibers, from about .375 to 1 inch in length. From genetic tests, we know that both *barbadense* and *hirsutum* are ancient, natural crosses between Old World varieties and still-existing wild New World forms (which produce no fiber, only small seed hairs). It's not clear how the New World and the Old World plants came together in the 5 to 10 million years since cotton evolved, but theories range from continental drift to seeds floating thousands of miles on ocean currents. Because the two American types produce more abundant and higher-quality lint, both *barbadense* and especially *hirsutum* are now generally planted around the globe. Today upland constitutes over 95 percent of the world's cotton harvest.

—— · ——

It's late February, and Zack is anxious to start this year's crop of *hirsutum*. The truth is that he doesn't need to plant as early now as he once did, because the new varieties mature faster. He can afford to let the weather moderate so he doesn't risk losing the seed and having to replant. But like many farmers, Zack has a baseball player's passion for regularity. He's already circled a planting date on his calendar and constructed a mental timetable leading up to it, and he doesn't want to get behind plan. There's more to this anxiety than superstition. He wants to plant as early in the year as possible, so the cotton can take advantage of the spring ground moisture and get established before the worst of the dry summer heat, and so it will be ready to harvest ahead of the late fall rains. The soil must be sixty-five degrees for cottonseed to germinate, and the air has to be warm enough that the emerging seedlings aren't chilled and weakened. These conditions are generally met in the Delta around the end of April. When they arrive, Zack wants to be ready.

He still needs to prepare the land before planting, but this winter has been too rainy. The weight of the equipment would compact the wet soil, ruining its texture and creating ruts that Zack would have to contend with all season long. He's already overhauled the tractors and other equipment for the work ahead.

Ever since deer season ended, Zack has been trapped inside with nothing to do, like one of those "deadbeats" he worries about becoming. Too many *Leave It to Beaver* reruns, too many iced teas in the Rib Depot, too many late-night poker games with his younger neighbors. Lately he's taken to pacing his new family room. Now he gets up from the table, goes to the window, and peers outside, as though he could will the weather to clear. "If the ground doesn't dry out soon . . ." He can't bring himself to finish the thought. All that remains is to watch the unconstructive days click by, each one putting him further behind where he hoped to be.

TWO

The Machines

On this hazy February morning, Zack and I are in his truck, making the undulating twelve-mile drive from Lexington in the hills to Tchula in the Delta. Zack spends a dozen hours a day in his pickup and pays a thousand dollars a month for gas to keep it running. It's a Ford F–150, which seems to be the workhorse of the Delta. I once asked Zack why that model was so popular here, and he told me that Chevys ride better but Fords stand up to the abuse of farming. Zack's F–150 is the special King Ranch edition. He says he bought it because he liked the way the leather seats smell; they remind him of sitting in a saddle.

Zack still remembers his first truck, a bright-blue '59 Chevy pickup with round fenders and chrome trim. It belonged to his parents—the only new truck they ever had—and Zack inherited it when his mother died. He kept it for years. But in the early

'70s, when he was just starting to farm and money was short, he sold it so he could repaint his '65 Mustang. The Mustang had a vinyl top and dual pipes out the back, and it would turn heads when he pulled away from a stop sign. "That car would talk to you," Zack says. But he still thinks about the Chevy. The truck is on the road even now, pampered as a classic, and he wishes he'd held on to it. For that matter, he'd still like to have the Mustang.

Zack's pickup is more than transportation. Of all the machines he uses to farm his cotton, none is more important than this truck. Loaded with a huge toolbox in back, it's a mobile workshop. And it's his office, the place where he manages his business. One morning when I drive up to the area Zack calls his "shop," a wide site with a large garage on one side and a tall, open shed for storing field equipment on the other, he's sitting in the cab, writing checks on the broad center console that doubles as his desk. He also uses the truck's telephone and two-way radio to keep in touch with his crew and the consultants he hires—his soil man, his crop duster, his irrigation specialist. Often he has business meetings in the truck, pulled alongside another pickup in the middle of the road, conferring with his entomologist on the best way to kill thrips, or with another farmer about the weather forecast. But the truck is also his sanctuary; though he generally likes to talk, Zack can be laconic behind its wheel, listening to George Strait on the radio and driving for miles without saying a word.

Like any office, Zack's reflects the personality and interests of its occupant. He has a pair of spurs hooked over the parking brake pedal, in case he has time to ride one of the half dozen horses he keeps. On the backseat are a carton of paper shop towels, a box of saltines, an empty sardine can, and a child seat for ferrying his grandbaby; on the floor is a case of shotgun shells. Riding in the truck bed, stretched out beside the toolbox, is the ever-present Duke. Just as the pickup is Zack's home away from home, it's also the dog's, though the retriever's arthritis now prevents him from climbing in and out by himself.

Zack's pickup is white, by far the most popular color for trucks in this area. It seems an impractical choice on these dusty roads, but Zack says it's so you can lean on the hood or door without burning your arm in the summertime. Though most of the other pickups we pass are indistinguishable to me, he can differentiate them at a thousand yards. As we drive this morning, he uncurls his left hand from the steering wheel and lifts two fingers at other vehicles as they approach in the opposite lane. Zack seems to know everybody in these parts, and at first I think he's acknowledging neighbors. But when he signals to a car with out-of-state plates, I realize that he waves to everybody. All the while, he continues his conversation, seemingly unaware of these habitual greetings or whether they're returned.

When we reach Tchula, Zack turns off the highway, drives through the deserted business district, and crosses the concrete bridge on the south edge of town. He follows the bend of Tchula Lake for a couple of miles, then pulls off the road beside one of his cotton fields. Zack's 1,700 acres are divided into four parcels— these 350 outside Tchula, another 350 along the Yazoo River, 800 up the road on the old Hyde Park plantation, and 200 acres out on Horseshoe Lake. The last, including the land that used to belong to his parents, is the only piece he owns.

We climb out of the truck. The air this morning is balmy, springlike, but there's still a tang you can feel on the tip of your nose. The rainy January left the ground soaked, but February has been dry, and Zack is finally preparing his land for planting. He's palpably relieved to be outside and occupied, but the work hasn't been enough to dissipate his restless energy. Every morning he's taken to walking two and a half miles before sunup, out on the highway near the abandoned landing strip. Such activity isn't common here, and passersby often stop to ask if he needs help. When he tells them no, they give him a strange look and drive on.

Zack started exercising because he decided he needed to lose some weight. But the walks also give him time to think. With the start of every season come new decisions and worries. When you're beginning to work the land, he says, you're mulling over last year, wondering how you can do better this time and coax a little more cotton out of the ground. But Zack ponders more than farming on these predawn walks. After thirty years of marriage, it looks as if he and Pam are about to separate. Zack doesn't know what he would do without her business acumen, which has saved him from more than one financial scrape, or without her moral support, which has always helped him through the hard times. His normally healthy appetite has fallen off in recent weeks, and he's losing more weight than he intended.

This morning, with the weak February sun to our back, we position ourselves on the side of the road, hands stuffed in our jacket pockets. It sometimes seems that not much has altered in the Delta over the past century, but one thing that has surely changed is the technology. As we stand in front of Zack's cotton field, it's not mules that are working the land but a pair of bright-green John Deere 4960 tractors. Thanks to chemicals and machines, Zack can work his farm with two full-time employees and two part-timers, instead of the dozens of hands it would have taken a hundred years ago. One of Zack's convictions, born of years of experience, is that you can't manage your operation sitting in a tractor cab all day, so he hires men to run his equipment while he shuttles from field to field supervising.

Each tractor has two six-foot-tall driving wheels in back and two smaller steering wheels in front. The engine, with 280 horse-power, burns between four and eight gallons of diesel fuel an hour, depending on what's being towed. (Like boats, tractors measure their wear and tear in hours of operation, not in miles on an odometer.) Each machine has an air-conditioned cab, power steering, an ergonomic console bristling with knobs and buttons, and a computer display that gives instantaneous readouts on the functioning of the tractor and whatever it's hauling. The rig is as far from the little open-air tractors seen on farms only a couple of decades ago as Zack's extended-cab pickup is from the '59 Chevy. Zack remembers his first tractor, an old McCormick whose transmission would get so hot that the metal floorboards would burn his feet. Unlike the Chevy, the tractor evokes no nostalgia.

Out in the fields, the earth retains the same hills ("rows" to a farmer) and furrows ("middles") that Zack formed last year. But the ground has become compacted by rain and machinery, with the rows beaten down and the middles silted up. Before this year's crop can be planted, the soil needs to be loosened. For centuries, the process has been called "breaking the land," and even today the term captures the farmer's adversarial relationship with the earth, as though it were a wild animal to be tamed anew each year.

This morning the tractor is pulling a green metal frame known as a paratill. The low implement has six vertical shanks extending earthward, one for each row to be worked. Each shank is about two feet long and bent at the bottom to form a forty-five-degree angle. As the paratill moves over the ground, the shanks sink about a foot into the soil, skimming off the hardened upper crust then dropping it intact, like a layer cake that's been sliced through the middle.

Next Zack's workers drag a piece of equipment called a middle buster over the land. Like the paratill, this is a metal frame with descending shanks, but at the end of each is a V-shaped blade with high, concave sides. The blades turn over the earth, burying the stubble from last year's crop as they reshape the rows and raise them up to their full height. After the middle buster passes, the freshly turned earth has a fecund smell, and it looks dark and fresh and ready. This model plows only six furrows at a time, because opening the ground is heavy work that taxes the tractor's engine.

Zack used to take more extreme measures to prepare his land for planting, breaking the ground so thoroughly that the rows were obliterated and had to be raised back up. But now he does this only where the fields have become rutted. For one thing, he doesn't want to disturb the ground unnecessarily, which increases erosion and encourages weeds. He also likes to make sure his rows are in the same place every year, so the plants can take advantage of any fertilizer that may be left in the soil.

Zack doesn't want to use his tractors more than he has to. Their weight, which can run over ten tons, compresses the ground and crushes the small pores holding the air and water that plant roots require for growth. To restore the soil, Zack needs to loosen the compacted earth with a harrow or a cultivator (frames fitted with metal spikes or discs). Thus the price of running equipment over the fields is having to run yet more equipment over them. With each trip costing labor and expensive diesel, there is a strong incentive to minimize the to-and-fro. As Zack says, the fewer passes you make with your tractor, the more money in your pocket.

At the edge of the field, a second John Deere tractor is cleaning out one of the trenches that runs diagonally across the rows to channel away excess water. Just as crucial as getting moisture on the crop, Zack explains, is getting it back off. "Do you know the three most important things about farming?" he asks. "Drainage, drainage, and drainage." So before planting and periodically during the season, Zack will clear away the silt that accumulates in the trenches using a furrow plow, whose metal paddles scoop out the earth and scatter it over the field in a high, twenty-five-foot arc.

As I watch the tractors' back-and-forth across the earth, I'm struck by how the everyday of farming often seems more about the equipment than the plants. The growing cotton makes plenty of demands, of course—for water, fertilizer, protection from weeds and insects. But provided with the proper conditions, it goes ahead turning sunlight and water and nutrients into stems and leaves and flowers. But all season long, not one process of any significance—not tilling, or planting, or fertilizing, or spraying, or harvesting—will be accomplished without the aid of a big, noisy, complicated, expensive machine.

A small farmer like Zack can't afford the time or money to be calling a mechanic every time something refuses to work the way it's supposed to, so coddling all this cantankerous equipment is largely how he occupies his time. Another day that I spend in the fields with him, every machine that he and his men touch (with the exception of the pickup) has to be repaired—a balky hydraulic hose cleared, a tire changed, caked fertilizer loosened, a pin reinserted in a spraying rig's arm. And it is on these chores that Zack's background as a John Deere mechanic proves invaluable. As I watch him attack these bedeviling but to him routine problems, I'm impressed not only by the depth of his knowledge but by his feel for the machines. When one of his workers has trouble connecting the hydraulic line, Zack takes the nozzle and guides it in with a sure touch. When the tractor-trailer's wheel begins to squeak, Zack has a hunch it's not a bad bearing, as Keath supposes, but a sticky brake shoe—which turns out to be the case when the huge tire is removed and the wheel examined. It's not that Heath and Keath don't know their way around cutting torches, compressors, and other mechanical things. But Zack addresses the devices with an uncommon sensitivity, like old friends whose quirks he knows. That's not to say he's afraid to take a sledgehammer to a piece of equipment if need be. In fact, that's how he finally manages to get the pin back into the arm of the spraying rig.

Among all the field equipment that Zack owns, none is as rugged or versatile as the tractor. Other than his picker, everything working his land—plow, planter, sprayer, fertilizer spreader, boll buggy, module builder, shredder—is towed by one of these vehicles, from which it draws its power. Tractors get their name from the Latin *tractus*, which means "pulled." But the earliest tractors weren't even equipped with wheels. Developed around 1850 as a portable power source for machines such as threshers (devices to remove the grain from its husk), these first models had to be hauled into position in a horse-drawn cart. It would be another decade before they became self-propelled and were put to work towing an expanding collection of farm implements.

The earliest tractors were powered by steam. But even after being fitted with wheels they were cumbersome and understandably slow to find a market. Then in 1892 Iowa blacksmith John Froehlich built the first successful gasoline-fueled tractor. Much lighter and easier to operate, this improved model reduced the need for labor and allowed farmers to accomplish their chores more quickly, so they could take advantage of good weather. Still, draft animals were cheaper to buy, easier to maintain, required no expensive fuel, and even produced fertilizer. Thus it was only when farmers' standard of living rose and they could afford the new equipment, and when farms became too big to work with animals, that the advantages of tractors outweighed the cost and trouble. In much of the developing world, the equation is still weighted in the other direction and mules and bullocks remain the principal source of farm power.

Even in the United States, there were only six hundred tractors operating by 1907. By 1920, the First World War had pushed that number up to 246,000 by simultaneously increasing the demand for food and fiber and decreasing the supply of horses. All these vehicles still had steel wheels, since Firestone didn't introduce rubber tires for tractors until 1931. By 1940, there were more than 1.5 million tractors in the country, but it wasn't until the mid-1950s that they outnumbered horses and mules.

In Mississippi the tractor was particularly slow to catch on, since by the early twentieth century most farmers were poor and most landholdings were small. In 1920, even after the wartime boom, there were only 667 tractors in the state, less than 0.3 percent of the U.S. total, even though Mississippi's economy was overwhelmingly agricultural. In 1950, mules were still widely used for plowing and other farm chores.

Today there are over 5 million tractors working the fewer than 2 million American farms. Crucial though they are to modern agriculture, tractors have their disadvantages. One is their price. New, each of Zack's tractors costs about $125,000. Another drawback involves safety. From the beginning, they have been equipped with power take-offs, or PTOs, used to run other pieces of equipment. PTOs are a tremendous tool but also a hazard, since they operate by means of an exposed rotating shaft. Many a farmer has been maimed or even killed when a thread from his clothing has caught in the spinning PTO. Zack has been lucky so far. He once had a shirt ripped off his back, but no body parts followed into the whirling machinery. In recognition of the danger, some tractors sound a warning tone when the driver leaves the seat with the PTO in operation. Be careful, it's saying, it's dangerous back there.

But the history of cotton and the history of machines have far more in common than the tractor, or the various accoutrements it pulls, or more recent equipment such as the crop duster or the picker. Even though the cotton fields remained one of the least mechanized backwaters of American agriculture for many years, the chronicle of cotton over the past two centuries has largely been the story of mechanical invention. Machines to plow, plant, and harvest would come later. The first innovations were made at the end of the process, in the weaving of cotton cloth.

In the mid-1600s, cheap, handmade cottons from India (called chintz from the Hindu word *chint*, for "multicolored") became popular in Britain, owing to their bright hues and floral designs even more than to their greater comfort. Also, because cottons were available in various qualities and a range of prices, they were within reach of virtually everyone. Fearing for the venerable wool industry, Parliament passed a series of measures to stem the flood of imports. In 1689, it legislated that cotton garments could be worn only in summer, and in 1701, it forbade the importation of all printed cottons from the Far East.

The latter law backfired, as English weavers began to copy the now prohibited Indian designs. Because the British didn't know how to spin cotton yarn strong enough to form the fabric's warp, or lengthwise threads, they had to substitute linen, which wasn't as pliable. Their designs also didn't have the fine workmanship of the imported cloth. Still, the knockoffs sold briskly, leading Parliament to restrict the domestic production of cotton fabrics in one way or another for the next five decades. But there was no appeasing the public's demand for inexpensive, comfortable, fashionable cotton, and eventually it supplanted both wool and linen as Britons' fabric of choice.

Like all cloth at the time, the new cottons were spun and woven by hand. But by about 1725, traditional methods could no longer meet the demands of a growing, more affluent population, and entrepreneurs began searching for ways to speed production. Eight years later, Englishman John Kay made the first break-through by designing a shuttle (the part of the loom that carries the crosswise threads, or woof, back and forth among the warp) that could "fly" from side to side by use of spring-loaded boxes.

By greatly increasing the efficiency of the loom, the flying shuttle created a new problem. Spinning technology hadn't kept pace, and now sixteen spinners were needed to supply the thread used by just one weaver. Briton James Hargreaves solved the chronic shortage in 1765 when he invented the spinning jenny, which by setting the spindles in an upright position, was able to turn eight of them, and later as many as eighty, off a single wheel. (The device was named for Hargreaves's daughter, who suppos-edly gave him the idea when she knocked over the family spin-ning wheel and set its spindle revolving on the floor like a top.) The year of Hargreaves's invention, less than 500,000 pounds of cotton thread were spun in England; two decades later, that figure had grown to 16 million.

In 1769 another Englishman, Richard Arkwright, introduced his water frame, which used rollers to produce stronger thread, making it possible for the first time to weave 100 percent cotton cloth by machine. Five years later, Parliament finally conceded to reality and allowed domestic production of pure cotton fabric. In

1775, Samuel Crompton's spinning mule combined the virtues of the jenny and the water frame, turning out thread of exceptional fineness and strength. Then in 1787, Edmund Cartwright invented a practical power loom, operated first by oxen and later by steam. Other improved looms followed, and the formerly wool-weaving district of Lancashire, some two hundred miles northwest of London, became the world's leading manufacturer of cotton cloth. By the turn of the nineteenth century, the Lancashire mills were employing nearly a quarter million operatives laboring in notoriously difficult and dangerous conditions.

But the advances in spinning and weaving created a shortage of raw material. In 1783, England imported 9 million pounds of cotton, mostly from Brazil, the Caribbean, the Middle East, and India, but there still wasn't enough of the fiber to supply the new mills. Demand also burgeoned on the other side of the Atlantic after 1790, when Moses Brown (whose family founded Brown University) built the first American cotton spinning mill in Pawtucket, Rhode Island, using plans smuggled from England. In 1813, Francis Cabot Lowell and Paul Moody also copied British designs to build the first power loom on American soil, and soon Lowell, Massachusetts, became as synonymous with textiles in America as Lancashire was in England.

One reason for the worldwide scarcity of cotton was botanical. Each boll contained not only the valuable lint but, anchored to it, dozens of seeds, which made up about two-thirds of the harvested cotton's weight. Since at least the first century, wooden rollers had been used in Africa, Asia, and the Americas to coax cottonseed away from the fiber. In Britain's New World colonies, variations on this method had been employed since the 1600s, and throughout the following century these roller gins (short for "engines") grew in size and speed. They were still inefficient and temperamental, but the alternative, cleaning the cotton by hand, was incredibly slow. Whereas a slave could pick an average of two hundred (and sometimes as many as four hundred) pounds of cotton a day, he or she could produce only one pound of cleaned fiber in the same period. But in 1793, the shortage of cotton fiber, brought on by the new spinning and weaving devices, would be solved by the invention of yet another machine.

The man who would revolutionize the cotton industry was born in 1765 in Westboro, Massachusetts, the oldest child of a prominent patriot farmer. It can be challenging to distinguish fact from fiction about Eli Whitney's early life, thanks to mythologizing nineteenth-century biographers, but it appears that young Eli showed a prodigious mechanical and entrepreneurial aptitude early on. At age fifteen, he opened his own business to produce nails. Then when demand dropped due to cheap imports from England, he switched production first to hat pins, then to walking canes. He later taught school before persuading his father to send him to Yale College, where at twenty-three he enrolled as the oldest member of his freshman class.

In New Haven, Whitney befriended Phineas Miller, a well-connected New Englander just a year older. Miller managed a Georgia plantation outside Savannah called Mulberry Grove, and when Whitney graduated from Yale in 1792, his friend found him a tutoring position on a nearby estate. The idea of returning to teaching didn't appeal to Whitney, but, deep in debt and with no other prospects, he prepared for the voyage south. In New York, Miller introduced Whitney to his own employer, Carolyn Greene, the charming widow of Revolutionary War hero Nathanael Greene. She lent Whitney money for the passage, and the three embarked together.

On his arrival in Georgia, Whitney discovered that there had been a misunderstanding and that his tutor's salary would be only fifty guineas a year, half what he'd expected. Instead of taking up the position, he lingered at Mulberry Grove, where Miller and Mrs. Green encouraged him to apply his obvious mechanical talents to the problem of separating cottonseed from fiber. Typical of the myths that grew up around the inventor, one version has it that he got the idea for his new gin while watching slaves tease cotton away from the seed by hand; another says his inspiration came after he saw a cat leap at a chicken and catch only feathers in its claws. As he himself told the story, he finished the device after just ten days' tinkering.

Whitney had never seen a cotton gin, and instead of rollers to pinch the seed away from the fiber, he introduced a single cylinder, turned at first by a hand crank and later by animal or water power. Set into the cylinder were wire hooks, which caught the cotton and pulled it through a metal grille. The seeds, being too large to pass through the bars, remained behind, where they were swept away by a rotating brush. With Whitney's gin, one horse and three workers could clean an astonishing half ton of seed cotton daily, producing more than three hundred pounds of usable fiber. In contrast, the best roller gin of the time, known as a barrel gin, required a horse and twenty-five slaves to operate, turning out only about two hundred pounds of cleaned lint per day. Whitney's gin was also particularly suited to the obstinate green seeds of upland cotton, which grew best in the humid climate of the southern United States. Recognizing the commercial potential, Miller offered to underwrite the invention's manufacture, and the two friends went into business, obtaining a patent the following year.

Though the early history of Whitney's gin reads like something out of a Horatio Alger fable, it soon degenerated into a cautionary tale for any would-be entrepreneur. Determined to maintain control of the new technology, Miller refused to license farmers the right to construct their own gins. Unhappy with the size of the ginning fee, which Miller set at one-third of the cleaned cotton, some growers began building copies of the ingenious but easy-to-make machine, while others circulated rumors that the gin, by tearing the seeds away from the fiber, damaged the lint, making British mill owners in particular reluctant to accept cotton processed by the new invention. As a result of the rampant counterfeiting, Whitney and Miller were embroiled in lawsuits for more than a decade. By the time their patent expired in 1807, Whitney figured he had received $90,000 for the gin, virtually all of which had gone for manufacturing costs and legal fees. But in time, the new machine's economy and speed wore down the resistance of mill owners and Whitney's so-called saw gin (rotating blades had by now replaced the wire hooks) supplanted its older rivals.

Though Whitney hadn't "invented" the cotton gin, his device, by being more efficient to operate and easier to maintain, helped satisfy the huge international demand for the fiber. By 1825, England was importing 228 million pounds, mostly from the United

States. And from 1790 to 1830, American cotton production increased from just over 3,000 bales (under 1.5 million pounds) to more than 730,000 bales (over 350 million pounds).

As early as 1806, Judge William Johnson, who presided over the Whitney patent infringement case in Georgia, extolled the inventor's contribution to the regional economy: "The whole interior of the Southern states was languishing," Johnson wrote. "Individuals who were depressed with poverty, or sunk with idleness, have suddenly risen to wealth and respectability. Our debts have been paid off, our capital increased; and our lands are treble in value." Whitney's invention quickly became the object of national pride. In 1814, Assistant Secretary of the Treasury Tench Coxe, who is known as the father of the American cotton industry for his early promotion of the crop, reminded the world that "the invaluable saw gin was invented by a citizen of the United States" and that "by our own invention" Americans now had the means "to facilitate the manufacture of a staple production of our soil." Whitney was a certified hero, and a hagiographic biography published in 1832 by Denison Olmstead, professor of mathematics and natural philosophy at Yale, set the tone for later works.

Scholars have argued that Whitney has been given too much credit for expanding the American cotton industry. The Industrial Revolution itself spurred the rise of cotton more than any single invention, it's been pointed out, and improved roller gins were used more widely and more effectively than the traditional story allows. But the debate is over the degree of Whitney's influence. There is no disagreement that the saw gin, by easing the final bottleneck in the manufacture of cotton cloth, played a major role in the antebellum cotton boom. In the early 1800s, cotton became a vital engine of both the northern and southern economies, bringing in much-needed foreign capital and providing the raw material for the young nation's expanding factories. In the coming decades, cotton would fuel the Industrial Revolution on two continents, inspiring Karl Marx's claim (in 1846) that "without cotton, there would be no modern industry."

Despite his personal setbacks, Whitney's career didn't end with the cotton gin. In 1798, as his patent infringement suits were creeping through the courts, Whitney, still badly in need of money, signed a contract to manufacture 10,000 muskets for the U.S. Army in the ridiculously short period of two years—even though he didn't have a single gunsmith in his employ. That didn't concern him, because he didn't intend to hire any.

Having returned to his native New England, Whitney saw that the North lacked the skilled workers needed to produce manufactured articles such as guns. Since there was no simple way to increase the supply of laborers, he set out to remake manufacturing methods so as to eliminate the need for them. His solution was a widely copied (this time Whitney didn't even bother to apply for a patent) "milling machine," which, as he explained, "reduced a complex business, embracing many ramifications, almost to a mere succession of simple processes." In a system that would remain essentially unchanged for 150 years, relatively unskilled operators clamped templates onto sheets of metal and cut them out using a sawlike machine of Whitney's design. Because the parts were produced from a pattern, they could be made much more quickly and cheaply than with the traditional method, in which each piece was crafted entirely by hand. Since all the components were (at least theoretically) identical, it would also be easier to replace broken or defective parts to repair the guns.

As with Whitney's cotton gin, these improved industrial techniques didn't emerge out of a vacuum. A quarter century before, British economist Adam Smith had advocated just such a division of labor, and in France and the United States manufacturers had produced muskets and pistols through similar methods. Whitney's contribution was rather one of scale. Though he didn't deliver the final batch of muskets until 1809—nine years after the contracted delivery date—he did succeed in applying existing ideas to an operation more complex and better coordinated than any of his predecessors'. In the process, he also managed to achieve the wealth that had eluded him in his venture with the cotton gin.

By the time of his death in 1825, Whitney was hailed as the inventor of the "American system" of manufacturing. Applied in the coming decades by competing gunsmiths and makers of sewing machines, clocks, and other precision instruments, the system would play a crucial role as the North grew into an industrial power in areas other than textiles. Thus, even as cotton was sustaining the South on its slave-holding, agricultural course during this period, improved manufacturing techniques were speeding the northern states along their chosen path of industry and free labor. In the thirty-five years following the inventor's death, this sectional schism would grow only more bitter and violent.

In Tchula, the sun is setting early on this chilly February afternoon. There were no equipment problems today, and Zack's machines have managed to plow 150 acres. Even at that rate, it will be eleven more workdays before all his land is ready to plant. But after weeks of worry about his schedule, it's a good start. If the weather holds and the tractors don't break down, Zack should be ready to sow his corn in March, his soybeans in early April, and his cotton toward the end of that month. In the meantime, he'll have to work out the financing and decide how many acres to devote to each crop. Tonight he watches the tractors clamber out of the field and turn back toward the shop, their yellow warning lights flashing in the twilight. Then he climbs into his Ford pickup, cranks the engine, and begins the twelve-mile drive home to Lexington.

THREE

The Seed

On this April morning, Zack Killebrew is halfway through planting his cotton. He's had a good week for it. The weather has been dry for the past several days, and now the sky is milky blue, the air warm and moist on the skin. But as he stands on the road outside Tchula, watching his tractors crisscross the land, Zack's fists are working nervously in his jeans pockets.

Planting is like no other moment of the year. Later in the season there will be drought and storms, weeds and insects to contend with. In September will come the exhilaration and fatigue of picking, the culmination of months of effort and expense and worry. The harvest may be met with disappointment, if the crop doesn't live up to expectation. But now in the spring, all is unspoiled potential, a blank page unblotted with frustration or setback. Like any farmer, Zack needs to be an optimist to do what he does, and planting is the quintessential occasion for hope.

That doesn't mean it's an easy time. Even under the best of circumstances, planting is the most stressful period of the year. Zack has already been sowing his cotton for several days, and he has several more to go before it's done. It's been a frenetic stretch of early mornings and long evenings, of unwavering purpose and focus. But it's not the work that makes it so tense; it's thinking about everything that can go wrong, now and in the months ahead. As Zack says, "You got all the pressure on you when you're plantin'. You're worryin' like a cat on a hot tin roof. You're worryin' about the weather. Or what if you plant too deep? What if you plant too shallow? Every year's not the same." Over the course of these two weeks he'll spend tens of thousands of dollars as he lays his bets and realizes decisions—what to plant, when, where—that will govern the success or failure of the entire season.

There's something else making this planting season particularly difficult. A few weeks ago, Zack and Pam separated. He's moved out of the brick house in Lexington with the brand-new family room and kitchen and is now renting a more spartan place here in Tchula, just across the road from where we're standing. It's been thirty years since Zack has lived alone, and it's not an easy adjustment for somebody with his gregarious temperament. Little wonder he's on edge, worrying over the details, eager that everything go right out in the fields. Patience isn't one of Zack's more obvious virtues, and as the work progresses, his forbearance is likely to be tested further.

In February, flush with the success of last year, Zack decided to put 1,000 acres, or nearly two-thirds of his land, in cotton, as

much as he's ever wagered on that crop before. This field outside
Tchula and the one on Horseshoe Lake will be entirely in cotton,
and the ones along the Yazoo River and on the old Hyde Park
plantation will have a mix of cotton, corn, and beans. Planted
last month, the three hundred acres of corn are already three feet
tall. Sown about a week ago, the four hundred acres of beans
have just poked through the earth, looking like the sprouts you'd
put on a sandwich.

Old-timers used to exhort, "Plant your cotton when you still
need a coat," but today it's hot despite the early hour. Dressed in a
Confederate flag T-shirt and blue jeans, Zack glances out over the
waiting ground, reading the land the way other men read a newspaper. The Delta's deep, well-drained earth, rich in organic matter, is ideal for growing cotton. But even here, not all soil is
created equal. Of the parcels that Zack farms, these acres outside
Tchula have the most felicitous texture, belonging to a category
known locally as "ice cream land" for its smooth, light consis-
tency. But he also plants some "gumbo," which when wet becomes
rubbery as chewing gum; it's sometimes called "alligator clay" because when it dries it can harden up like its namesake's hide.

Each tractor is towing a drag, a flat metal frame fitted with four
rows of diabolical teeth and trailed by a series of horizontal metal
plates, to give the soil a final dressing before planting. Ahead of
the machines, the foot-high rows of earth are rough topped, the
soil the color of café au lait. Where the tractors have already
worked, the rows' little peaks appear flatter, more inviting to a
seed. Cotton is particular about how deep it's planted, and a nice
flat bed means that all the seeds will be placed at the same depth.
The earth is several shades darker where the drags have passed,

because the freshly exposed soil contains more moisture. The deeper color gives the dragged ground a richer, more fertile look, but Zack is eager to husband whatever water the soil contains, not expose it to evaporation.

Zack's third tractor, a bright-red International Harvester MX270, is hooked to the other essential piece of equipment he will use today, his International Harvester planter, an intricate device supported on narrow rubber tires and stretching across eight rows of earth. Before horse-drawn planters became popular, about 1900, farmers would take seeds from a bag around their neck and drop them into the earth by hand, then run a mule-pulled harrow over the rows to bury them. The first four-row, tractor-pulled planter was marketed in 1945, and for years the technology remained essentially unchanged. At its simplest, the planter opens a hole in the ground, releases a seed, and covers it. On the back end is a double line of hoppers, two for each row to be planted. Beneath each pair of hoppers is a mechanism for dropping the seeds. In front are two metal discs to carve a trench in the soil, in the rear two more discs to close it. Zack sets the machine for how many seeds he wants to sow per acre and for how deep they will be buried.

Planters used to rely on gravity to drop each seed onto a rotating horizontal plate with a hole in its center. When the seed reached the opening, it would fall onto the soil. It was a relatively simple mechanism, but sometimes the hole might pass with no seed in it, and sometimes more than one would slip through. As a result, the number of seeds planted could vary significantly along any given row, or from one row to the next.

Now planters are much more sophisticated. They still have two pairs of discs to open and close the earth, but the metal plates that disperse the seed operate by vacuum pressure, which is more reliable than gravity. Three depressions in each plate form a triangle, with each hollow about the thickness of a pencil lead. A vacuum hose fits on the side of the rotating plate, sucking a seed out of the bin and into one of the depressions. As the disc continues to spin, the seed encounters a brush, which knocks it off the plate and through an opening onto the ground. The result is a much more consistent seed count in any given row, which translates into less waste. With cottonseed costing around $7.50 a pound (it's actually sold by count, not weight), Zack will spend nearly $70,000 on this item alone. Not only do the new machines conserve seed, they're fast, covering more than 150 acres a day. Like the ex-mechanic he is, Zack has a deep appreciation of the new equipment. "It's just like a dream," he says.

The seeds that go into the planter are as high-tech as the machine. Zack has chosen three different strains, each identified by number, to meet differing conditions in his various fields—"444" on his four hundred acres of ice cream land, "555," or "Triple Nickel," on four hundred drier acres, and "5599" on two hundred acres of wetter, more marginal ground. He orders his seed from the supplier up the road, specifying the exact blend of fungicides and insecticides that will coat each batch. The seeds are about the size and shape of a navy bean but with a point on one end. Naturally they are dark brown or green, but the commercial product has been given a bright-blue chemical jacket bearing little resemblance to anything in the plant kingdom. They also have been genetically modified to resist certain caterpillars as well as the herbicide Roundup.

Today Zack will be putting down eight and a half to nine pounds, or about 35,000 seeds, per acre. Exposed to the proper conditions of moisture and temperature, the cottonseed uses its stored energy to force a slender stem upward through the soil. Once it has broken the surface, the stem unfurls two tiny temporary leaves, which capture the energy of the sun to fuel further development. Because the ground still has good surface moisture this early in the year, the cotton will be sown at about five-eighths of an inch. Generally speaking, cotton is planted more shallow when the earth is damp, because germination is slower in the moist soil's cooler temperatures and the seed is more prone to fungus attacks. A couple of weeks later in the season, when the weather is hotter and the ground is drier, Zack would plant a little deeper. The idea is to bury the seed just deep enough that it doesn't dry out. If planted any farther than an inch, the seedling may expend excess energy on its journey, arriving too exhausted to get a good start. Or it could run out of nutrients before breaking the surface at all, especially in the Delta's silty soil, which is prone to forming a crust after a heavy rain. If the ground has become too hard, the delicate stem might snap before reaching the surface. On the other hand, if the seed is planted as shallow as conditions will allow, it will still have plenty of energy left after its comparatively short trip to daylight. Then, "when that little stinger comes out of the seed," Zack says, "it's ready to take off."

Ideally Zack would have started the planter immediately behind the drags this morning so as to minimize the time the soil was open and losing moisture. But there's a last-minute snag with

enveloped in the rumble of the engine. But the cab is so well
sulated that it allows in only about as much motor noise as a
esel pickup. Willie and I have no trouble talking over the sound,
d I can clearly hear the crackle of the two-way radio. As the
ctor eases into gear, I brace myself for the lurch, but again I'm
prised. Willie pulls on the hand throttle to accelerate and the
tor accelerates smoothly, like a small truck with a manual
smission. There are fifteen forward gears and four in reverse,
with the planter behind us, we won't get higher than ninth
today; top speed will be six miles an hour. Is it hard to learn to
a machine like this? I ask, looking at the complicated con-
"Not really," Willie answers. "It's like anythin'. Some people
easy and some learn hard. It's easy to learn if you want to."
llie expertly guides the tractor into position at the end of a
hen presses a black plastic button. There's a high-pitched
, like a jet engine, as the fan powers up the vacuum sys-
he business end of the planter is below and behind us, and
for the new noise I can't immediately tell that anything
ening. But as the tractor moves on and the first eight
rows emerge, their smoothness contrasts with the sharper
of the unsown rows to their right.
e work our way down the field, Willie starts punching
beside the computer monitor, but the display isn't giving
information he wants. Last night, the men hosed down
ter, and he suspects that the water caused a short circuit.
can't check whether he's putting down the right number
er acre, or whether their depth matches what's been set.
Zack on the radio and alerts him to the problem.

one of the air hoses and it's ten-thirty before the problem is re-
solved. Two of Zack's hands, Johnny and Charlie, now start to fill
each of the plastic seed hoppers on the back of the planter.

Like generations who worked the Delta before them, Charlie
and Johnny are black. Johnny is the oldest of the four-man crew,
and one of Zack's two year-round employees. His goatee is flecked
with gray, but it's hard to guess his age; maybe in his fifties, he
looks older. Johnny is tall and thin but not a healthy thin, and the
whites of his eyes are creamy instead of clear. This morning when
I shake his hand, I smell alcohol on his breath. He was born a little farther up the Delta, he tells me, in Sunflower County. Though
he's been farming for thirty-six years, he's never planted any land
of his own. Addressing Zack, Johnny is deferential. But he stands
erect and seems to hold himself slightly aloof, as though observing
and judging everything from a distance. When Zack berates another worker, I sense the beginning of an ironic smile playing over
Johnny's lips, threatening to expose his gold tooth.

Charlie is the one being rebuked, in what I soon recognize as a
pattern. Unlike Johnny, Charlie works for Zack only during peak
periods such as planting and picking. Like Johnny, Charlie is lanky.
Younger, maybe forty, he too seems prematurely aged. His front
teeth are missing, and a speech impediment makes his words un-
intelligible to me. But Zack understands well enough; earlier this
morning, Charlie tells him, he didn't see a tree stump in the field
and knocked the steps of his tractor out of kilter. It is this accident
that is drawing Zack's ire.

After the dressing-down, Charlie and Johnny carry two five-
gallon buckets to the back of Zack's pickup, where a big green
hopper bears the legend HELENA SEED BOX. The hopper holds half

a ton of cottonseeds, and Zack watches as the two begin to trans-fer them, pailful by pailful, into the planter's plastic bins. Holding his white bucket in one hand, Charlie pulls a lever with the other, and turquoise cottonseeds clatter down the metal chute. But as he struggles with the increasingly heavy receptacle, he fails to release the lever in time, and a couple of cups spill to the ground. This earns another rebuke from Zack, who reminds him that the seeds cost ten cents apiece. (He's exaggerating; they're about a tenth of a cent each.) When Zack threatens to dock his pay, Charlie silently sinks to all fours and starts to pick the seeds out of the dirt. Zack watches him for a few seconds, then softens. "Get up out o' there," he says. "Just be more careful next time." After that, Zack operates the chute while the men hold the buckets with both hands.

When the planter's seed hoppers are full, the crew loads its eight smaller bins with aldicarb, a pesticide that will be applied during the same pass of the tractor. The grayish granules have to be handled with extreme care. Zack once saw a dog swallow a small amount of the chemical. In its death throes, the animal defecated copiously, and when a cat came along and sampled the feces, the secondhand dose proved fatal to it as well. To protect the workers, the pesticide is now distributed in plastic "lock 'n load" bottles that can't be opened except when inserted into the planter's hoppers.

Next Johnny and Charlie fill the yellow, 250-gallon tanks on either side of the tractor with water and the liquid herbicide Mirage, which will be sprayed on areas where Johnson grass is already sprouting. Cotton farming is a chemical-dependent busi-

ness, and Zack will spend much of his time between the fields and the seed store, ferrying Inside the firm's corrugated metal shed, which ton gin, dozens of fertilizers, insecticides, and on pallets, their cases stamped with muscul Armor and Touchdown. There is also a pan lounge with a soda machine, coffee pot, TV minal where customers can check the wea latest commodity prices. The lounge serves local farmers, especially since the Rib Dep weeks ago.

When the planter is loaded, Zack goe chine and checks the sprockets on the side to side, confirming the depth setting he signals to his other year-round worke tractor. Willie is of average height and boyish face. In his mid-thirties, he's Z guys my age don't know how to handl plains, "because they didn't grow up o grandfather was a farmer, and his fath outside Tchula. Willie has been in years old, when he would chop cott his school clothes. Later he tried jo fish plant, but since finishing high time. He's married now, with three

As Zack's most trusted employ of pulling the planter. I climb up the passenger seat. As I slam the

When we've completed the first pass and worked our way back up to the road, Zack is waiting for us. Bounding out of his pickup without bothering to turn off the engine, he drops to his knees and gingerly digs in the row with his penknife until he uncovers a couple of the blue seeds. His expression lightens. The depth and spacing seem right, and he tells Willie to continue while he tries to get the IH repairman on his cell phone.

Zack's fourth hand, Ben, rumbles up on his John Deere tractor. He's finished dragging and has changed that equipment for a set of heavy metal rollers. Wearing close-fitting sunglasses and a black do-rag, Ben seems hard and muscular. With a coffee complexion and a broad face, he appears to be nearly forty. But Ben is a talker, as I discover when I climb into the jump seat to ride with him for a while. He was born up North, he tells me, and came to Tchula a couple of years ago because of a woman. "It's all right here" is the extent of his enthusiasm for the place. But as we sit together in the glass cab, Ben proceeds to make his views known on the present administration, the war in Iraq, and other issues of national and regional concern.

When the slower-moving planter has enough of a head start, Ben puts his tractor in gear and follows with the roller, breaking up the remaining clods and tamping the soil over the seed. The resulting rows are about six inches high, with flattened tops. The blackbirds see the difference from the air, and now they swoop down to see whether anything edible has been turned up by the morning's activities.

By lunchtime, the first field has been planted, and the crew moves beyond the turn row, the narrow strip of land left vacant so machinery can get in and out of the field. The soil here is drier, lighter in color. The clods are also noticeably larger than in the ice cream land down the way, Zack says because he made the mistake of tilling when it was too wet. The men repeat the same process of dragging, planting, rolling. Because this field isn't as naturally rich, they fill the planter's auxiliary hoppers with a sulfur-based fertilizer the size and shade of smallish lentils. Again the tractors pursue each other over the flat ground, and by early afternoon this part too is sown.

Now Zack casts a practiced eye heavenward. The sky is streaked with the high, wispy clouds known as mare's tails, which he tells me may indicate a change in weather. And he doesn't like how the breeze has been picking up all morning. "'Wind out of the southeast is good for neither man nor beast,'" he recites.

He knows there isn't enough daylight left to finish seeding his property near Horseshoe Lake today. He'd like to push on and accomplish as much as possible, but he doesn't want to get the parcel half planted if there's going to be a heavy rain. A shower won't make any difference, but if the storm is severe, it could keep him out of the fields for days, by which time the sown portion might have sprouted. He can't afford to have the same acreage at various stages of development, requiring different dates for spraying and maybe even for picking. For the rest of the season he could be in the awkward and expensive position of having to move his machinery to the same field twice in order to complete a single task. And the situation would be made worse by the fact that Horseshoe is several miles from the rest of his holdings—a considerable distance for a slow-moving, diesel-scarfing tractor. Zack considers the sky again, then decides to take a chance. He radios the men, tells them to shift the equipment to Horseshoe, and to begin planting there after lunch.

———•———

Late in the afternoon, I make the twenty-five-mile drive from Tchula back to Yazoo City. As I recross the quiet Delta, I find myself mulling over Zack's reprimand of Charlie. Though the incident was brief and perhaps already forgotten by both of them, I can still hear Zack's preemptory tone and see Charlie on his hands and knees in the dust. I suppose one could put it down to the usual tensions that flare up between employer and employee everywhere. But here in the Delta, things are rarely that simple.

Zack's biggest headache, he's told me, is finding reliable workers. "If I had good help, I could cope with the rest of it. If I had people who would show up on time and do their work and do what I tell them to do, oh man, farmin' would be a dream." But sometimes his hired hands don't show up, sometimes they need to be bailed out of jail, sometimes they spot Zack's truck in downtown Tchula and jump on the running board to plead for a salary advance, which, more often than not, he grants. Far from the straightforward association he would like, his relationship with some of his workers is messy and seems suffused with shared resentment and distrust as much as mutual need. But these complications are nothing new. Even more than the story of machines, the history of American cotton has been the story of labor, especially the shifting methods used by southern planters to guarantee enough workers in the fields. At first, landowners solved their need for hands in the most direct, brutal way imaginable—they bought them.

Slavery came to North America virtually with the first British settlers, and by the end of the seventeenth century the practice had spread throughout the colonies. Though there were a few early critics, most people didn't question the morality of slavery until the mid-1700s, when Enlightenment concepts such as natural rights and human dignity inspired Europeans and Americans to take a more skeptical look at society. During the Revolutionary War, the irony wasn't lost on English author and wit Samuel Johnson that every third colonist was a slave. "How is it," he asked, "that we hear the loudest yelps for liberty among drivers of Negroes?"

Most signers of the Constitution were slaveholders. Thomas Jefferson elected not to manumit his servants even on his death. "We have the wolf [slavery] by the ears, and we can neither hold him, nor safely let him go," he rationalized. "Justice is in one scale, and self-preservation in the other." George Washington also owned slaves, and his attitude is revealed in these instructions to his overseer: "Every labourer (male and female) does as much in the 24 hours as their strength, without endangering their health, or constitution, will allow. . . . If the Negroes will not do their duty by fair means, they must be compelled to do it."

Rather than putting an end to slavery, the Constitutional Convention suggested that it be allowed to die a gradual death. And in the early years of the Republic, the practice did seem to have reached its natural limits. Most wealthy urban northerners owned house slaves, and the large farming estates of New York, New Jersey, and Pennsylvania employed slave labor. Yet slavery was not central to the northern economy, which was dominated by family farms and increasingly by industry, and in 1804 New Jersey became the last state above the Mason-Dixon Line to mandate eventual abolition.

In the Upper South, factors such as exhausted farmland, falling tobacco prices, and the unprofitability of rice and indigo caused a shift away from large plantations and toward smaller farms growing a variety of crops. As a result, planters in Virginia, Maryland, and parts of North Carolina found themselves with a surplus of slaves to feed and clothe. Though rice cultivation sustained the demand for slave labor in the Carolinas and Georgia and sugar plantations spurred the slave market in New Orleans, in the 1790s, slavery was confined to a relatively narrow band along the southern coast. By 1800, the price of a field hand had fallen to half of what it had been twenty-five years earlier. A number of southern states even enacted laws encouraging owners to free their slaves.

The rise of cotton changed all that. As demand for the fiber surged in the early 1800s, mill owners in Great Britain and New England looked to the South to satisfy their requirements. Cultivation expanded westward to Georgia, Alabama, Mississippi, Louisiana, and Texas, and cotton became the only American crop whose production doubled in each decade from 1800 to 1860. At the start of the nineteenth century, the United States produced fewer than 100,000 bales of cotton; by the outbreak of the Civil War, that figure had increased to 4 million bales, or nearly 2 billion pounds, representing three-quarters of the world's harvest. By then, cotton was the United States' chief product, accounting for more than half of exports and paying for 60 percent of all imports. With the fate of the world's manufacturing nations in their grasp, southerners believed themselves invincible. "No power on earth dares . . . to make war on cotton," South Carolinian James Henry Hammond famously bragged on the floor of the U.S. Senate in 1858. "Cotton is king."

With the expansion of cotton came the need for more hands to plant, hoe, and pick it. Since laboring on a plantation was not the first choice of free men, landowners relied on slavery. The importation of slaves had been outlawed in 1808, but in the antebellum years the trade in human beings became a huge business within America's borders. Between 1790 and 1860, an estimated 1 million persons of African descent were transported from states such as Maryland and Virginia, the majority to work the cotton plantations of the Deep South. At the beginning of the nineteenth century, nearly 75 percent of American slaves lived between the Delaware and Savannah Rivers; by the start of the Civil War, that figure was less than 40 percent. By 1860, the Union included fifteen slave states, stretching from Delaware to Texas. That same year, there were 3.9 million slaves, nearly 13 percent of the population and far more than in the rest of the New World slave nations (Brazil, Cuba, Puerto Rico, and Dutch Guiana) combined. It's uncertain whether slavery would ever have died of its own accord, but the bargain had been struck. Without King Cotton, slavery would not have taken hold so firmly in the Deep South, and without slaves, there would have been no cotton plantations.

In Mississippi, it wasn't until the early 1830s, only after the soil in neighboring states and the surrounding hill country had become depleted, that white settlers began to push out the native peoples and settle the Delta. (Indeed, by 1860, only 10 percent of the Delta was cleared for planting, and even by 1900 that figure was just 30 percent.) From the beginning, there were huge disparities of wealth here, springing not just from the greed of the property owners but from the character of the land itself. The same rivers that had formed the Delta had to be tamed before the soil could be cultivated, and the same rich earth that was a boon to agriculture had given rise to dense forests that had to be cut. Only those who were already rich—and were prepared to risk their fortune in an isolated, unforgiving wilderness—came to the Delta to establish plantations. Including the expenses of clearing and draining land and acquiring slaves, animals, equipment, and other necessities, the cost of creating a thousand-acre plantation circa 1855 was $150,000, or nearly $3 million in today's dollars. Much of that money was spent on slaves. By 1840, there were more blacks in Mississippi than there were whites. By 1850, slaves in the Delta outnumbered free men by five to one, in some areas by nearly fifteen to one.

Eager to recoup their huge investment, Delta planters were known for driving their hands especially hard. As one proprietor put it, "Land has to be cultivated wet or dry, negroes to work, hot or cold." But even after clearing forests and constructing levees, the early Delta planters were by no means assured of success, due to two factors as potentially ruinous as they were unpredictable—drought and floods. Still, the marriage of cotton and slavery created fortunes for many. Mississippi became the country's leading cotton producer,

with 387,000 bales annually, or about 90,000 tons, the great majority of which originated in the Delta. By 1860, the state was harvesting nearly a quarter of all the cotton grown in the United States,
and Natchez was said to boast more millionaires than any other city
in America. If it had been a separate nation, the South would have
been the fourth richest country in the world on the eve of the Civil
War, ahead of France and Germany.

But even as the southern states were amassing great wealth,
their economy was not modernizing. Per capita income in 1860
was only 73 percent of that in the North. On antebellum plantations, slaves generally represented the bulk of their owners'
wealth, appraised more highly than the land and everything else
on it. When planters had excess cash, they would invest in more
property and more slaves; although this may have made good
short-term sense in light of the booming cotton market, it left
little capital for building railroads and factories. Before the Civil
War, though the South had 42 percent of the nation's population, it could claim only 18 percent of its industry. As a result, the
region imported two-thirds of its clothing and other manufactured items from the North and exported the lion's share of its
cotton there for milling. Northern production of cotton cloth
jumped from 4 million yards to 308 million in just twenty years,
and the city of Lowell, Massachusetts, produced more cotton
cloth than all the southern states combined.

Even after the North abolished slavery, it continued to profit
from the practice—as it had from the start, when ships from New
England participated in the African slave trade and when many
northern exports such as lumber, fish, grain, livestock, and rum

were exchanged for slaves to work the southern plantations. Slave-grown cotton still filled the New York docks, and the millions of dollars' worth of food and factory goods that the North shipped southward each year were paid for mostly with cotton. Northern bankers and commodities brokers also made fortunes from the cotton trade, and by extension from the slavery that supported it. "Our whole commerce except a small fraction is in the hands of Northern men," complained an Alabama businessman. "Financially we are more enslaved than our negroes."

Beginning about 1830, the Protestant religious revival known as the Second Great Awakening intensified the moral argument against slavery. Abolitionism gained new force, and under growing pressure to justify the practice, southerners adopted increasingly strident arguments in its defense. Many touted slavery as more humane than the North's expanding capitalism. One correspondent went so far as to argue in the popular journal *American Cotton Planter and Soil of the South* that it was the ideal system of social organization: "In all countries, where 'peculiar' institutions like our own do not exist, there is a conflict—a constant unremitting struggle for the mastery between *capital* and *labor* . . . which not unfrequently . . . [results in] 'strikes,' mobs, bloodshed and revolution. . . . But is there no remedy for this state of things? . . . We answer yes . . . [in] a system of labor such as the South is blessed with—a system which proclaims peace, perpetual peace, between the warring elements. Harmonizing the interest betwixt capital and labor, Southern slavery has solved the problems over which statesmen have toiled and philanthropists mourned from the first existence of organized society."

The two-thirds to three-quarters of white southerners who didn't own slaves also endorsed the practice. Slave labor may have depressed their own wages and standard of living, but it was the undeniable basis of the southern economy. Besides, slavery guaranteed less affluent Caucasians that someone else would occupy society's bottom rung. The practice provided not only the economic but also the social linchpin of the South, the hallmark by which both southerners and outsiders defined the region. Over the first half of the nineteenth century, as cotton spread slavery throughout the Deep South, the "peculiar institution" became the central, viciously disputed issue in American life.

Exacerbating the crisis between North and South were the vast western lands to be settled and added to the Union as either slave states or free. The issue had come to the fore as early as 1803 with the Louisiana Purchase, and for five decades Congress had tried to smooth it over with a patchwork of legislative compromises. After vicious guerrilla warfare broke out between pro- and anti-slavery factions in the Kansas Territory, it seemed increasingly unlikely that the country would be able to resolve its bitter sectional rift peacefully. In May 1856, after Charles Sumner of Massachusetts delivered a polemic against "The Crime of Kansas" in the U.S. Senate, he was beaten nearly to death on the floor of the chamber by Congressman Preston Brooks of South Carolina. "Has it come to this," challenged the New York Evening Post, "that we must speak with bated breath in the presence of our Southern master? . . . Are we to be chastised as they chastise their slaves? Are we too, slaves, slaves for life, a target for their brutal blows, when we do not comport ourselves to please them?"

North and South had come to tread decidedly different social, economic, and political paths. As a Savannah planter phrased it, Yankees and southerners had been "so entirely separated by climate, by morals, by religion, and by estimates so totally opposite of all that constitutes honor, truth, and manliness, that they cannot longer exist under the same government." And underlying this schism—beneath the reliance on agriculture and the rejection of industrialization, beneath the battle for the new western lands, beneath the institution of slavery and the illusion of noble aristocracy—lay cotton, the seed from which other regional disparities grew. When Republican candidate Abraham Lincoln was elected president in 1860 on a platform of halting the spread of slavery, southern states didn't wait until Inauguration Day to begin announcing their secession.

Recognizing King Cotton as their most potent weapon economically and diplomatically, the new Confederate government brandished it toward England, where cotton textiles were now the most important industry. Britain obtained three-quarters of its fiber from the southern states, and without it, Senator James Hammond had boasted, England "would topple headlong and carry the whole civilized world with her, save the South." In March 1861, on the eve of war, the Confederacy sent envoys to London to appeal for intervention, then launched a boycott of cotton exports to force England's hand. Diplomats were also dispatched to Paris, where Napoleon III was eager to reclaim the New World empire that Napoleon I had sold to the United States. But the French needed British naval support; if the English could be persuaded, France most likely would act as well.

Though the British upper classes were generally sympathetic to the aristocratic South, the government was reluctant to assume the risk and expense of another conflict with the United States. There was also widespread resentment of the Confederates' voluntary embargo of cotton, even though record crops in 1859 and 1860 had created a glut in English warehouses and mills. It wasn't until summer 1862, when British inventories had fallen to a third of their usual level, that the economy began to suffer. Still, English factory workers tended to support the free-labor North against the slaveholding South. Predicted riots by idled mill operatives never came to pass, although three-quarters were either laid off or put on short hours. Then cotton inventories began to improve the following spring, as countries such as India, Egypt, and Brazil increased production.

After September 1862, when Lincoln's Emancipation Proclamation couched the war in terms of human liberty, it became even more awkward for England (which had abolished slavery in its own colonies in 1833) to justify intervention. And after Confederate losses at Gettysburg and Vicksburg the following July, the South's military fortunes were indisputably on the ebb. At the same time, a series of European grain failures made England more dependent on Union imports, causing wags to crow that King Corn had trumped King Cotton. When it became clear that England and France would not join their cause, Jefferson Davis expelled the British and French consuls from Confederate territory.

Desperate for cash and supplies to maintain the war, the South ended its voluntary boycott of cotton. But the Union had initiated a coastal blockade in April 1861 to prevent Confederate fiber from being exchanged in friendly ports such as Bermuda and Havana. With an average of 150 ships at any given time patrolling the South's 3,500-mile coastline, the northern navy at first intercepted only about one in every twelve of the agile blockade runners. But starting in summer 1862, when most of the South's principal ports had been either captured or put out of service, the blockade proved more effective. By 1864, one in three of the runners was being halted, and over the course of the war about 1,500 were captured. Though some 8,000 successful runs were made through the blockade, the South managed to ship out only half a million bales of cotton during the war, compared to 10 million in the last three years of peace.

With labor shortages and other wartime disruptions, and with more land in desperately needed food crops, Confederate cotton production dropped steadily throughout the fighting, from about 4.5 million bales in 1861 to 1.6 million in 1862, 450,000 in 1863, and 300,000 in 1864. Cotton manufacturing was the largest industry in the North, as in England, and virtually every Union cotton mill was forced to close during the war, laying off more than 100,000 workers. But other businesses thrived. Woolen mills saw their sales double, thanks largely to contracts for army uniforms. Shoes and leather goods, the North's second largest industry, also prospered, as did arms makers, wagon factories, and iron and coal producers, among others. By 1864, Union industry had actually grown by 13 percent over 1860, despite the shuttering of its most important component.

The Confederacy outlawed the sale of cotton to the North, but after Union troops captured the Mississippi Valley in 1862, smuggling became commonplace. The "mania for sudden fortunes made in cotton," wrote Charles A. Dana, managing editor of the *New York Tribune*, "has to an alarming extent corrupted and demoralized the [northern] army. Every colonel, captain, or quartermaster is in secret partnership with some operator in cotton; every soldier dreams of adding a bale of cotton to his monthly pay." Mississippi planter James Alcorn reported seeing forty bales displayed for sale on a riverbank, with some fifty bidders in attendance, and he himself sold ninety-five bales for more than $15,000 in U.S. currency and gold. By March 1864, an average of five hundred bales of contraband were passing through the Mississippi River port of Vicksburg every day.

In the Delta, the worst of the fighting took place in 1862 and 1863, as federal troops laid siege to Vicksburg. There were numerous skirmishes, widespread property destruction, and frequent confiscations of food and animals by both sides. Confederate troops routinely burned cotton to keep it from the Yankees, while Union soldiers seized all the fiber they could find. Fully understanding their stake in the conflict, slaves took advantage of the universal disorder and began to assert their independence, especially as Union forces approached. Many deserted, and those who stayed behind were, in the words of James Alcorn, "no longer of any practical value in this vicinity."

Then came peace, and with it defeat and devastation. The plantations that had been the basis of the southern economy were in ruins, the fields fallow, the levees breached. With wartime shortages driving the price of cotton to nearly three times its prewar level, planters were desperate to make the land productive again. But after Emancipation, they could no longer order their former slaves into the fields with a bullwhip. A more insidious means of binding the workers to the land would be required.

———•———

As I continue my drive from Tchula, where Zack is planting his cotton, I see that the thin, high mare's tails have given way to a brooding overcast. Within the hour, the lowering sun is obscured by an advancing wall of leaden clouds, rendering the spring day prematurely dim. Later that evening, we're watching television in Yazoo City, when a tornado warning for our area crawls across the bottom of the screen. The town's tornado siren blasts and alarming gusts rattle the old frame house. On the ten o'clock news from Jackson, the storm is the lead story, and we learn that the wind lifted the roof off a public housing project just a few blocks away from us. That same night—the night after Zack sowed his cotton outside Tchula, the night after he decided to partially seed his remote field at Horseshoe Lake, the night after he decided to take a chance that the coming storm wouldn't be too severe—tornados also touch down in Holmes County. In Tchula, it rains five inches.

FOUR

The Hands

Zack sleeps fitfully the night of the storm, even though the rain ends long before bedtime. The next morning, he's up before dawn. While the coffee is brewing, he parts the blinds in his rented house and peers outside. In the half-light he can see Tchula Lake lapping several feet higher up the backyard's grassy slope. He slips on his blue jeans and boots and walks stiffly across the road. By now the sky has brightened, and he can make out the long, unerring rows of his cotton field. But as he looks over the ordered expanse, he sees nothing but narrow silver ribbons running all the way to the river. Zack is not immune to the haphazard beauty of cotton farming, but this morning he can't appreciate the shimmer of standing water. "Shit," he exhales, the word coming out as two syllables in his Mississippi drawl. There will be no planting today or tomorrow or the day after. Worse, Zack knows what this silty land is capable of after a soaking rain, especially when it's followed by intense heat. The fine soil particles can bind together to form a crust impenetrable to cotton seedlings. Later that morning, the April sun rises big and red and fierce.

Zack drives to the "chemical place," which is what he calls the seed store. Several of his neighbors have congregated in front of the coffee pot, including the man who rents him the land at Tchula. Zack tells them of his fears, but the other farmers, who are in the same position with their own fields, resist.

"You can't make no money replantin'," somebody chides. "You're jumpin' out there too quick. Give it some time."

"I ain't got time," Zack shoots back. "I got to get out there and get with it. I know I'm goin' to lose the seed money, but I can't just say the hell with it." The property owner is inclined to agree. He used to farm that land himself, and he knows the soil at least as well as Zack does.

Zack checks his fields a hundred times over the next few days. The beans are already an inch tall; they'll be fine. The cotton on the Yazoo and at Hyde Park was first to be planted, and it had already poked its two tiny leaves through the soil before the storm. It's withstood the rain well, and will even benefit from the soaking, as long as the sun continues to shine. In the Tchula field and the part of Horseshoe planted the afternoon of the deluge, things are different. The pale green shoots should be visible by now. But all Zack can see is brown Mississippi soil, turning progressively paler as it dries out from the rain. He knows there's a problem, he says, just the way a mother knows when something is wrong with her child.

Zack pulls his white pickup off the road and into the turn row. He throws the truck into park, then, not bothering to close the door or turn off the engine, jumps out and drops to all fours. With the truck's door alarm pinging, he takes his penknife out of his pocket and jabs at one of the rows. The hard soil lifts up in a flat clod. Digging a little deeper, he uncovers one of the cotton seeds. It's sprouted, but instead of pushing its way through the earth, the white stem is bent double, broken. Zack prods a little farther up the row and finds the same thing. "Damn," he mutters.

He straightens himself and stands for a long time in the hot sun, considering the planted but barren field and doing some calculations in his head. Then he climbs into the pickup and drives to the chemical place, where he learns that some seed has been returned by a farmer who ordered too much. Zack tells them to set aside two tons for him, enough to replant 450 acres, or nearly half his crop. The seed will cost about $5.50 a pound, or better than $22,000; with diesel and extra labor, he figures the cost of replanting at close to $30,000.

The next day, Zack has his new seeds, the 444, the 5599, and the Triple Nickel, all coated bright blue and redelivered in their green hoppers. By now the fields have dried out enough to withstand the weight of the equipment. First the crew runs the cultivator, a tractor-pulled rig with metal tines, to loosen the crust and dig up the doomed seedlings. They follow with the planter, which Zack calibrates to bury the seeds a little deeper this time, in consideration of the rapidly warming weather. Then come the rollers to flatten the tops of the rows and settle the seeds into the soil.

Whereas the first planting was undertaken in a hopeful frame of mind, this time Zack works resolutely, "sulled up," he says, like a traveler forced to retrace territory he thought he'd already put behind him. "But it's all part of the game," he rationalizes. "It's frustratin', but the Good Lord must have had other plans for me. He must have wanted me to replant, because it wasn't my fault, it was the weather's fault. There was nothin' in the world I could have done anythin' about." Still, he can't stop thinking about how he could have spent that $30,000.

By now his neighbors have also conceded the necessity of replanting. But Zack got out there first, and he's glad he did, since his cotton will have more time to establish itself before the summer heat. He works his crew particularly hard in the coming days, meeting them before sunup to get the equipment ready, then staying in the fields until it's too dark to tell the rows from the middles. The men grumble over the long hours, but they're happy for the extra pay. Even Charlie shows up on time. Working sixteen-hour shifts, eating lunch in the tractor cabs, they get the 450 acres of cotton replanted in three days. Several mornings afterward, Zack walks across the road from his rented house and stands in front of his field. He won't really relax until the cotton is picked, some five months from now, but as he gazes out over the land he permits himself a smile. In the early light, he can just make out a welcome green fuzz on his resown acres.

Zack's sons Heath and Keath also had to replant some of their cotton, though not as much as he did. Partnering on 2,400 mostly leased acres, the twenty-eight-year-old brothers have about half their land in cotton, with the rest in soybeans, corn, and rice.

Zack is proud they managed to outmaneuver the full brunt of the storm. He's proud of his sons, period. Of medium height, like their father, but wiry, the twins look clean-cut, even preppy, in their blue jeans and the long-sleeve oxford cloth shirts they favor. Quiet and conscientious, they exude a seriousness out of proportion to their years. They love farming and hope to end their careers doing exactly what they're doing now. That's why they try to add some new land every year, to expand their operation and stay competitive. That's also why they've suggested going into partnership with Zack, which would give the three of them a total of 4,100 acres to plant.

The twins often ask the advice of their father, whom they call either "daddy" or "sir." But they also have their own ideas about farming. It's not so much that they have a different philosophy, Heath explains one day. It's just that sometimes they have different ideas about how to achieve a particular goal. There's no one right method, he allows, and every farmer seems to have his own way of doing things.

Heath and Keath are close even for identical twins. As business partners, they work well together, anticipating each other's moods and unspoken signals. Usually their division of labor is loose, with each doing whatever needs to be done on that particular day or at that particular moment. But they also agreed early on that each would have a primary area of responsibility, Keath for the cotton and Heath for the soybeans. They've taken on a lot for their age, jointly running a multimillion-dollar operation in a notoriously risky enterprise, and there's stress to be managed. Sometimes, Keath admits, they fuss at each other just to blow off some steam.

Since their bachelor days, the twins have been not only business partners but next-door neighbors on some of their rented
land outside Tchula, just up the road from where Zack has been
staying since his separation from Pam. Not wanting to be both-
ered with the much bigger house next door, Heath took the modest ranch built by local planter J.P. Love in the 1960s. Keath
moved into the grander place. Put up by J.P.'s son Jimmy, it's a
brick McMansion with white columns flanking the entrance,
stone lions guarding the iron gate, a circular drive, wide lawn,
and a swimming pool overlooking Horseshoe Lake. Jimmy died of
a heart attack the same year the house was finished, and now
both places belong to one of Heath and Keath's principal landlords, Kenny Goodman. Before Keath moved in, the big house
had been vacant for a long time, and there were cows grazing beside the algae-covered pool. Though the imposing residence may
have embodied Jimmy Love's planter fantasy, neither Heath nor
Keath has any such illusions. Like their father, they're "farmers,"
and like him, they drive Ford pickups. Their wives have organized a Friday-night dinner club, but the brothers would generally prefer to be in the woods with a rifle.

Heath and Keath have already accomplished a lot. But eighteen months ago, they thought their farming careers might be
coming to a premature end. That October, their landlord Kenny
Goodman was charged with illegally collecting more than $11
million in federal price support payments, in the largest farm-
subsidy fraud case in U.S. history. Indicted along with his wife,
Stephanie, his brother Gray, and their accountant, W. Benoit
Holloway, Goodman was charged with forty-two counts stemming

from his involvement in sixty-four corporations and fourteen part-
nerships, which for the past three years had made him the biggest
recipient of federal farm aid in the state of Mississippi.

Because a portion of the government subsidy is determined by
the number of partners, not by the number of acres farmed, the
more members in a partnership, the more money they may be
eligible for. To protect against abuse, the law requires that each as-
sociate contribute land, capital, or equipment as well as either his
own labor or active management of other workers. But Goodman
was charged with recruiting outsiders as dummy investors, then
creating false minutes for the various companies to give the impression that they were legitimate business concerns. Of the $11.2
million paid, Goodman reportedly kept $1.9 million, while the
rest went to the other partners.

Goodman pleaded not guilty, and his trial was scheduled for
the following spring. The Killebrews waited anxiously through
the intervening months, hoping the case wouldn't end with the
government seizing his property and turning the twins off those
impossible-to-replace acres and even out of their houses. Along
with many people in the area, the family likes the man and describes him as generous. One day Heath expresses the oft-heard
comment that Goodman got a raw deal, that he'd just grown too
big too fast and that the government was trying to knock him
down to size. There's also a widespread feeling in the Delta that
Goodman didn't do anything different from anybody else, only
on a larger scale, and some farmers are said to worry that the case
will direct attention to their own business dealings. In Goodman's hometown of Yazoo City, some readers complained that the

local paper, the *Herald*, was trying to whitewash the case through underreporting, while someone else threatened the managing editor for supposedly giving it too much coverage. Then last June, just before the trial was to begin, Goodman's accountant pleaded guilty and agreed to testify against the other defendants. As part of the plea bargain, he was sentenced to seven months in prison and ordered to pay a $20,000 fine.

When the trial finally started in the federal courthouse in Jackson, U.S. Assistant Attorney John Dowdy's hourlong opening statement laid out the situation in stark simplicity. "This case is nothing but lies," he told the jury. "Lies to get the money and lies to cover it up." On an oversize pad he wrote: "Lies + Lies + Lies = $11 million."

In its own opening argument, the defense countered that Goodman was only trying to help farmers who had gotten into financial trouble, so they wouldn't lose their land and livelihood. Then the prosecution began calling its witnesses, starting with a trio of employees of the USDA Farm Service Agency, whose testimony stretched on for three days.

On the third day, the remaining defendants entered a surprise guilty plea. Kenny Goodman admitted to just one of the forty-two counts against him, while his brother pleaded guilty to misprision of a felony—having knowledge of a crime but failing to report it. Under the terms of the deal, the charges against Kenny Goodman's wife were dropped. He remained free on $10,000 bond, and sentencing was delayed until November to give him time to harvest his crops.

The next five months were even harder for the Killebrews, as they waited to learn what would become of Goodman's holdings.

In the end, he was sentenced to five years in prison and ordered to pay $11.2 million in restitution. But Heath and Keath were lucky: The government was prevented from seizing Goodman's property in Tchula, and the brothers weren't forced out of their homes or off their land.

———•———

As April continues and his replanted cotton grows, Zack rides alongside the fields in his pickup, worrying over the plants like a first-time father. Are all the seeds germinating? Do the shoots look good and strong? And not only does he inspect his own fields, he examines his neighbors'. To Zack, the identification of a farmer with his crop is so complete that one day, passing through an unfamiliar corner of the county, he asks, "Who's that over yonder?" meaning, "Whose cotton is that?" As we drive, Zack will note whose plants are growing well, whose are weedy. "God dawg, that's some pretty cotton," he might say. Or, "Somethin's wrong with that there cotton. It's all chewed up like it's been run over by a truck." He looks for telltale ridges and ruts in other farmers' fields, and he's not above getting out of his cab to dig up a seed on a cousin's property to check how deep it's been planted. As we leave a neighbor's impeccably neat farm, Zack tells me, "That's how you want your shop to be. You feel good drivin' up on your place when it's lookin' like that."

Another day we're in the truck when Zack looks at the sky and says, "It's gonna do somethin'. You look at those mare's tails. There's some wind up there, buddy." Sure enough, the spring rains return in the coming days. As I make my daily drive up the Delta to work with Zack, the trees on the horizon are bathed in a misty greenish gray, and the cars speeding toward me are streaming long tails of vapor. By now the replanted seedlings are up. Cotton comes along slowly at first and needs sunshine to grow. Zack wishes the skies would clear, but more than ten inches of rain fall in the month of May.

The Delta's warm, humid climate is a paradise for weeds, and this year's wet weather produces a bumper crop. First come the heart-shaped leaves and blue, trumpet-like flowers of the morning glories. Next to appear are the broad-leafed prickly sida (also known as teaweed) and the grasses—signal grass, barnyard grass, crabgrass, nutgrass, and worst of all, Johnson grass, which author James Agee claimed "takes hell and scissors to control."

None of these pests is a stranger to Zack, and neither are the cockleburs, careless weed, velvetleaf weed, or many of the two hundred other botanical pests that cotton is prone to. The difference this year is their luxuriance. In places the Johnson grass is already poking higher than the crop. Doing nothing is not an option, because the young cotton can't compete with the fast-growing invaders for light, water, and soil nutrients. If left unchecked, an infestation of weeds early in the season will stunt the plants and drastically reduce their yield.

When Zack began farming, the only way to get rid of weeds was hoeing, bitterly hard work performed in the merciless Delta heat. First a tractor towing a cultivator would pass through the field, getting as close to the cotton plants as possible and tearing up the weeds in the middles. Then an army of hand laborers would move systematically down each row, gently chopping away the remaining weeds. Before leaving for his job at John Deere, Zack would drive stakes into the ground, marking out for his workers the area he expected them to finish that day; then on his way home that night he would drive by the field to inspect their progress.

"Chopping is a simple and hard job," James Agee describes, "and a hot one, for by now the sun, though still damp, is very strong, hot with a kind of itchy intensity that is seldom known in northern springs. . . . It is done with an eight-to-ten-inch hoe-blade. You cut . . . with a short sharp blow of the blade of which each stroke is light enough work; but multiplied into the many hundreds in each continuously added hour, it aches first the fore-arms, which so harden they seem to become one bone, and in time the whole spine."

Today all this work is accomplished with chemicals, especially Roundup. Since its introduction by Monsanto in 1974, Roundup has become the world's herbicide of choice. The active ingredient, gylphosate, disrupts a plant's ability to synthesize an enzyme called EPSP synthase, which is needed to manufacture proteins. When sprayed on green, growing leaves, the liquid is absorbed and the plant begins to wither and die in a few days. Transported internally down to the roots, the chemical also kills those tissues, preventing the plant from regenerating. Roundup's nonselectivity used to pose a problem for farmers, since spraying the herbicide over a growing crop would have killed the desired plants along with the weeds. But in 1997, Monsanto introduced Roundup Ready cotton, which is genetically modified to resist the effects of the herbicide. (There are also Roundup Ready corn, soybeans, and other crops.)

So now when farmers like Zack buy their cottonseed, they pay Monsanto an additional "technology fee" of about $2.00 per pound, which is a license for the genetic engineering that went into it. (That's why the seed to replant cost Zack about $5.50 a pound instead of $7.50, because he didn't have to pay the technology fee a second time.) The farmers also agree not to save any seeds from year to year, since they're only renting the technology, not buying it outright. For Monsanto the arrangement has been a bonanza, since the company profits from the licensing fee as well as the enhanced market for its herbicide. But Zack has benefited as well. Roundup is relatively cheap (about $7.00 an acre) and easy to use, sprayed right over the cotton. By controlling weeds, Zack gets a better yield from his crop. And because the chemical reduces tilling, it also saves him time and fuel, as well as reducing soil runoff. So even with the technology fee, Zack still comes out ahead. In fact, over 90 percent of cotton grown in the Delta is now Roundup Ready. More than any other recent innovation, the herbicide has changed the way the crop is grown.

Not that Roundup is perfect. For one thing, it's not effective on all kinds of weeds, which means that Zack sometimes has to spray with other chemicals as well. And although the problem hasn't been reported in Mississippi yet, farmers in other states have found that certain weeds are developing a resistance to the herbicide, leading some to believe that Roundup, at least in its current formulation, is not a permanent solution.

Roundup is also controversial among environmental groups. Greenpeace has expressed concern that the product is killing endangered wild plants. Some critics fear that cross-pollination between genetically modified and wild species could create "biological pollution," including superweeds that are impervious to herbicides. A researcher at the University of Pittsburgh believes that Roundup poses a hazard to amphibians. And there have been reports of Roundup proving deadly to other species, including insects and birds, and, when accidentally swallowed, to humans.

But the U.S. Environmental Protection Agency considers glyphosate relatively safe when used as directed. For one thing, the enzyme it disrupts is not present in animals or humans. Because it binds to soil particles, the chemical does not move easily through the ground, and it is broken down comparatively quickly into harmless components by bacteria, water, and sunlight. The agency considers glyphosate noncarcinogenic and has placed it in category III, Low Toxicity (with category I the most toxic and category IV the least). For humans, the EPA finds, the greatest threats are eye and skin injuries due to splashing while pouring or mixing.

One afternoon I drive to the Delta Research and Extension Center in Stoneville to talk to Charles E. Snipes, Ph.D., whose job is to conduct research and advise local farmers on how to control weeds. Snipes is among those who think that, beneficial though Roundup has been, farmers have come to rely on it too heavily, and that other herbicides should be reintroduced to the antiweed arsenal. He believes that herbicides in general have gotten a "big black eye" among the public, and unfairly so. "We are not polluting the world with these chemicals," he says. For one thing, herbicides are safer now than they've ever been, thanks to stringent oversight by the EPA. He estimates that a new product costs between $50 and $70 million to develop and market, and at those prices chemical companies can't afford to waste resources on herbicides that might not win EPA approval. Today's chemicals break down faster in the environment and are less toxic to people and other species. They're also applied in much smaller doses than in the past, instead of a pound or two per acre, perhaps now only an ounce or two—the equivalent of a packet of sugar being sprinkled over a football field. "If it weren't for these herbicides," Snipes says, "we would not be able to afford the labor costs to produce enough food for a growing population. These herbicides are terribly important."

Zack doesn't need a scientist to convince him of Roundup's benefits. In May he generally fills his spraying rig with the chemical and goes after the burgeoning weeds. But this year, that's not possible. With all the rain, the fields are too waterlogged to take the weight of a tractor. So Zack calls his neighbor Ricky Davidson of Southland Flying Service and arranges for him to put down the Roundup. Zack would have preferred to save Southland's application fee of a little over three dollars an acre. "But I know one thing," he confesses. "Without that airplane, we'd be up the creek this year."

Crop dusters saw their first widespread use in 1922, when U.S. Army planes treated 3,000 acres of cotton for boll weevils in Tallulah, Louisiana. From early on, dusters also worked the Mississippi Delta. The world's first commercial crop-dusting operation was Huff Daland Dusters, the company that later grew into Delta Airlines. Founded in 1924 in Macon, Georgia, the company moved the following year to Monroe, Louisiana. In 1929 the airline made its first commercial flight, from Dallas, Texas, to Jackson, Mississippi.

The first dusters tended to be cheap army surplus biplanes, and the early pilots made Wild West cowboys seem like milquetoasts. But today the field belongs to 2,200 professional agricultural pilots flying sleek, single-wing planes. Ricky Davidson's father bought his first aircraft, a Boeing Steerman biplane, for $800 and rigged the chemical hopper himself. Ricky began working with him at age eleven; by eighteen he had his pilot's license and the next year his ag certification. Now Southland's two planes are chrome-yellow Turbo Thrush S2R's, with a fifty-four-foot wingspan and the cockpit set rakishly aft of the wings. The placement gives the plane an aggressive, modern appearance, but it's not for looks; it's to make room for the tank holding liquid chemicals, which have replaced the powders that gave the early dusters their name. The nose is sharply pointed, but this isn't for show either. Because the engine is so light, only 350 pounds, it has to be placed farther forward to offset the heavy tank, the way a skinny kid has to lean farther out on a see-saw to balance a pudgy playmate. The engine's light weight also means that the plane can accommodate double the payload of the older models, or four hundred gallons of chemicals. And a side benefit of the pointed nose is that the aircraft is more aerodynamic and faster, with a top working speed of about 140 miles an hour.

The engine that makes all this possible is a turboprop, the same type used on small airliners. Representing about $350,000 of the plane's $650,000 cost, the turboprop is basically a jet engine; but instead of expelling the gases into the air to produce thrust, the turbine is used to turn a propeller. A regular jet engine would generate too much speed for the type of flying that crop dusters do, but the turboprop captures the advantages of that design while preserving maneuverability. Not only are the turboprops lighter and more powerful than the old radial engines, they're much simpler, which means they're easier to maintain—and less prone to midair breakdowns. Both Ricky and Southland's other pilot, Bill Crandall, have had to make forced landings after radial engines cut out on them, and Bill once broke his back in a crash. But they've never had a problem with the turbine.

The engine isn't the only high-tech device on the planes. Whereas old-timers had to rely on their eyes and memory to tell them where they'd already dusted, pilots now have satellite-directed global positioning systems to track ground speed, remember where they've been, and show exactly when to begin releasing chemicals from the stainless steel tube mounted under the wings. Limited time and expensive fuel make efficiency even more crucial for pilots than for tractor drivers, and like farmers working the land, Ricky and Bill plot their route to make as few turns as possible. They also work their way upwind to avoid flying through their own chemical spray, even though the Thrushes have sealed, air-conditioned cockpits.

Since the rate of application can now be as little as three gallons of solution for every acre, the pilots can cover quite an area before having to land and fill up again. That, combined with the aircraft's speed, means that on a good day a single plane can treat 2,000 acres of farmland. The turboprops are so efficient that they've reduced the number of crop dusting businesses, as well as the number of planes flown by the companies that remain.

A surprising amount of physical strength is necessary to handle a crop duster's stick, especially when the plane is fully loaded. And even with GPS, the pilot is constantly occupied in the cockpit, watching the light bar mounted on the fuselage to see when to release the chemicals, monitoring wind speed, making sudden changes in altitude, watching for electrical wires. With the Delta's dwindling population, power lines are less numerous than they used to be, but they still pose the greatest threat to the low-flying dusters, since the slender wires are impossible to see from the air. Ricky and Bill know this patch of Delta well; in fact, they've never taken their Thrushes more than twenty-five miles from home. Even so, every time they fly, they clip in the cockpit a photocopied map of the field they're working, with all electrical lines marked in heavy black ink. Complacency or a moment's inattention can spell disaster. So they try to take Sundays off to help them stay sharp, especially in the busy season of March and April, when they apply herbicides to winter grasses; June, when everyone is spraying for plant bugs and worms; and September, when they put down defoliant to strip the leaves from the cotton plants.

About twenty-five years ago, Zack thought to become an ag pilot to supplement his farming income. For two years, he took lessons whenever he could, logging sixty-five hours in the air and even soloing. But one day, as he was taking off alone in the cockpit, his wheel strut clipped the top of a pecan tree beyond the runway. The plane seemed to stop in midair, he recalls. It regained momentum, but he'd ripped the top out of the tree, and a limb four feet long and several inches thick became lodged in his landing gear. Though Zack managed to bring the plane down, dragging the branch behind him, the thought of his wife and family put an end to his flying career. "I just figured I wanted to live a little longer," he says.

Ricky and Bill still use the strip where Zack had the near accident, located on the edge of his Tchula field. Known locally as the "airport," it's owned by Southland, whose planes are the only ones using it on a regular basis. There's a corrugated metal building that serves as a combination hangar and office, and next to the runway there's a shed where workers mix the chemicals and fill the planes' hoppers. Actually there are two runways side by side, one concrete and the other grass. The concrete is used for takeoffs, when the tanks are full and the planes are heavy; the wider grass one is used for landings. Not only is it easier to hit, it saves wear and tear on the tires.

Nationally, crop dusters apply up to a quarter of all agricultural chemicals. But a relatively new piece of field machinery, the RoGator, has taken some business away from the planes. Like its less versatile predecessor the highboy, the RoGator is a spraying rig built far enough off the ground that it can be driven right over the tops of plants, letting farmers treat their own crops all season long. But the RoGator's six-figure price tag has discouraged many smaller operators, including Zack. Also, farmers who irrigate with pipe laid in their fields can't use land-based sprayers, and even RoGators are useless when rain makes the ground too wet to drive over. But the dusters' principal advantage, Ricky says, is speed. They can put down chemicals quickly, which can be critical in the case of an insect infestation or a rapidly closing weather window. Seventy-five percent of Southland's business is spraying cotton, and most of its clients are now larger operations.

The major players have too much territory to cover by ground, and there are fewer small growers in business. As Bill says, echoing a statement often heard in the Delta, "The little farmers are getting bigger, or they're getting out of it."

———•———

Abruptly, spring balminess yields to summerlike heat. The cotton is eight or nine inches tall, and its branches are showing their characteristic whorled pattern, tracing a spiral as they grow around the plant's central stem. The first leaves to sprout are on the bottom of the plant and have a roundish shape. Those farther up the stalk have three large lobes, a little like maple leaves but with an underside of fine white hairs. From the road, the plants have a scrubby look, and you can tell the cotton by its dusty, yellow-green color, in contrast to the more compact shape and the darker, bluer leaves of the soybeans.

Now that the crop is well under way, Zack has only two full-time hands, Willie and Johnny, though Charlie and Ben still fill in from time to time. One Thursday, a payday, Zack is expecting Ben to come and plant some late-season beans. He doesn't show, and Zack's irritation builds as the morning passes. Finally, at eleven-forty, Ben pulls up in a cherry-red Cadillac, wearing a cherry-red suit over a black nylon T-shirt, with a cherry-red beret. Clearly he hasn't come to plant soybeans. Leaving the car running, Ben goes into the shop to pick up his pay for work he did earlier in the week. Zack heads in after him, and when he comes out, he's sputtering.

Why didn't he come to plant the beans? I ask.

"He don't have to give a reason," Zack answers testily. "He just don't show up if he don't feel like it."

The other part-timer, Charlie, often serves as the lightning rod for Zack's frustrations as well. One afternoon Charlie is bush-hogging, towing a cutter attachment behind his tractor to trim grass around the margins of the fields, when he runs over something. The cutter uses the tractor's power takeoff, and the obstruction instantly freezes the blade. But the PTO keeps spinning, and the shaft snaps with a *thunk*. The accident will require a troublesome repair, which Zack ascribes to Charlie's carelessness. He chews him out, then walks away shaking his head and muttering that he needs to find some decent help.

It is a lament heard since Emancipation. After the Civil War, planters simply hired back their former slaves at wages averaging from $8 to $15 a month, plus housing and food and sometimes clothing and medical care. When some balked at tilling the same land they had worked as slaves, many landowners restricted their freedom of movement, forced them to sign labor contracts they couldn't read and didn't understand, and reverted to the old methods of violence and threats of violence.

Assuming the presidency after Lincoln's assassination in April 1865, Andrew Johnson set such lenient terms for the readmission of the Confederate states that the new southern governments were controlled by former secessionists with little interest in protecting their erstwhile slaves. In November of that year, Mississippi (along with the other Confederate states) began to enact the notorious Black Codes. Despite the cynical title of one of the measures, An Act to Confer Civil Rights on Freedmen, and for Other Purposes, the laws were intended to limit, not protect, black rights, including the ability to rent land, participate in the legal system, carry weapons, drink alcohol, and even conduct religious services. Bragged one Alabama landowner, "The nigger is going to be made a serf, sure as you live. It won't need any law for that. Planters will have an understanding among ourselves: 'You won't hire my niggers and I won't hire yours.' Then what's left to them? Whites are as much the masters of blacks as ever." Still, blacks didn't prove quite as tractable as freedmen as they had been as slaves, and they wrested whatever small concessions they could from the landlords, refusing to work on Saturday afternoons, for instance, and withholding labor contracts unless certain demands were met. Lamented the *Vicksburg Times*, "Emancipation has spoiled the Negro."

Johnson's lax policies, which made the Black Codes possible, were rejected by congressional Republicans. In 1867, Congress passed the first Reconstruction Act, later supplemented by three others. Declaring the existing governments illegal in the former Confederate states, the law divided the region into five military districts, called for new state constitutional conventions, and stipulated ratification of the pending Fourteenth Amendment as a prerequisite for reentering the Union. The amendment, which took effect the following year, conferred on the freedmen citizenship and equal protection under the law.

As they met the requirements of the Reconstruction Act, the former Confederate states reentered the Union, with six admitted in 1868 and four, including Mississippi, in 1870. That same year, the Fifteenth Amendment extended the franchise to blacks, who began to play an important role in state and local politics throughout the South. In Mississippi, four former slaves were elected sheriff in the predominately black Delta, thirty freedmen were sent to the state legislature, four went to the state senate, and one, Hiram Revels, became the first black man ever elected to the U.S. Senate.

The prospect of being governed by their former slaves was more than southerners could contemplate. As Charleston matron Emma Holmes confided to her diary, "Oh, my God, when will the dark days end which seem enveloping our stricken land in deeper and deeper gloom, day by day. . . . The ferocious Black Republicans [are making the region] an almost unlimited military despotism, holding the South as conquered territory—by granting 'universal suffrage' to the negro who now is the curse that clogs us at every step. . . . Despair is laying its icy hand on all."

Among the many groups formed to oppose freedmen's progress during these years, the most prominent and longest-lived was the Ku Klux Klan, which was founded by Confederate veterans in Tennessee as "an institution of Chivalry, Humanity, Mercy and Patriotism." It's been estimated that over a three-year period, the Klan murdered 20,000 southern blacks, in addition to beating untold numbers and destroying uncounted homes and churches. To curb Klan activity, Congress passed legislation in 1871 that allowed persons to sue in federal court if they believed their civil rights had been violated. But the measure failed to end the brutality, and Republican influence began to wane in the South. In Coahoma County, Mississippi, 1,300 votes were cast for Republicans in 1873; in 1875, there were only 230. In Yazoo County, 2,500 votes for Republicans were recorded in 1873; two years later, just seven.

For most northerners, the task of reconstructing the nation had always been more pressing than the plight of the freedmen, and congressional Reconstruction policies had never enjoyed tremendous popularity. During the 1870s, national resolve eroded in the face of southern recalcitrance, the death or retirement of Republican leaders, disclosures of government corruption, and a general yearning for reconciliation. Then in 1873 the country plunged into the worst economic depression it had ever experienced. Beginning with the collapse of overextended railroads, the panic soon spread to banks and brokerage houses. Credit dried up, factories furloughed employees, and over 10,000 businesses failed. Agriculture suffered more than industry, and the South more than the North. Between 1872 and 1877, the value of farmland plummeted and the price of cotton fell nearly 50 percent. Planters were forced into bankruptcy, along with the merchants who depended on them, and southerners' income fell to one-third that of their northern counterparts. The hard times helped sweep away Reconstructionist governments in the South, and after Republican Rutherford B. Hayes won the White House in the disputed election of 1876, he withdrew the last federal troops from the region.

In the ensuing "Redemption," southern whites moved to reclaim their previous advantage. Given the postwar labor shortage, a primary goal was keeping the freedmen in the fields. The landowners didn't prove adept at managing free labor, and the former slaves, paid a set fee, had little incentive to work at full capacity. Still, most planters preferred the wage system for the undisputed control it conferred over the land and the harvest, as well as the inarguably inferior position in which it placed the laborers. But freedmen pushed for another arrangement, and tenant farming became widespread.

In its simplest permutation, the tenant paid the landowner an annual fee, provided his own seed, fertilizer, equipment, and other essentials, and assumed all responsibility for the crop— essentially what Zack and most other Delta farmers do today. The freedmen generally preferred this system, because although it entailed the highest risk, it also offered the widest measure of independence and the greatest potential for profit. But few former slaves had the cash or credit to pay rent and buy supplies before the cotton was in. And recognizing that leasing land might offer former slaves the quickest means of bettering themselves, many whites took exception to this practice, paying lower prices for black farmers' cotton, shunning neighbors who rented fields to freedmen, and sometimes even burning down the landlords' houses. For all these reasons, outright leasing was relatively limited among blacks.

The most infamous form of tenant farming was sharecropping. Under the typical arrangement, known as "working on halves," the tenant supplied only the labor, while the property owner furnished the house, seeds, animals, fertilizer, and all necessary tools, with the two parties theoretically dividing the crop equally. For most freedmen, sharecropping was an attractive alternative to working for wages, since it implied that they were in partnership with the landowner, sharing in the profits of a successful harvest—

which they dreamed would one day allow them to buy land of their own. White owners, not surprisingly, played down the aspect of collaboration and tended to view the sharecropper as a tenant paid in kind rather than cash.

Though not their preferred system, sharecropping offered landlords certain advantages, as it laid some of the risk for the harvest on the tenant, who would receive no payment for a failed crop. It also had the benefit of reducing the flow of very tight cash. Though the landlord advanced some money during the season, no wages were paid till the cotton was made and ginned, if then. The fact that the settlement came after the harvest also meant that workers were effectively bound to the land until the end of the year. Sharecropping quickly became established in the Delta, and strong cotton harvests in the late 1860s and early 1870s encouraged both owners and tenants to feel satisfied with the compromise they had made. Maintaining control of the land, whites had preserved their political, social, and economic prerogatives, while blacks had achieved a degree of autonomy and at least the hope of betterment.

Because it limited the landlord's risk, sharecropping became even more appealing during the Panic of 1873, and the practice expanded. In the 1880s, cotton recovered along with the rest of the economy, but rather than restrict sharecropping, the boom only served to entrench it further, since landowners were especially eager to ensure enough workers in the fields. In the Mississippi hills, many poor whites found themselves sharecropping. In the Delta, by 1890 more than 42 percent of the land was cultivated by sharecroppers, and by 1910, 92 percent of the region's farms were operated by tenants, 95 percent of whom were black.

By 1930, fewer than 3 percent of African American farmers in the Delta owned their own land. That year throughout the South, there were 8.5 million tenant farmers spread across the ten principal cotton states.

For the overwhelming majority of tenants, sharecropping wasn't the hoped-for first rung to landownership and social advancement. It was in the landlords' interest to keep tenants poor and dependent, so as to bind them to the cotton fields. As a Georgia man explained, "The Nigger, when poverty stricken . . . will work for you—but as soon as you get him up and he begins to be prosperous, he becomes impudent and unmanageable."

Living conditions were notoriously harsh for sharecroppers, white and black. Shoes were scarce, and clothes were often sewn from flour sacks. Food consisted mainly of flour, cornmeal, dried peas, canned beans, and a little pork, supplemented with vegetables from the garden. Housing was far substandard, and as late as 1900, a third of all southern black farm families were still living in one-room cabins.

The necessity of tending the cotton meant that sharecroppers' children attended school irregularly, if at all. And though an underemphasis on education would hamstring the southern economy for decades to come, this fact worked to the landowners' short-term advantage. As Mississippi Governor and U.S. Senator James Kimble Vardaman, "the Great White Chief," put it early in the past century, "Educate a nigger, spoil a good farm hand."

Having seen their hopes for a piece of their own land slip away, sharecroppers soon lost much of their prized independence, as landlords instituted systematic management based on an industrial model of close oversight and cost control. Sharecroppers wanted to work as big a plot as they could handle in order to maximize potential profits. But to allow for easier supervision and to limit tenants' earnings, the average Delta sharecropper's field was reduced to just over twenty-three acres. And virtually every decision, such as when to plant and what time to start and quit each day, was dictated by the owner. Most merchants who advanced seed and other essentials insisted that only cotton be grown, since that cash crop was considered the best protection for their investment. As a result, the fortunes of a huge swath of the South rose or fell according to the harvest of and market for one staple. Southern farming was slow to diversify, and even though the region was primarily agricultural, it imported food from northern states.

Sharecroppers objected to their loss of control, though they were helpless to stop it. Nate Shaw was the pseudonym of Ned Cobb, an Alabama activist for tenants' rights whose story is told by Theodore Rosengarten in his book *All God's Dangers*. "It's stamped in me," Shaw said, "in my mind, the way I been treated, the way I have seed other colored people treated—couldn't never go by what you think or say, had to come up to the white man's orders. . . . Showin me plain he ain't got no confidence in me."

Crop lien laws made the growing cotton the property of the landowner, which meant the tenant couldn't use it as collateral for loans to support himself until the harvest. His needs for food and clothing during the season were met either by independent merchants or by the plantation store, both of which often sold shoddy, overpriced goods at interest rates of up to 35 percent, all of which had to be recouped as part of the end-of-year settlement. In addition to the inflated prices and usurious interest rates, fraudulent bookkeeping was widespread.

The sale of the cotton offered even greater opportunities to cheat the illiterate, innumerate sharecropper, in the weighing, pricing, and accounting. Not only did such ruses enrich the land-lord at the expense of the tenant, they served to tie the worker to the land. Many times the year-end settlement wasn't sufficient to discharge the tenant's accumulated debt, and in that case the law prevented him from signing a new contract with another landlord. Sharecropping thus often became a form of peonage.

"Cotton," wrote James Agee, is "the symbol of [the sharecropper's] privation and of his wasted life." It is the crop "in which the landowner is most interested; and it is . . . the one of which the tenant can hope for least, and can be surest that he is being cheated, and is always to be cheated. . . . It has the doubleness that all jobs have by which one stays alive and in which one's life is made a cheated ruin . . . as if the plant stood enormous in the unsteady sky fastened above them in all they do like the eyes of an overseer."

William Faulkner also excoriated sharecropping, referring to it in his novella *The Bear* as an "edifice intricate and complex and founded upon injustice and erected by ruthless rapacity and carried on even yet with at times downright savagery." Even apologists such as Mississippi planter and author William Alexander Percy recognized the ease with which tenants could suffer at the hands of owners: "Share-cropping is one of the best systems ever devised to give security and a chance for profit to the simple and the un-skilled," he wrote in his classic memoir *Lanterns on the Levee*. "It has but one drawback—it must be administered by human beings to whom it offers an unusual opportunity to rob without detection or punishment. The failure is not in the system itself, but in not living up to the contractual obligation of the system—the failure is in human nature."

Given the bitter realities of life here, it's not surprising that the tortured howl known as the blues arose in the Mississippi Delta, among the first American blacks born in nominal freedom. From the beginning, slaves had enriched mainstream culture in areas such as music, dance, language, religion, folk crafts, and food, and their descendants would contribute sermons, books, poems, and plays to the American canon. But the blues were in a category all their own. The practitioners had no real training, and rather than Western musical traditions, they took their inspiration from African forms such as the field holler, a kind of call-and-response work song. Intense and hypnotic, the blues sounded different from anything heard before, thanks partly to its raw vocal style and the so-called blue note, a flattened, wavering tone obtained by bending the guitar's strings. The lyrics sprang directly from the musicians' own experiences, giving vent to despair and cynicism, brooding over subjects such as poverty and death, and dealing with love and sex with a gritty new frankness. The first original musical form in this hemisphere since the days of the Indians, the blues would inspire virtually all American music, including ragtime, jazz, swing, gospel, rock and roll, and all their permutations. And as those styles came to dominate popular music, not just in the United States but around the world, there wouldn't be a place on earth within reach of a portable radio that was untouched by these humble sounds of the children of slaves.

Not surprisingly, many blues songs were about escape, from love gone bad, from poverty, or from planting crops on other men's land, as in this one by Big Bill Broonzy:

Plowhand have been my name,
Lawd, for forty years or more.
Lawd, I've did all I could
Tryin to take care of my so-and-so.

I ain gon raise no mo cotton,
I declare I ain gon raise no mo corn.
Gal, if a mule started runnin away with the world,
Oh, Lawd, I'm gon let him go ahead on.

I wouldn't tell a mule to get up,
Lawd, if he set down in my lap.
Lawd, I'm through with plowin,
That's what killed my old grandpap.

I done hung up my harness, baby,
Lawd, I done throwed my overalls away.
Lawd, now good-bye, old plow,
Big Bill is goin away to stay.

With international trade in cotton cloth booming before the turn of the century, labor-short landowners began to recruit African Americans from the nearby Mississippi hill country, where their forebears had also worked as slaves. By 1890, Delta blacks outnumbered whites seven to one, in at least one county by more than fifteen to one. Between 1900 and 1930, the black population of the Delta would increase by almost another 50 percent. Yet as more blacks arrived, whites feared a mass uprising by the exploited sharecroppers, just as they had once feared a rebellion by their slaves. In 1889, in the Delta county of Leflore, a black man named Oliver Cromwell received death threats for organizing sharecroppers, and local blacks retaliated with a letter warning that they had the support of "3,000 armed men." Fearing an insurrection, local whites hunted down and murdered two dozen blacks, including a young girl who was beaten to death.

But whites recognized an even greater threat to their hegemony than armed revolt, and one that required no violence or illegality—black suffrage, which had been guaranteed by the Fifteenth Amendment in 1870. Now that planters had secured the large labor force their cotton demanded, they systematically began to neutralize the political power implied by those same workers. In 1890, Mississippi called a constitutional convention with the express purpose of disenfranchising African Americans, through establishment of a poll tax and a literacy test as requirements for registering to vote; blacks were also excluded from juries, which were selected from voter registration rolls.

The new constitution had the desired effect. In the elections of 1888, 29 percent of adult black male Mississippians had voted; in the elections of 1895, their participation was virtually zero. Similar documents were written throughout the South, and for Nate Shaw, like other blacks, this wholesale disenfranchisement had deep implications. "As I growed to more knowledge, I thought that was as bad a thing as ever happened—to disenfranchise the nigger. Tellin him he didn't have a right to his thoughts. He just weren't counted to be no more than a dog." Meanwhile, in 1896 the infamous Supreme Court decision in *Plessy v. Ferguson* upheld the doctrine of Jim Crow (the name comes from a stock character in nineteenth-century minstrel acts), and the ruling would make racial segregation an unquestioned part of southern life for the next three-quarters of a century.

Despite disenfranchisement and segregation, planters found that control over their black workers wasn't complete. Sharecroppers still created labor problems by migrating from plantation to plantation when possible, in search of better working conditions or just to demonstrate their independence. Later they would seek to escape the South altogether. But for workers who became too troublesome, whites had the ultimate weapon—lynching, which they employed on the average of twice per year in the Delta between 1900 and 1930.

By the turn of the twentieth century, Delta planters had achieved their goal of an abundant but politically neutralized labor force. As the U.S. Census of Agriculture concluded in 1900, "The plantation system is probably more firmly fixed in the Yazoo-Mississippi Delta than in any other area of the South. The fertile soil and climatic conditions favorable for cotton raising, together with the large negro population, make the plantation the dominant form of agricultural organization in the Delta." In 1910, the Illinois Central Railroad, seeking to recruit more planters, could rightfully claim, without hint of irony or shame, "Nowhere in Mississippi have antebellum conditions of landowning been so nearly preserved as in the Delta." With white domination restored, the burgeoning region was once again a cotton kingdom presided over by a nobility of wealthy landowners.

Thirty years ago, when I first came to the Delta, the landscape was still punctuated with the relics of sharecropping—unpainted shacks with their roofs stove in and their flimsy porches buried in kudzu, faded plantation stores with names barely legible above the doors through which so many tenants had passed in anticipation and dread. Though you have to look a little harder to find them now, these memorials remain.

Here it sometimes seems that cotton has touched every family, every past. Zack's mother, Ethel, grew up the child of sharecroppers working both the Delta and the Mississippi hill country, along with her sister (my wife's mother) and their eight siblings. It was a childhood of unimaginable privation, when your earliest memory was watching your father slide down the side of the chicken coop and die of a heart attack at the age of forty-three. When your all-time favorite Christmas present was a plain rubber ball. When you spent blazing afternoons chopping cotton in ground so hard and dry that each strike of the hoe would jolt your teeth. You'd subsist on rabbits and squirrels, biscuits with "doodle gravy" concocted from lard, water, and flour, with a tomato thrown in if you were lucky enough to have it. You wouldn't see a loaf of bread until you were grown, and you'd be twenty before you graduated from high school because the cotton, and survival, had to come before education.

Growing up, the descendants of these white sharecroppers, like my wife, considered their forebears' past a badge of shame. Half a century further on, safely in the middle class, they find their relatives' way of life alien, unimaginable. "My mother was a sharecropper," they might say in the wondering tone used for some distant nightmare: "My mother had polio," or "My father was on Iwo

Jima." Yet for some of Zack's workers, children of the Delta's black sharecroppers, what's so striking is not how much has changed over a generation but how little. Like their parents, they may still derive their small living from working cotton on white men's land—and no longer even as tenants, but as wage workers, having reverted to the practice rejected by their predecessors. The early black sharecroppers at least had the hope of one day buying some land of their own. But the currrent generation is more apt to share the later tenants' view that for them, nothing is about to change for the better.

And it often does seem that not much has altered in the Delta in the past half century. Just as it was cotton that spread the essential inequality of slavery throughout the Deep South, it was cotton and sharecropping that perpetuated racial disparity for decades. Today the much-loathed system is gone, but its legacy persists in places like Tchula, forming an unspoken and perhaps unrecognized bond between the descendants of white and black tenants. For those who have become employers, like Zack, this inheritance comes in the struggle to find reliable workers, which he considers his greatest impediment. For his part-time hands like Ben and Charlie, its effects are seen in the broken-down trailers clustered along the highway, in idle hours spent congregating at the convenience store, in intangibles like resignation and despair. Meanwhile, many of those with the ability and the means continue to leave the Delta, realizing the escape that their sharecropping forebears yearned for nearly a century ago.

PART II

Summer

FIVE

The Water

Zack lifts his hand, signaling for his employee Willie to raise the backhoe's loader. The big scoop jerks a few inches higher. The wheel hub, chained to the loader, is now too far above ground, and Zack and I can't lift the heavy tire onto the waiting lugs. Zack motions downward, and the scoop drops. But the backhoe wasn't engineered for such sensitive maneuvers, and now the hub is too low again. Breathing heavily, Zack straightens up in the 90-degree sun.

It's four o'clock on a hazy Wednesday in early June, and we're in Zack's cotton field outside Tchula, trying to change the flat tire on an irrigation pivot. Almost all of Zack's fields are outfitted with these giant sprinklers, steel trusses fifteen feet high and sometimes more than half a mile long, supporting a six-inch-wide perforated pipe. One end of the pivot is connected to a wellhead and the other is free to swing in a huge arc, bumping over the rows of cotton on outsized, deep-grooved tires. When I ask Zack how you keep the pivot from running over the plants in its path, he replies matter-of-factly, "Well, you don't."

With a price tag of more than $100,000 apiece, the pivots are costly insurance policies. And like any policyholder, Zack would prefer not to have to use them. For one thing, the energy needed to operate them is expensive. Those with diesel pumps burn five gallons of fuel per hour; the ones powered by electricity are no less expensive to run, and the enormous arms can take up to a hundred hours to complete a full circuit in a single field. Also, the pivots are only a stopgap, since they can't put down enough water to match a good, soaking rain. But being able to supply the cotton with moisture when it needs it can be critical, and the man from the irrigation company has pages of figures showing how the pivots pay for themselves in improved crop yields. He's given Zack a proposal for putting one on the Yazoo parcel, and though Zack believes the numbers, he's having doubts about the six-figure price tag.

What Zack would truly like to see in his fields right now is water pooling after a cloudburst. As we drive by, sunlight reflects hot and white off the cotton leaves, and clouds of coffee-colored silt billow up behind pickups on the unpaved roads. It's not that the heat bothers the cotton. The plant likes it hot, and it prefers its soil well drained. But young cotton needs water, about four inches in each of its first three months, while it's still putting down its fibrous side roots and the long, tough taproot that will eventually penetrate the earth three times as deep as the plant is tall. If it doesn't get enough moisture, the stems will grow short and spindly, and the plants will drop leaves and produce fewer bolls. So Zack spends considerable time early in the season making sure that the cotton has the moisture it needs. The issue is especially critical this year, he tells me, because the heavy rains of April and early May have encouraged the plant to grow shallow roots and thick, water-hungry stems.

The weather has been hazy all week, and I wonder aloud if the moisture is getting ready to condense into rain. No, Zack says, it can't rain if there's haze in the air; it has to clear first. Like much of Zack's weather lore, this bit of information baffles me, but I've come to trust his pronouncements. Have I noticed that the wind is out of the north? he asks. As a matter of fact, I haven't. A northerly breeze may feel good on human skin, Zack explains, but all it's doing for the cotton is robbing moisture from the ground.

Yesterday morning we parked the pickup beside the Tchula field and hiked the quarter mile through the rows to the irrigator's fixed end. Before Zack can use the pivot, he has to connect it to a well, which has been sunk about a thousand yards away in the center of the field. The pivot's control panel is mounted on the superstructure, inside a tall red metal box. Opening the lid, Zack fiddles with a couple of switches, then presses the black plastic toggle marked RUN. We listen for the sound of water gushing from the well and into the wide pipe. Nothing. He rocks the toggle back and forth. Still nothing.

At first Zack thinks the main switch has been turned off at the power pole beside the road. But when he pushes another toggle, the pivot's giant arm jerks into motion; it isn't electricity that's lacking, but water. We trudge back to the pickup to get some tools, then head for the pump box. But this time, rather than make another trek through the field, Zack drives the truck through the drainage ditch and right up the middles, over several rows of cotton that have been overdosed with herbicide and are turning brown anyway.

At the wellhead, he takes a voltmeter out of his toolbox, opens the pump's gray metal cover, and tests the connections. The needle jumps: It's getting power. The problem could be as simple as a loose wire, or the pump's point might need to be lifted from deep inside the well and replaced. Zack is supremely confident with mechanical things, but electricity is something else again. He stares at the tangle of colored wires, then slams the box closed.

On the truck's cell phone, he raises the irrigation company repairman. He has some other calls to make this afternoon, the man says, but he'll try to stop by before the end of the day. Zack isn't happy thinking about his cotton going without the water it needs. And he's irritated, because he had the pump's electrical system repaired just this spring, after a mouse gnawed through the underground power cable. Why didn't the company make sure everything was working before they left?

While he's waiting for the technician, Zack drives Keath to one of the twins' fields. The earth here is especially parched, owing to its composition. In addition to stones and plant matter, soil is made up of tiny particles that have eroded from rock. The smaller the particles, the more total surface area for water to cling to, and the more moisture the soil can absorb. The smallest particles (less than .004 millimeters in diameter) are called clay, and they hold water tenaciously, becoming sticky when wet and baking hard when dry. The next-largest particles are known as silt (from .004 to .0625 millimeters), which also bond well to water. The largest particles, sand (from .0625 to 2 millimeters), are too big to hold moisture effectively, which is why this type of soil is notoriously dry.

Nutrients also adhere well to tiny bits of clay and silt, but soil benefits from some sand, which lightens the texture and creates pockets to hold air and water. The soil called loam has a balance of all three—clay, silt, and sand—and makes an ideal medium for growing plants. But in the Delta the loam leans toward clay and silt, whose smaller particles were transported more readily by the flowing water that created the region. Their high concentration is also what makes the earth here so fertile.

Cotton likes a reasonable amount of sand, because the lighter texture makes it easier to push down those deep roots. But owing to some ancient accident of geology, this field of the twins' is unusually sandy. A pivot wouldn't do any good here, since the moisture would drain into the earth before the plant roots could soak it up. Fortunately the land's consistent, gentle slope makes it possible to irrigate with a more effective technique—a controlled flood. To this end, Heath and Keath have unrolled a long, soft polyethylene tube along one edge of the field, running perpendicular to the rows and resembling thousands of sky-blue garbage bags glued end to end. There are small holes punched every couple of feet, and when water is pumped from the ground, it fills the fat hose and shoots out the openings, eventually washing down to the far corners of the field. Pipe irrigation is much cheaper than building pivots, and Zack would happily have used this same method, except none of his parcels has the required grade.

However, the lightweight poly tubing has sprung leaks in several places, and as we drive up we can see unintended waterworks splashing in the sunlight and irrigating the road instead of the cotton. The solution is simple. Keath has a bag of orange plastic plugs, about the size and shape of baby pacifiers, and when we reach a puncture, he jumps out of the truck and inserts one into the poly. Because the plug is wider than the hole, the plastic stretches over it, creating an instant seal. In ten minutes, all the leaks are stanched.

Afterward Zack and I ride by the Tchula field, but there's no sign of the repairman. When there's no answer on the man's cell phone, Zack leaves a message for the company's owner, and we head toward the field at Horseshoe Lake, where another pivot problem is waiting. Like the pump in Heath and Keath's sandy field, this one is powered by a diesel tractor engine. Last week it blew a head gasket, and the cylinder head was sent up the Delta to Indianola to be rebuilt. In the meantime, this cotton hasn't been getting any irrigation either. But the part has just come back, and Zack is anxious to put it in and get the system running. This pivot is strategically placed on the border between his field and one planted by a neighbor, which allows the two to share expenses and maintenance, including this repair. Early this morning, Zack and a couple of the neighbors' hired hands hoisted the heavy header into place, and they made plans to meet again to reassemble the engine.

This piece of land at Horseshoe Lake used to belong to Zack's parents. When the house where he grew up burned to the ground several years ago, it was replaced by a mobile home occupied by Zack's aunt and her grown son, who writes computer programs. Turning left at the trailer, we drive down an unpaved road until we come to the pivot. Zack steers the pickup onto the grass next to the engine, where three men are already working.

Rob is in charge of the group. In his forties, he is a powerfully built, good-looking black man who projects an easy authority. His helpers are two older black men, Jim and Sam. As we pull up, Zack gets a call on his truck's cell phone, and I climb down alone. Holding a piece of paper printed with the engine schematic, Rob is directing Jim, who appears to know motors, while Sam lends a hand where needed.

Zack ends his phone call and walks over to the engine. The others have just finished bolting on the head, and there's some question about the order in which the valves are to be adjusted. Reading to Zack from the schematic, Rob seems confident about how it's supposed to be done. But Zack, who admits he hasn't re-placed a head in a good number of years, remembers something different. He goes to the truck, calls the shop that rebuilt the part, and double-checks. When he comes back and admits that he was wrong, I think I see a look of satisfaction flash across Rob's face.

While the others are reassembling the motor, Zack and I drive to Tchula to pick up an oil filter, a case of coolant, and other parts needed to finish the job. Located on a side street off the main highway, the store is presided over by a tall, fiftyish woman with curly white hair. Zack tells me she's only been working there a few years, but she rattles off inventory numbers like a veteran. And in her smoke-thickened voice, she talks like a trucker. She clearly enjoys the banter with her customers, and I suspect that the more she likes you the harder a time she pretends to give. She doesn't let up on Zack from the minute he enters to the moment he leaves.

Back at the pivot, we find that Rob and the other men have left to get some lunch. For another hour or so, Zack continues putting the engine back together, reconnecting the diesel line and the electric system. I serve as his helper, holding parts and passing tools. Afterward my hands are as greasy and my tractor cap is as streaked with sweat as Zack's. Still, I can't help feeling like an imposter as we drive up the road and walk into Mr. T's Sports Bar & Grill, a local lunch spot filled with farmers. Although I'm a resident of Mississippi and I pay taxes and vote here, every time I open my mouth, I betray my urban, Yankee origins. Once when I stopped at a country store to buy a sandwich, the owner asked, "You from around here?" I knew what he really meant was, "You're not from around here, are you?" But today, the counter lady hands me my unsweetened iced tea before I've even ordered it, and I feel like a regular.

Mr. T's is the kind of place where the lunch special, with dishes like fried pork chops, collard greens, cornbread, pinto beans with hog jowls, and Jell-O pie, is apt to be sold out by one o'clock. The wide, square room has a white linoleum floor, light gray paneling, a painted plywood ceiling, and a pool table. Along one wall is a short counter with a few stools; to the left is the open kitchen. We take a seat at a table to wait for our food. Zack knows everyone, of course—the young man playing pool went to school with Heath and Keath; the fellow in the polo shirt works at the John Deere concession in Yazoo City; the slight man with glasses manages the cotton gin. While we wait for our lunch, the talk is about the heat and lack of rain. The subject is on everyone's mind, because in the Delta the weather doesn't affect just the farmers but all the businesses that depend on them, from the crop duster to the fertilizer salesman to the man who installs irrigation systems, to the stores and restaurants and all other places where people spend their money.

The only women in Mr. T's are behind the counter. With few exceptions—like the wisecracking saleslady at the parts store—Zack inhabits a purely male world during his working hours, surrounded by hired hands, his sons, other farmers, assorted salesmen and technicians, pilots, weed men, bug men, soil men. And now that he's separated from Pam, there's no respite even when he goes home. It's a masculine environment with its own customs, where certain conventions have been dropped by tacit agreement. If Zack's hands ever heard him say "please" or "thank you," they'd probably talk about it the rest of the day. This morning Sam, one of the hands on the Horseshoe pivot, said, "Mr. Zack, your temper is down," meaning that Zack is mellowing. Even so, when they screw up, the men expect to be not simply corrected, but hollered at. And the same no-frills directness holds true not just between employer and employee, or between white and black. Every interaction comes with a plainspokenness that can take the uninitiated by surprise, whether it's a good-natured ribbing delivered across the table at Mr. T's or a six-figure business proposition pitched in Greenwood's fanciest restaurant.

Another inescapable aspect of this masculine world is guns. They say that hunting is on the downswing across the United States, but I see no evidence of that in Mississippi, where every pickup seems to boast a rifle rack and every closet a camouflage suit. Each year more than 200,000 Mississippians purchase hunting licenses. A million and a half doves are killed in the state annually, along with half a million ducks, 400,000 rabbits, 300,000 deer, 150,000 quail, and lesser numbers of other creatures, including squirrel, raccoon, opossum, bobcat, frogs, geese, and crow. The limit on bobcat is five per day; on frogs, twenty-five; on doves, fifteen; there's no limit on crow. Every year a dozen or so sportsmen are also killed. Most are shot by other hunters, although occasionally someone falls out of a tree stand.

After lunch, Zack takes me back to Horseshoe, to a shed he's built on the banks of the muddy, cypress-dotted oxbow. As we stand in the shade of the building's narrow front porch, he tells me how when he was a boy his family used to build bonfires here on the shore of the lake. Then he says he has something he wants to show me. Unlocking the shed's door, he motions me inside. The interior is about ten feet by ten, paneled with handsome cypress boards. On the walls hang an American flag, several racks of deer antlers, a purloined street sign for Zack Road, and an old framed photo of downtown Tchula, with ranks of antique cars parked head-in on the unpaved street. Centered on the wall opposite the door is a gray safe, about five feet high and three feet wide.

Zack goes to the safe and turns the dial. As the thick door swings open, he steps aside to reveal the contents—about forty rifles, shotguns, and pistols, all carefully arrayed in racks and on wooden shelves. "These are my jewels," he says. "Guns are to men like jewelry is to women. It just makes me feel good to be able to hold them."

He takes out a .22 and hands it to me. "This was my first rifle. I got it when I was eleven." Another is a 1954 Winchester twelve-gauge shotgun that used to belong to his father. There's a Remington six-gauge automatic, a gift from his uncle Lawrence, which Zack used to kill his first deer at age thirteen. Now he takes only about ten of the guns hunting. The others he keeps for sentimental value, or just for looking at.

Stacked on the floor of the safe next to the pistols are a couple of boxes of shotgun shells with old-timey type. Zack lifts one of the cartons and opens the lid. "Look a here. These aren't like the shells they sell now. These have paper cartridges. They're like the ones we used to have when I was a boy." He removes one of the old shells and rubs a stubby finger over it. "Sometimes I like to take one out and just feel it," he says.

In Mississippi, hunting is still a family affair, with young sons, and increasingly daughters, following their fathers into the woods. More than the test of skill or the companionship or the love of the outdoors, I realize, it's this sense of continuity that keeps Zack and the others hunting. To sit in a duck blind or a deer stand for a few hours is to maintain a connection—to the forebears who settled this land, to departed family, to their own youth. Some might call it tradition and others might call it nostalgia, but in the end, it doesn't seem all that different from the impulse that sends cotton farmers back into the fields every spring. Inside the cypress-paneled shed, Zack replaces the old cartridge in its box, lays it in the safe, and closes the heavy steel door.

Late that same day, we see the irrigation company's truck parked alongside the Tchula field, where Zack has the problem with the electric pump. The technician, a large man drenched in sweat, is just putting away his tools. The problem was only a loose wire, he tells Zack, breathing hard from his walk through the cotton rows. Zack is relieved it's a simple fix, but he's still irritated that the service call was necessary. He doesn't want to set the pivot tonight, in case there's another problem, but at least it will be ready to go first thing tomorrow.

The next morning, Wednesday, we retrace our steps through the growing cotton. Zack is putting his feet down gingerly. He isn't used to so much walking in his pointed boots, he explains, and yesterday's hike to the pump raised some blisters. At the control box, he confidently opens the lid and presses the toggle switch. But instead of water rushing into the pipe, the only sound is the drone of a distant crop duster. He flips another switch, and like yesterday, the pivot starts its slow rotation. The problem is still with the pump.

"Of all the wop-sided, cock-sided . . ." Zack stalks off, tracing the underground pipe toward the wellhead. This time he walks not up the middles but straight across the rows of cotton. Whereas I'm careful to sidestep the plants, Zack plows through them. About a third of the way to the wellhead, he stops and sets his hands on his hips. There's water bubbling from the ground. Judging from the size of the pool, the pipe has been leaking all night. Zack wanted to see water standing in his field, but not like this. "Those sapsuckers!" he mutters.

He means the men from the irrigation company, who repaired the electric line earlier this spring. Zack thinks they punctured the water pipe running alongside but the problem went unnoticed until the pump was turned on for the season. He wades into the muddy, shin-high water and uproots a dozen cotton plants to mark the source of the leak. As we drive toward the shop, he's as angry as I've ever seen him—apparently his temper isn't down as much as Sam supposed. When he can't reach the owner of the irrigation company, he leaves an annoyed voice mail. But even as he fumes into the cell phone, Zack lifts his fingers from the steering wheel to greet the oncoming cars.

Today the preoccupation in the Delta is getting enough rain during the long Mississippi summers. But for most of mankind's tenure in the region, the far more pressing worry was too much water. In one of the earliest accounts of the Mississippi, historian Garcilaso Inca de la Vega describes a deluge that de Soto's expedition encountered. "The great river . . . came down with an enormous increase of water, which . . . little by little rose to the top of the cliffs. Soon it began to flow over the fields in an immense flood, and as the land was level, without any hills, there was nothing to stop the inundation. . . . It was a beautiful thing to look upon the seas that had been fields, for on each side of the river the water extended over twenty leagues [60 miles] of land, and [in] all of this area . . . nothing was seen but the tops of the tallest trees."

Three centuries after de Soto, as white planters and their black slaves ventured into the Delta, flooding remained a constant threat. In *Life on the Mississippi*, Mark Twain recorded a European

observer's sinister impression: "It is a furious, rapid, desolating torrent, loaded with alluvial soil. . . . It is a river of desolation, and
instead of reminding you, like other rivers, of an angel which has
descended for the benefit of man, you imagine it as a devil."

By the late 1850s, settlers had constructed 4,000 miles of
earthen levees along the lower Mississippi to protect their towns
and crops from rising water. Yet 1858–1859 brought the worst
flooding to that date, and between then and 1927 there were a
dozen major inundations. The flood of 1882 submerged 34,000
square miles—half the size of New England—and the one in
April 1922 left 20,000 homeless in six Delta counties. But it was
the Great Flood of 1927 that would be called (at least until Hurricane Katrina) the greatest natural disaster in American history
and the worst calamity to strike the South since the Civil War.

The rains began in August 1926, and as they continued into
the autumn, there was widespread flooding in the Midwest. During the last three months of the year, the Ohio, Missouri, and Mississippi Rivers were running at their highest levels ever recorded.
In Vicksburg, the river had never been measured at more than
thirty-one feet in the month of October; in 1926, it was at forty.
In December another huge storm struck the Mississippi Valley
from Montana to Tennessee. By Christmastime, Nashville and
Chattanooga were under water, and flooding had suspended railroad traffic throughout the state of Mississippi. The freakish
weather continued into early 1927, with heavy snows in the Upper Midwest and record rainfalls farther south. As the Mississippi
continued to rise, thousands of black sharecroppers were forced,
often with billy clubs and guns, into the dangerous, exhausting

work of reinforcing the levees with sandbags. Occasionally one would lose his footing and be swept into the river, but work went on uninterrupted.

By early April more than a million acres had been inundated along the river's tributaries, and 35,000 people were homeless as far north as Pittsburgh. Meanwhile the Mississippi was pressing ineluctably on its levees. On April 15 an astonishing fifteen inches of rain fell on New Orleans, filling the streets with up to four feet of water. The following day, the levee at Dorena, Missouri, collapsed, flooding 175,000 acres; levees in Missouri, Illinois, and Arkansas followed. The *New York Times* reported, "Somebody's house passed through Memphis today en route to the Gulf of Mexico. . . . In St. Louis thousands of weary men tonight continued to struggle to strengthen the levees against what threatened to be the greatest and most damaging flood in the history of the lower valley. Other thousands of men, women, and children were refugees under the care of the Red Cross."

Still the rains continued. At Mounds Landing, Mississippi, twelve miles north of Greenville, the levee made a perilous 90-degree turn, exposing it to the brunt of the current. Thousands of black workers struggled in 40-degree weather to shore up the earthen dam, but the river was rising faster than the rows of sandbags, sweeping along animal carcasses and entire trees. A two-mile-wide wall of water began to spill over the top, inundating the workers. To one of them, the edifice "felt like jelly. The levee was just trembling" under the tremendous force of the water.

At six-thirty on the morning of April 21, a break two feet wide and a foot deep appeared in a low spot of the earthworks. More workers were forced to the breach at gunpoint, but the crevasse continued to widen. According to one witness, "You could see the earth just start boiling. A man hollered, 'Watch out! It's gonna break!' Everybody was hollering to get off. It was like turning a hydrant on." Then the levee "just seemed to move forward as if one hundred feet of it was pushed out by the river."

A torrent three-quarters of a mile wide surged into the Delta, carrying twice the volume of Niagara Falls. One planter described the approaching water as "a tan-colored wall seven feet high, and with a roar as of a mighty wind." "When that levee broke," another witness reported, "the water just come whooshing, you could just see it coming, just see big waves of it coming . . . You didn't have time to do nothing, nothing but knock a hole in your ceiling and try to get through if you could. . . . It was rising so fast."

A woman who had managed to reach a surviving part of the barrier watched someone who wasn't so fortunate: "A lady was coming to the levee, had a bundle of clothes on her head and a rope around her waist leading a cow. She and the cow both drowned. . . . Just as we got to the levee we turned back and saw our house turned over. We could see our own place tumbling, hear our things falling down, and the grinding sound. And here come another house floating by. The water was stacked. The waves were standing high, real high. If they hit anything, they got it. Every time the waves came, the levee would shake like you were in a rocking chair."

The ruptures upstream took some of the pressure off New Orleans' levees, and the city's defenses held. But in the Delta there was devastation. The crevasse at Mounds Landing left nearly

200,000 people homeless and submerged houses sixty miles away in Yazoo City. Though that was the worst breach, there were dozens of others along the river. By the end of April, an area thirty miles wide and a hundred miles long was lying under as much as thirty feet of water. The flood left more than a thousand dead and three-quarters of a million people without homes, and inflicted an estimated $400 million in property damage (about $4.7 billion in today's dollars). When the water finally receded, not until September in some places, residents found everything buried in foul-smelling mud up to eight inches deep. Near Mounds Landing, the river had carved out a lake that remains to this day.

The cleaning and rebuilding went on for months. "We were tired out," wrote William Alexander Percy, who was in charge of relief efforts in Greenville. People "grabbed. Everyone wanted what was coming to him and a little more . . . everybody criticized everybody else. . . . Here and there we discovered simple undiluted dishonesty. It was a wretched period." In this climate of exhaustion and misery, relations between the races deteriorated. Black residents were furious at their forced labor on the levees and in the cleanup, and they resented the widespread discrimination in the distribution of food and other aid. Whereas whites received fresh meat and luxuries such as canned peaches, blacks were given only the most basic foodstuffs, and not much of those. Worse, they were herded into camps patrolled by armed National Guardsmen and were prohibited from leaving except with written permission of their employer.

A rash of lynchings broke out from Tennessee to Louisiana. In Louisville, Mississippi, two blacks accused of killing a white farmer were burned alive. In Yazoo City, the bullet-filled body of a black man thought to have attacked a white girl was found hanging from a tree. As John M. Barry points out in his authoritative history *Rising Tide*, the Great Flood of 1927 "shattered the myth of a quasi-feudal bond between Delta blacks and the southern aristocracy, in which the former pledge fealty to the latter in return for protection." Henceforth, landowners would find it even more difficult to hold on to their labor.

When they were eventually released from the camps, many blacks fled the South for good. The First World War had already lured about half a million African Americans northward in search of factory work. But the decade of the '20s saw a net outflow of nearly twice that number, especially to Chicago, where they hoped to find better jobs and less racial tension. Most of the emigrants left by train, inspiring the arch observation that it was the Illinois Central, not Abraham Lincoln, that finally freed the slaves. In the Delta, it's been estimated that as many as half of all black laborers migrated north in the years immediately after 1927. Always covetous of their workers, landowners were deeply troubled by the exodus. As one Mississippi politician pointed out, "Delta lands without labor . . . are as useless as an automobile without an engine."

Devastating as it was for the South, the Great Flood's effects were felt far beyond cotton country. For one thing, the disaster generated widespread admiration for Commerce Secretary Herbert Hoover, the director of flood relief, known as "the Great Humanitarian." After garnering front-page headlines for months, Hoover made a successful bid for the White House the following year.

Moreover, as the nation struggled with how to avoid a similar catastrophe in the future, Americans' idea of the role of government began to change. For decades, the Army Corps of Engineers, responsible for flood control along the Mississippi, had insisted that it was possible to contain the great river with levees alone. The deluge had proved them wrong, and it was clear that a system of floodways and reservoirs needed to be constructed to siphon off water during periods of emergency. Levees would also have to be fortified, and the course of the river would have to be straightened to speed the movement of water through the huge system. Such measures would require that some land be sacrificed, making the structures' location a problem as much for politicians as for engineers. Because of the political sensitivities, as well as the overwhelming size of the undertaking, it was decided that the federal government would assume responsibility for the river. On May 15, 1928, President Coolidge signed a package of $325 million for flood control programs in the lower Mississippi, the largest single appropriation Congress had ever made, and the most money the nation had ever spent for any purpose except the First World War.

As a result of the enormous project, years in the realization, today the threat of rising water is all but gone along the Mississippi's southern course. Yet eight decades later, the legislation's effects are still being felt in other ways. By accepting responsibility for managing the river, the federal government assumed unprecedented control over matters previously considered the province of the states. In the coming years, Americans would increasingly look to Washington to solve overarching issues such as unemployment and poverty, and within a decade, this new idea of government would culminate in the historic programs of Franklin Roosevelt's New Deal, ranging from agricultural subsidies to the minimum wage to Social Security.

It was a philosophy of expanded, activist government that some have railed against ever since, and it continues to shape policy debate today, as conservatives seek to undo decades of such programs and to redefine government in more narrow terms. Ironically, some of these voices emerge from Mississippi, a beneficiary of this first intervention and the recipient of so much federal largess in the intervening years. However the argument over these conflicting philosophies is decided, one thing is clear: The Delta is still influencing the nation's political landscape out of all proportion to its own size or population.

———•———

Late Wednesday afternoon, Zack and I drive to the Tchula field again. The irrigation company has called to say that the water line is fixed, and we're going to try to set the pivot. As we retrace our steps through the rows, walking alongside the quarter mile of elevated pipe, Zack happens to glance to one side, then stops.

"Oh, man!"

I follow his gaze toward one of the pivot's wheels. We've walked by this tire half a dozen times in the past twenty-four hours, and neither of us had noticed that it was flat. Without another word, Zack spins and strides toward the truck. Using the radio, he raises Willie, who's been spraying for insects, and tells him to meet us.

Zack speeds to the shop, an open area littered with equipment and the detritus of farming—two tractors, a backhoe, a planter, fifty-gallon drums, cases of chemicals, abandoned tools. Walking to the back, we find an oversize tire lying on its side. We stand it up and inspect it, and Zack pronounces it sound.

Willie appears towing the spraying rig, its long green arms folded upright like a referee's. Climbing down from the tractor cab, he switches to the backhoe, and when he rumbles up in front of us, we tip the bulky tire into the scoop. Then we take off in the pickup, with Willie following somewhat more slowly in the other vehicle.

At the cotton field, we carry a fat chain and a wrench out to the flat tire, and Zack sets to loosening the lug nuts. As he's finishing, Willie arrives. The only way to the pivot is through the cotton. The new wheel is too heavy to roll up one of the middles, but the backhoe is too low to maneuver through the field without brushing the foot-high plants.

"How's he going to get the tire out here?" I ask.

"I hope he's gonna drive it," Zack answers.

As I watch, Willie pulls the backhoe into the rows of cotton. When he reaches us, Zack and I bounce the tire from the bucket and roll it into position. Zack wraps one end of the chain around the pivot's wheel hub and the other around the backhoe's loader, and with both of us holding the bulky tire upright, we begin the delicate process of lining up the openings in the wheel with the lugs on the hub.

After several tries, we manage to slip the tire on, and Zack begins to tighten the lug nuts. We maneuver the old tire into the scoop, and Willie lumbers over the field in reverse. As he goes, I notice that the backing-up has partially resurrected the cotton that was flattened on the outward trip. I point this out to Zack, but he doesn't seem concerned. The plants like to be mistreated, he tells me. "Some people whoop it with a stick so it'll make more cotton. A lot of times, where it gets torn up by the tractor, it makes more bolls."

By now I realize that farmers don't share gardeners' sentimental attachment to individual specimens. If Willie needs to flatten a couple of rows to get the spare tire out to the pivot, or if the pivot's heavy wheels trample some plants as they trace their wide arc, what can you do? When your fields are filled with hundreds of thousands of plants, you can't worry about each one. At their core, farmers are Darwinists: The survival of the group is what's important, not the longevity of every individual.

Zack tightens down the last lug nut, and we hike up to the pivot's control box. He presses the toggle to RUN, though more tentatively than before. This time the thick metal pipe begins to shudder, and we hear a distant gurgling. In another minute, water pushes up through the pivot's vertical tube and begins spitting through the perforations. The breeze blows some of the mist back on us, and it feels good in the late-afternoon heat. But Zack isn't celebrating yet; he only peers up at the long pipe, watching the water work its way out toward the far end. As it does, the huge metal scaffold starts rocking over the rows, jerking like an alien contraption from an old science fiction movie.

After several minutes, the water has nearly reached the end of the quarter-mile arm. We're too far away to hear anything, but we can see a sudden downward gush.

"Damn it!" Zack yells, turning back toward the control panel and jabbing the toggle again. The pivot's motion ceases, as does the sound of surging water. As we trudge along the dripping pipe, Zack explains what has happened. The pivot has a plug at the low point of each segment, so the system can be drained. Over the course of the winter, one of the plugs has come loose, and the pressure has blown it right out.

When we reach the area, water is still cascading out of the drain hole. The cotton plants under it are flattened from the force, and a wide pool has already accumulated on the ground. Zack wades in and retrieves the large metal plug. Then he goes to the truck and fetches a pipe wrench. He scrambles up the pivot's tall frame and, wrapping his wet legs around a strut for balance, reaches over to screw the cap back into place. In the meantime, he orders me up to the control box.

After a few minutes, Zack climbs down from the pivot and raises his hand. I press the toggle. Again there is the sound of rushing water, and again a fine mist floats over the field. Walking beside the arm of the pivot, I follow the spray's progress, which is faster now because of the residual water in the pipe. The flow passes Zack's repair, and by the time I reach him, the nozzle on the end is slapping rhythmically, tossing water one hundred feet past the end of the structure.

After two days of effort and frustration, the pivot is working. Arms crossed, Zack scrutinizes it. Then he sighs, the only expression of satisfaction he will allow himself for this twin victory over nature and machine. Enveloped by the hissing of the pivot, we stand for a time and watch the drizzle settle over the field. The sun is still hanging big and orange over the Delta horizon, but the artificial rain is finally falling on Zack's cotton.

SIX

The Predators

It's mid-June, and summer has closed over the Delta. Daytime highs are hitting ninety, and the air is still thick with the haze that Zack says will keep the rain away. There's been only about a fifth the rain of last June, and Zack begins to wonder whether he should have installed that new irrigation pivot in the Yazoo field after all. But his crops are coming along. The corn is now six feet tall, and the soybeans have set their tiny violet blooms, poking out from the hairy notches between the stems.

The cotton leaves have grown as large as a lady's hand. The plants have also put out their first flower buds, known as pinhead squares. "Pinhead" is in reference to their initially tiny size. But "squares" is a misnomer, since they actually resemble diminutive pyramids wrapped in three fringed, specialized leaves called bracts, which meet in a point. About twenty-five days after its appearance, each pinhead produces a blossom.

The flowers first show themselves toward the base of the plant, close to the main stem. In the coming weeks, they will emerge in an out-and-up pattern, spiraling toward the edges of the branches. The process is so orderly that if you know when the branch below bloomed, you can predict the exact date when the one above will flower. With five petals and a prominent center stamen, the cotton blossom resembles the hibiscus, its relative in the mallow family. The flower opens at dawn and on the first day is buttery yellow. By the second day, it's the color of rosé wine, and by the third it's begun to wither. In another couple of days, the blossom falls. The brief period of bloom wouldn't leave much opportunity for insects or even wind to pollinate the plants, but no such help is necessary. Cotton flowers can fertilize themselves, dropping their large-grained pollen from the stamen directly onto their own stigma, whence it is carried down to the ovule at the base of the blossom.

Once fertilized, the blossoms begin to develop into bolls, the fruits of the cotton plant. Like flowering, this process unfolds in an orderly ascending spiral, but being influenced by air temperature, it isn't so spectacularly predictable. By the end of July, oblong green bolls form toward the base of the plants, while flowers are still blooming toward the top. If allowed, the cotton plant would continue blossoming until frost, although the flowers that open first are most likely to set bolls. Even on normal, healthy plants, about 60 percent of the squares will drop off before maturing, probably a natural check to prevent the plant from producing more fruits than it can bring to maturity.

One morning, a heavy-set man with a salt-and-pepper goatee rumbles up on a motorcycle and stops beside Zack's field. Getting off the bike, he wades into the cotton and begins swooping a long white object under the plants. The man is Virgil King, and he comes bearing a degree in entomology from Mississippi State University and a cone of cotton cloth three feet long and fifteen inches wide at the mouth, mounted on a wooden stick like a butterfly net. After making a predetermined number of passes—say, a hundred—in a given area, Virgil carefully rolls back the cone and records the insect pests he finds. Dividing the number of pests by the number of passes, he arrives at a ratio of bugs per swoop, which he enters into a handheld computer. (To Virgil and other entomologists, a bug is a specific kind of insect, a member of the order *Hemiptera*; but here I'll use *bug*, as most people do, as a synonym for "insect.")

Virgil marks the precise location of each sample using a global positioning system, then repeats the process for every fifty-acre section of Zack's fields, twice per week early in the season and about every week and a half later on. (When the plants have grown too close together to swoop under them with a net, Virgil spreads a white, three-foot-square drop cloth between the rows and gives the plants a good shake with his hands to loosen whatever is clinging to them.) The data are downloaded into a computer in Virgil's office, which produces a map of Zack's fields showing the insect population of each section. Usually Virgil relays his findings to Zack over the phone or in one of those pickup-to-pickup meetings in the middle of the road, but sometimes the two confer at church, before Virgil begins teaching his Sunday school class. As part of his services, for which he receives a flat, per-acre fee for the season,

Virgil recommends what chemicals to use to control the pests he's found. Often he suggests doing nothing at all, when the level of infestation isn't great enough to justify the expense. That's fine with Zack. With margins as slim as they are, he doesn't want to spend any money he doesn't have to.

Virgil King's services are in demand because the same subtropical climate that makes the Delta a paradise for weeds makes it heaven on earth for insects. In this part of the world, summer belongs to the bugs. The creatures multiply with the hot weather—cicadas piercing the long afternoons with their metallic chatter, mosquitoes and moths invading the muggy nights. They say that the average square mile of earth is home to 26 trillion insects, and driving a convertible through the Delta on a warm summer night, I can believe it. The bugs seem to be everywhere, swooping in the headlights, thudding against the windshield. The next morning, there's a grayish stubble on the car's painted bumper, like two days' growth on an old man's chin.

By sheer force of numbers, insects have to be considered the most successful life form on the planet. For every human being, there are some 200 million bugs. Of the million or so known animal species, about 85 percent are insects—and it's thought that several million more are waiting to be discovered. Fossil evidence shows that many haven't altered their basic design in hundreds of millions of years. Adults generally have a hard outer skeleton, a segmented body, six jointed legs, and two pairs of wings. But most members of the class develop through four vastly different stages over the course of their life. First comes the egg, followed by the voracious, wormlike larva, the quiescent pupa, and finally the adult, which is preoccupied mainly with reproduction.

Only about fifteen species of insect feed on cotton plants, but that's more than enough. Marvels of the animal kingdom that they may be, Zack can't bring himself to appreciate bugs. And for good reason. With an ever-changing selection of delicacies to choose from—leaves, stems, flowers, fruits—cotton offers an irresistible smorgasbord for insects, from the moment the plants stick their tentative leaves from the soil until the last of the fiber is picked.

Among the first to appear in spring are the thrips, slender black bugs that use their specialized mouthparts to inject saliva into the seedlings, then suck out the partially digested cells. Though less than a sixteenth of an inch long, thrips inflict disproportionate damage on the cotton, because they feed on the terminal bud, the topmost structure where the leaves and other plant parts first develop. When the affected leaves emerge, they're crinkled and silvery, and the cotton's growth may be stunted; heavy infestations can kill the seedlings outright.

About the same time as the thrips, the plants are assailed by the cutworms, inch-long caterpillars that burrow in the soil by day but crawl out at night to feed on the cotton's main stalk, often severing it at ground level like a felled tree. Along with some other pests, cutworms have increased in number in recent years because farmers are using more chemical herbicides, rather than tilling, to rid their fields of weeds in the spring; as a result, the weeds stand longer in the field, giving the insects a hospitable environment in which to grow.

In late June or early July come the aphids, tiny, voracious insects that suck the cotton's sap. Because plant juice is mostly carbohydrates, the invaders need to ingest huge quantities—as much as their own body weight *every hour*—in order to get the protein they need. The heavy feeding weakens the plants, and their growth may be stunted. And since most of the sap is excreted as undigested sugars called honeydew, the fiber is apt to stick together at the mill.

Early summer is also the season for stinkbugs, large insects with a wide, flat back that when disturbed exude a foul smell from a gland on either side of their body. After feeding on the corn and soybeans, they invade the cotton fields, where they eat the developing seeds inside the bolls. Even more numerous and more damaging are the tarnished plant bugs—brown, squarish insects that can strike the cotton at any time of the season, feeding on flower buds and squares.

Also with summer arrive hordes of so-called worms (actually caterpillars—the larval stage of insects, in this case, moths). Loopers, with their characteristic, inchworm-like way of moving, feed on leaves, stripping a crop in a matter of days. The beet armyworm, a green, hairless caterpillar that also eats foliage, leaves behind only a transparent network of veins. But historically, the two worst caterpillar pests have been the tobacco budworm and the bollworm. In both species, the female moth lays anywhere from 500 to 1,000 eggs, and the hatching larvae devour the squares and sugar-rich bolls, sometimes causing the loss of the entire crop.

This year isn't a particularly bad one for insects, maybe because the uncommonly wet spring has disrupted their reproductive cycle. Zack has already put down aldicarb at planting as a preventative against thrips. In June, when the pinhead squares appear, he hitches up his spraying rig and fills the tanks with a chemical called imidacloprid, which is related to nicotine, to counter thrips, aphids, and plant bugs. Then in the middle of July, he sprays for bollworms with a pyrethroid, the synthetic form of a poison found in chrysanthemums. In August, he may need to spray again, for loopers and beet armyworms.

With the advent of modern pesticides, cotton farmers have never had a more effective arsenal against bugs. But as with weed control, the biggest news in insect management over the past decade hasn't been in chemistry but in genetic engineering. In 1996, Monsanto, the company that introduced Roundup herbicide and Roundup Ready cotton, began marketing cottonseed genetically altered to resist bollworms and budworms. Sold under the brand name Bollgard, the seed incorporates genes from *Bacillus thuringiensis*, or Bt, a bacterium found in soil that produces a protein poisonous to the caterpillars. Unlike standard pesticides, Bt doesn't release any chemicals into the environment. In fact, the genetically engineered cotton has allowed farmers to reduce their total pesticide load by half or more.

That should be good news. But like Roundup Ready cotton, Bt has its detractors. Though the EPA has judged the new strain safe, some groups are concerned that genetically modified plants are being introduced without adequate testing to determine their long-term effects on the environment or workers' health. They also worry that the worms' natural predators are depleted along with the pests, and that the caterpillars themselves are becoming resistant to the bacterium. To counter this final possibility, federal law requires that all farmers using Bt cotton set aside 5 percent of their acreage as a "refuge" planted with a non-Bt variety and not sprayed with any pesticide. The idea is that the caterpillars hatched on this land will mate with any found on the Bt cotton, producing nonresistant offspring. But not everyone is sanguine about this strategy. Monsanto is currently testing Bollgard II, which incorporates two genes from the Bt bacterium instead of one, rendering it effective on a wider variety of insects and, it is hoped, making adaptation less likely.

Meanwhile, sales of organic cotton, from nongenetically modified varieties grown without the use of chemical herbicides or pesticides, have been rising, although products made from it cost 20 to 50 percent more (in part because per-acre yields are about half that of conventional cotton). About 7,000 acres of certified organic cotton are now planted annually in the United States, producing some 4 million pounds of fiber, or about 0.2 percent of the American harvest.

Genetically modified cotton isn't a perfect solution for the farmer, either. Though Bt has been very effective against the budworm, it's proven less so against the bollworm, which means that Zack still needs to spray for this pest if it appears. And other insects, such as tarnished plant bugs and stinkbugs, have become more prevalent, probably because of the generally lower levels of pesticide used. Also, Bt cotton hasn't reduced the cost of controlling insects. Zack still spends somewhere between $75 and $100 per acre on this item every year, including about $35 an acre for the technology fee to Monsanto for his Roundup Ready, Bt cotton, $30 for various sprays over the course of the season, and $12 for the aldicarb applied at planting. That's about the same as he was paying when he was making all those extra applications of pesticide. But Zack is now getting much better protection than before, since budworms are difficult to control by conventional means. For him, the Bt is worth it, and most other planters agree. Genetically modified cotton now makes up 95 percent of the crop in Mississippi, and Bt varieties have been introduced for corn, soybeans, and potatoes.

Though insecticide use is way down since the introduction of Bt, there are still a lot of chemicals being applied to cotton fields. Some environmentalists worry about water pollution and dangers to agricultural workers. One day I ask Zack if he ever wonders about how all these substances are affecting his health. "I reckon I'll just live till I die," he tells me. "I'd go crazy if I thought about that. I'm sure I'm going to get cancer someday, because I never was careful with that stuff."

To determine the validity of such concerns, in 1993 the National Cancer Institute, the National Institute of Environmental Health Sciences, and the U.S. Environmental Protection Agency began a study of 50,000 North Carolina and Iowa farm families to evaluate the risk posed by agricultural chemicals in the development of cancer and other diseases. But it's a long-term study, following the subjects over many years, and as yet no definitive conclusions have been published. In the meantime, farmers like Zack and their families can only continue to speculate.

———•———

One afternoon as Zack and I are riding in his truck, I point to the edge of his field. "What are those green things?" I ask.

Zack cocks his head and, betraying the extent of my supposed naïveté, answers, "Why, Gerry, those are cotton plants."

"No, I mean *those* green things," I clarify, indicating the row of plastic, space-capsule-shaped devices erected on wooden sticks along the side of the road.

"Oh," he says. "Those are boll weevil traps."

It's a testament to the creature's unique stature that it alone has inspired such defenses. After crossing the Rio Grande in 1892 near Brownsville, Texas, the weevil infested American cotton for nearly a century. By 1900, the pest blanketed half that state. In 1906 it reached Arkansas, and in fall of the following year it crossed the Mississippi River near Natchez and found its way into the Delta. By 1921, it reached Virginia, leaving a swath of destruction 1,100 miles long and 300 miles wide. Affecting 96 percent of the U.S. cotton crop, the weevil lowered yields by at least 30 percent, in some areas as much as 100 percent. Total losses in the United States have been estimated at some $22 billion.

Brownish or grayish in color and up to a quarter-inch in length, *Anthonomus grandis* is a member of the large order of insects known as beetles, which are characterized by biting mouthparts and hard front wings. Using its long proboscis, the female weevil lays one egg each in up to three hundred cotton squares or bolls. Then after hatching, the white larva consumes the seed and fiber inside. Three generations of weevil per year are average, but as many as eight have been recorded, which means that one breeding pair can produce millions of offspring in a single season. When cold weather comes, the surviving beetles take refuge in fallen foliage, slow their metabolism in a process called diapause, and even produce a kind of natural antifreeze. Then in the spring they emerge ready to begin the whole destructive cycle all over again.

Farms and entire towns were abandoned in the weevil's wake. Desperate growers paid bounties for them. Swindlers concocted useless preparations. Someone patented a boll weevil catcher, two mesh cages worn over the shoulders to scoop the insects off the plants. The state of Texas banned all bird hunting, hoping the predators would eat the pests. South Carolina declared a day of prayer. Blues songs were dedicated to the beetle, including one called "Boll Weevil":

> *The first time I saw the boll weevil,*
> *He was sittin on a square.*
> *Next time I saw the boll weevil*
> *He had his whole damn family there.*
> *Jus lookin for a home,*
> *Jus lookin for a home.*

> *The banker got half the cotton,*
> *The merchant got the rest.*
> *Didn't leave the po farmer's wife*
> *But one old cotton dress,*
> *And it's full of holes,*
> *And it's full of holes.*

> *The farmer went to the merchant then,*
> *Gonna get him a bucket of lard.*
> *"Cain't get nothing, farmer,*
> *The boll weevil got yo job."*

Some of the earliest commercial pesticides were developed for use against the weevil. After the First World War, the U.S. Department of Agriculture produced compounds such as copper acetoarsenite ("Paris green") and calcium arsenate, which were applied to cotton as a dust. At first the arsenic was shaken onto the plants from a sack, then by a mule-powered spreader, and later from the air by crop dusters. But the powder had to be applied at night or early in the morning, when it would adhere to the dew-wet leaves. Paris green also proved toxic to both animals and people, being implicated in cancer, nerve damage, liver disease, skin disorders, and other illnesses—and it was not particularly effective against the weevil.

Then in 1939 Swiss scientist Paul Müller discovered that the chemical DDT caused insects' neurons to fire spontaneously, resulting in spasm and death. During the Second World War, DDT was used to kill malarial mosquitoes in the Pacific, and in 1948 Müller was awarded the Nobel Prize in Physiology or Medicine. In subsequent years, DDT was used around the globe, and the World Health Organization estimates that it has prevented between 50 million and 100 million fatalities from malaria.

In the United States, the insecticide was used by cotton farmers to kill caterpillars such as bollworms and tobacco budworms. To control the boll weevil, DDT had to be mixed with another class of chemicals called chlorinated hydrocarbons, and this combination was used to keep both caterpillars and weevils in check. Soon after the introduction of these mixtures, cotton yields nearly doubled. But the insecticides not only killed the pests, they decimated the caterpillars' natural predators. As a result, budworms and bollworms rebounded after each application, proving nearly as destructive as the weevil itself.

Moreover, by the 1950s, the fast-reproducing weevil was evolving an immunity to the pesticide. The farmers' answer was to put down ever greater levels, which not only introduced more of the poison into the environment but further speeded the weevil's resistance. By the 1960s, enormous quantities of these compounds were being used, up to two pounds per acre *weekly*, and American cotton was being dusted with 60 to 70 million tons of chemicals a year.

Then in 1962, Rachel Carson published her landmark book *Silent Spring*. A former editor for the U.S. Fish and Wildlife Service and already a best-selling author, Carson levied an impassioned indictment against DDT, showing how it became concentrated in animal and human tissues and persisted in the environment for years. Although it now appears that some of Carson's claims may have been overstated, her basic point was irrefutable: DDT was a powerful poison with serious, unanticipated consequences, particularly to fish and birdlife. The book created a sensation, and its publication is generally considered the birth of the modern environmental movement. It also inspired a series of government investigations, and starting in 1972, the use of DDT was banned in the United States.

More recently the chemical has been controversial, ironically, not for being overutilized but for being underused. Citing environmental risks, for years the United States and other Western nations refused to fund DDT applications in the Third World, even though malaria still kills an estimated 2 to 3 million people annually. Experts from the World Health Organization and such staunch environmental advocates as Greenpeace and the World Wildlife Fund have called for a reversal of this policy, arguing that applying tiny amounts of DDT could save untold human lives without significantly degrading the environment. As a result, it looks as though DDT will be making a limited comeback in the Third World.

For cotton farmers, the shift away from DDT began before the publication of *Silent Spring,* not due to environmental concerns but because of increasing resistance in the bollworm and tobacco bud-worm. Some of the insecticides with which DDT was being com-bined in hopes of greater effectiveness belonged to a class called organophosphates. First isolated in the early 1800s and later em-ployed in the First World War as nerve gas, these chemicals, like DDT, attack the nervous system. One of the first organophosphates used on cotton was malathion, which was found to be effective against the weevil. The pesticide has received criticism from some environmental groups, which blame it for damaging brains, lungs, intestines, kidneys, and chromosomes in humans. However, mala-thion is considered one of the safest of the organophosphates for users and, since it dissipates relatively quickly in both water and soil, for the environment as well. Today about 17 million pounds of malathion are applied every year in the United States, on food crops, lawns, even Christmas trees. Pound for pound, organophos-phates are the most widely used insecticides on cotton and now ac-count for about half of all U.S. insecticide use, totaling nearly 40 million tons annually.

Over the past fifty years, the boll weevil has showed no resistance to malathion. However, after the experience with DDT, such adaptation was originally thought to be only a matter of time. So in the early 1960s scientists went to work on a new generation of chemicals, which they hoped would turn the weevil's biology against itself. It was discovered that when male weevils feed, they release pheromones, powerful substances that attract both females and other males. In 1969, a USDA researcher named James Tumlinson, working at the Boll Weevil Research Laboratory at Mississippi State University, succeeded in isolating this pheromone from weevil feces and creating a synthetic form, which he named Grandlure.

Traps baited with Grandlure were devised with the idea not so much of killing the insects (although any weevil that enters is killed by a pesticide-containing tape) but of monitoring the population. With these traps as the centerpiece, a comprehensive plan for eliminating the boll weevil was introduced in 1971 by a coalition of federal and state governments, universities, and the cotton industry. Under the program, farmers in a given region vote whether or not to participate. If a majority elect to do so, all cotton planters in the area are required to take part, paying an annual per-acre fee (in Zack's area, it was $24 in the first year but later reduced to $12 as the weevil moved closer to being eradicated). This fee, which includes all testing and any necessary spraying for weevils, represents about 70 percent of the cost of the program; the other 30 percent is funded by the state and the USDA.

In the first year of the plan, the crop is sprayed in the fall with malathion to kill any weevils that are overwintering. In the spring, the space-capsule-like traps are erected, and if any weevils are detected, additional applications are made to the young cotton. Thereafter the traps are monitored, and when two or more weevils are discovered in any given one, just that section of the field is sprayed. By the third year, there are typically two treatments with malathion, again only if the insects are found. Such low levels of pesticide are used (about ten liquid ounces per acre) that the applications are made not by the farmers themselves but by an independent company with special very-low-volume spraying equipment. And once the plan has been in effect for a few years, there is often no spraying at all. The program has been so effective that Mississippi's losses from the boll weevil are now considered to be zero.

But in the seventy-five years it took to control the weevil, the tiny insect changed cotton farming for good. During the teens, it was one of the reasons that half a million black sharecroppers abandoned the South. The weevil also prompted growers to switch to earlier-maturing varieties, providing the insect with a shorter season in which to wreak its destruction. It encouraged the expansion of cotton growing in Arizona, California, and New Mexico, where the pest didn't penetrate as readily. The weevil inspired other countries to increase production as well, reducing American dominance and setting the stage for today's international trade disputes over cotton. And in the South, it finally forced farmers to diversify into crops such as corn, oats, rice, dairy, and hogs. Enterprise, Alabama, was one of the first areas to abandon cotton for peanuts, with enviable success. In 1919, the town fathers even erected a statue of a maiden holding aloft a huge specimen of the bug, "in profound appreciation of the boll weevil and what it has done as the herald of prosperity."

The fact that the boll weevil has only one host—cotton—and therefore fewer places to hide was an important factor in its ulti-

mate control. But the pest is still more of a problem in the Mississippi hill country than in the Delta, because the hills' typically
smaller fields abut forests and other unsprayed refuges where the
weevil can overwinter. In general, hill country farmers are more
enthusiastic about the eradication program than Delta planters,
who are more likely to feel that they are receiving less bang for
their prevention dollar.

F. Aubrey Harris, entomologist and research professor at Mississippi State University's Delta Research and Extension Center at
Stoneville, believes that if the weevil ever makes a comeback, it
will be because of complacency on the part of growers. After all,
the weevil is not extinct. It is still thriving in Mexico and is even
extending its range in South America, neither of which has a prevention program comparable to that in the United States. Young
American cotton farmers who start their careers in 2010 will
never have seen a weevil, Harris points out, and the researchers
who developed the current weapons against it will have retired. If
planters let down their vigilance, the weevil will be poised to
make a comeback. Hence the fluorescent-green traps stationed
along Zack's fields, sentinels in the ongoing war against cotton's
most notorious pest.

―――――

By the first of July, Zack's cotton plants are almost knitting together over the middles, shading out any competitors that might
germinate among them. In the old days, when weeding was done
by hand, the final hoeing of the season, called "laying by," was
performed at this time. Today this work is done by chemicals, but

the old term is still used for the last application of herbicide. Though it no longer marks the end of backbreaking manual labor, laying by still constitutes a milestone in the progress of the crop, and Zack can tell you the exact date he laid-by for the past several years. This season, Willie mounts the tractor and makes the final spraying on July 10. It used to be, as James Agee explained, that after laying by the farmer was "hung as if on a hook on his front porch in the terrible leisure," knowing that "there [was] nothing more [he could] do. Everything [was] up to the sky, the dirt, and the cotton itself; . . . the cotton [was] making, and his year's fate [was] being quietly fought out between agencies over which he [had] no control." But now if Zack's crop needs any chemical applications before the end of the season, they can be made from the air.

In fact, the week after laying by, Ricky Davidson of Southland Flying Service is already buzzing over Zack's fields. He's applying a growth regulator, which will direct the plants' energy toward the developing bolls and away from the leaves and stems. Ricky is using a compound called mepiquat chloride, which was developed in the 1980s to reduce the plants' production of growth hormones. As a result, the cotton will have a shorter, more open form. The openness will allow more light and air into the center of the plant, reducing the possibility of boll rot and making for an easier harvest, with fewer leaves to strip before picking and less plant debris, or "trash," mingling with the fiber. The bolls will also ripen earlier, making the crop less vulnerable to late-season rains and insect pests.

It's fortuitous that fieldwork will ease for the next six weeks or so, because Zack is finding himself short on help. Johnny and Ben have quit without explanation, and Zack has heard they're work-ing for other farmers. One day Charlie doesn't show up for work, and Zack learns that he's in the hospital in critical condition, hav-ing been stabbed in the lung by a lady friend wielding a pair of scissors. Zack isn't sure what provoked the attack, and he doesn't know whether Charlie will be returning. So of the two full-time and two part-time hands Zack had at planting, only Willie re-mains. Zack's not heartbroken to see the others go, but he's con-cerned about lining up replacements before picking begins in September. As it did two centuries ago, the harvest makes the greatest demand for workers, and it can be hard to find reliable help. Even in the new, mechanized Delta, sometimes it seems that everything still comes down to labor.

Zack's own routine eases a bit now, and the Saturday following lay-by, he turns his attention from controlling insects to domi-nating another form of Delta wildlife: the catfish. "Hand grab-bing" (also known as "grabbling" or "noodling") the creature is popular enough in Mississippi that there's an official season, run-ning from May 1 to July 15. Traditionally hand grabbers wade into muddy lakes or rivers and locate a hollow log, where catfish like to nest this time of year. Without benefit of facemask or other equipment, the fisherman takes a deep breath, closes his eyes, and dives into the latte-colored water. Swimming into the log, he gropes for catfish, hoping not to encounter a water moc-casin curled up in an air pocket. If he finds a fish, he tries to seize it in both hands, then ease back out of the log and resurface.

The basic technique is unchanged, but now most hand grab-bers help nature along by providing their own nesting places. Zack and his friends build wood boxes with a hole in the top, then set them out in Horseshoe Lake, not far from shore. The catfish also apparently find the boxes more convenient than submerged logs, and they set up housekeeping. Even better, water moccasins don't nest in them, since there are no air spaces. But the oxbow is infested with the snakes, also known as cottonmouths, so hand grabbers still need to be alert, especially when wading under the low-lying branches where the brownish vipers, about as long and fat as a man's arm, like to sun.

Zack and his friends don't subscribe to catch-and-release, so they float two ice chests in the water, one for fish, the other for beer. But a wedding has decimated the ranks of the hand grabbers on this hot afternoon, and Zack and I are the only participants. We take off our shirts but leave on our blue jeans to protect our legs. Then, trading our work boots for sneakers, we wade into the cool, brown water of Horseshoe Lake. I search to the right and left for water moccasins, though I'm not sure I'd recognize one if I saw it. I glance at Zack to see if he's watching for the snakes, but he seems unconcerned. In chest-deep water, he locates the first submerged box with his feet, then wiggles a stick inside. A vigorous thumping indicates the presence of a fish. "That there sounds like a big one," he says.

Although the boxes are set in only four feet of water, a person needs to submerge himself in order to reach the bottom, where the catfish lurk. So Zack takes a deep breath, shuts his eyes, and dives. Bubbles mark the underwater battle, as well as a sharp banging as the fish strikes the sides of the box. Eventually Zack emerges, brandishing the wriggling, foot-long quarry over his head.

We work our way a little farther along the shoreline until we come to another box. Zack inserts the stick, and again there's a spirited thumping. "This one is yours," he tells me. He reviews the technique: You simply slip your arms inside, locate the fish, and grab it behind the head with both hands. Then you lift it out without losing your grip, letting it swim away between your arms, being bitten, or getting unduly scraped on the container's sides.

Sinking up to my shoulders, I take several deep breaths, not so much to fill my lungs but to stall for time. Twice I begin to submerge but hesitate before putting my face in the stagnant water. I review Zack's instructions. Finally I close my eyes and feel the coolness envelop me. I thrust my hands in the box, and there is more thumping. I feel the water swirling, but I can't locate the fish—until something hard closes over my right index finger. I leap back to the surface.

"It bit me!" I yelp. There's a wide red scrape on my finger, but no blood.

Zack laughs. "Let me get this one." He dives, there's more subsurface thrashing, and again he emerges clutching a good-size fish.

At the next box, it's my turn. Eager to redeem myself, I dive a little more readily. Fumbling inside, I feel the fish brush my hand. I pursue it around the box, but it's too quick and too slippery, and I can't grab it. Finally there's a flutter near my elbow, and the banging stops.

"He swam away," I tell Zack when I surface.

At the fourth container, Zack makes it look easy, now three for three. Approaching the next box with resolve, I spread my elbows as wide as possible to minimize the chance of escape. Again I grope in the darkness, but I can't close around the fish. Blocking the exit, I surface, take a quick breath, and dive again. Sliding my hands inside, I'm shocked to feel the fish in my grasp. In my hurry to stand, I run my elbows painfully over the rough sides of the opening. I have the fish by the tail, not behind the head, and as soon as I surface, it wriggles back into the water.

Such ineptitude would earn only ridicule for one of Zack's regular fishing buddies, but to me he says, "You got it up out of the water, that's what counts." As we dry off, he adds, "You know, I never could get the twins out here to do this with me. Said they didn't want to stick their hands in no water they couldn't see in. And my first time, I didn't catch nothin' at all."

I'm not sure I believe him, but I appreciate his generosity. Later Zack fillets the fish, breads them in cornmeal, deep-fries them with French fries and hushpuppies, and accompanies them with coleslaw, Bud Lite, and sweet iced tea. Wild catfish have a more pungent flavor than those raised on the fish farms now found in the Delta, the succulent meat still redolent of the muddy water from which the fish was plucked. Standing on the banks of Horseshoe Lake in the long summer twilight, my elbows rubbed raw and a full paper plate in my hands, I'd be hard-pressed to think of a finer repast.

PART III

Fall

SEVEN

The Picking

It's late August in the Delta. Wild white hibiscus have begun to bloom in the drainage ditches, and in Horseshoe Lake the cypresses are already assuming their autumnal rustiness. Zack's shop is so quiet this morning that you can hear doves cooing in the pecan trees and wind rustling the cotton across the road. In this season of shortening days, the entire Delta seems to hold its breath. The bulk of the year's work is done; all that remains is the picking.

Ricky Davidson's crop duster drones into the early haze. It swoops over a neighbor's cotton, then releases an opaque mist that hangs for a moment before settling onto the plants. At the end of the field, the plane banks high, then makes another pass. It's putting down defoliant, a chemical that causes the cotton to shed its leaves in preparation for harvest. Zack wishes his own crop were ready to be defoliated. The waist-high plants are filled with green bolls, about an inch and a half long and pointed on the end. But only a few toward the bottom of the stalks have opened to reveal their fiber. Inside the rest, the immature cotton is green and gummy. It's still three weeks away from being picked.

But the soybeans and corn are ready. Unlike cotton, these are "determinate" crops, meaning they don't grow indefinitely, but complete their preprogrammed life cycle, then die. After reaching about two feet in height, the spindly bean plants have withered to a lifeless brown, their slender, inch-long pods drooping from the stems. The nearby corn has grown about eight feet tall, putting out just one or two fat ears per plant, and now has ripened into dry stalks also waiting to be cut.

Soybeans and corn (like wheat) are harvested with a combine, so called because it combines the functions of a harvester (cutting the stalks) and a thresher (stripping the grain from the husk). About a story and a half tall, the boxy machine is fitted in front with a header, or "head," which is changed according to the crop. The head for corn has eight little pontoons that glide along the earth. The bean head is an open, six-sided cylinder two feet in diameter and twenty-eight feet long, like the paddlewheel of a diminutive steamboat. Both heads guide the plants toward a row of serrated blades set close to the ground. Then a screwlike auger feeds the cut stalks into an opening in the center of the machine. Inside, rollers squeeze the grain from the husks. It drops through metal slots and is conveyed to a hopper on top, while the husks and stalks are chewed up and excreted out the back in a brownish haze. When the hopper is full, a tractor maneuvers a cart alongside, a thick metal pipe is swiveled out from the combine, and the grain is transferred on the move, like an airplane refueling in midair. Then the cart carries the beans or corn to an eighteen-wheeler for the trip to the grain elevator down in Yazoo City.

Like most of his neighbors, Zack doesn't plant enough corn and beans to justify the six-figure investment in a combine. With their multitude of moving parts, the machines can also be a challenge to maintain, and in the cotton-focused Delta, it can be hard to find a mechanic to work on them. Zack is adamant about not wanting the nuisance and expense: "You couldn't melt one of those things and pour it over me," he says. So every September he hires someone to cut his corn and beans for him, paying about $30 an acre for the service. This year the man is a big, free-cussing Kansan, who has hauled his rig 650 miles on the back of a tractor-trailer to make some money in the Delta while waiting for his own corn to ripen back home.

Working alongside the Kansan is Zack's latest crew, the replacements for Ben, Johnny, and Charlie. Charlie came back briefly after his injury, only to be fired when Zack caught him driving a tractor into town to pay a midafternoon call on the same woman who had stabbed him. So operating the eighteen-wheeler today is Bill. Born in the Delta, Bill is in his fifties, with a long, leathery face and straight white hair falling to the middle of his ears. Easygoing and experienced, he often picks up a wrench when something goes wrong with one of the machines. Driving the grain cart is Harold. Pushing forty, lanky, with brown hair and beard, Harold has a loose-jointed walk and a perpetual grin. The youngest of the group is Zack's nephew Matt, who's in his early twenties. Raised in the Mississippi hills, he's just finished a degree in criminal justice from Delta State. He's applied for the coveted job of game warden and is helping Zack while he waits to hear whether he got it. Wiry and eager to please, Matt is often called on to climb into tight spaces in the machinery that no one else can reach.

Bill, Harold, and Matt are white, which means that Willie is the only African American left on the crew. I wonder how he feels about that, but the four work together well. Willie and Bill arrive in Bill's truck in the morning, and they often drive off to lunch together. As I've gotten to know Willie a little better over the course of the season, he's revealed a gregariousness and an ironic sense of humor that I didn't see earlier on. As they ready the cotton picker, he and Matt rag each other incessantly. One afternoon, Matt is working on top of the machine and Willie is below. "If I have to come down there," Matt mock-warns him over some alleged lapse, "I'm going to be one mad white boy." Willie only laughs and reminds the youngster of his general ineptitude. "Children! children!" Bill chides them both.

Zack's plan was to start by cutting the beans, since if left on the plants too long, the dry pods will crack open and spill their contents on the ground. But recent weather bulletins have caused him to think again. Over the past day or so, the late-summer sun has given way to ominous bands of gray. A weak hurricane named Katrina has passed over Florida and entered the Gulf of Mexico, where it has gained force and is now projected to hit New Orleans as a huge category-four or -five storm early tomorrow morning.

Though Tchula is three hundred miles north of projected landfall, the hurricane is powerful enough to be a threat even that far inland. The cotton should be all right, because only a few bolls have opened. The same for the beans, since a single heavy rain won't hurt them, and their low, thin stalks don't present much surface area to the wind. But the corn is another matter. Of the three crops Zack grows, the corn cobs, wrapped in their bulky husks, are most resistant to bad weather. But the tall stalks, with their wide, saillike leaves, could topple and become impossible to harvest. So that evening, when daylight fades, the Kansan switches on the combine's six halogen headlamps, and the men continue the work they began at dawn. They labor without pause through the blustery night, and by four o'clock the next morning, when the drizzle begins, they've managed to cut two hundred acres, or 80 percent of Zack's crop. The corn can't be picked wet, so there's nothing more to be done. They park the equipment at the shop, then drag themselves home to wait out the storm.

Home for Zack is no longer in Tchula. With the separation from Pam starting to look permanent, he's moved out of the rented house on the oxbow and bought himself a mobile home. He's set it just outside Lexington on a piece of property belonging to a boyhood friend named Bubba, grandson of Aunt Bea, the neighbor who gave Zack his start by renting him sixty-five acres on Horseshoe Lake. Zack has furnished the trailer in brown corduroy and dark pine, and over the tree-filled ravine in back he's built a nice two-level deck with a sink for cleaning catfish and a cooker for barbecuing meat.

Zack falls into his new bed, only to be awakened a few hours later by the wind. Though the hurricane is approaching from the south, its counterclockwise rotation means that the winds in Tchula actually come out of the north. They quickly reach fifty miles an hour, accompanied by sheets of blowing rain. In his three decades of farming, Zack has seen some powerful storms sweep across the Delta, but nothing like this. Trapped inside the trailer, he watches CNN and waits. Then at nine-thirty in the morning, the power fails, and for the rest of the day he can only peer out at the whipping trees. At five o'clock that afternoon, there's an enormous metallic crash. Running out onto the deck, he sees that an oak tree has fallen onto his aluminum carport, crumpling it over the front of his pickup. A limb has also poked a hole through the bathroom wall.

For the second night in a row, Zack doesn't go to bed but sits up listening for falling trees and thinking about what must be happening in his fields several miles away. By three the next morning the wind is easing, and at first light he ventures outside. He cuts the tree off the carport with his chain saw and discovers that the truck has sustained only some scratches on the hood and a good-size dent over the driver's door. Picking his way through debris-covered roads, he drives toward Tchula. He's surprised to see that the dry earth has soaked up most of the downpour and that flooding is limited to low-lying areas. But the cotton looks ragged and twisted, the leaves' silvery bottoms blown upward. The twenty-four-hour wind has also given them and the soybeans a decided southward tilt. But in the cornfield there is devastation. The remaining stalks have been knocked flat against the ground. As one farmer says, it looks as though a combine has been driven through the fields with its header up, trampling the plants without cutting anything. Zack takes in the destruction, then drives slowly back to the mobile home.

In Yazoo City, twenty-five miles south of Tchula, Katrina has also taken down trees and knocked over power lines. When the electricity comes back on the next day, we're transfixed by the unfolding disaster in New Orleans and the devastation along the Gulf. My sister-in-law Lisa and her husband, Joel, live in Picayune, Mississippi, not far from the coast. They haven't evacuated, and we fight off a deepening panic when we don't hear from them for five days. Finally Lisa manages to call from a borrowed phone. They were lucky, she tells us. They lost several trees and their roof will have to be replaced, but some nearby houses were much more severely damaged. For the next several weeks, they will help to clear wreckage from the neighborhood.

Katrina has replaced the Great Flood of 1927 as the worst natural disaster in American history, wreaking hundreds of billions of dollars in damage. Whereas New Orleans was spared in '27, now 80 percent of the city is inundated. The feeble relief effort has humiliated and enraged many and, like the Great Flood before it, has cast new light on the liberal–conservative debate over what citizens should expect from their government. Not least of all, the hurricane has exposed America's persistent racial disparity, which strands poor blacks in the path of disaster while better-off whites escape to safety. Many African Americans have even suggested that the city was flooded intentionally to rid it of "undesirable" elements.

In Tchula it's hard to know what the lasting impact of the hurricane will be. In a kind of agricultural triage, Zack decides to let the blown-over corn sit where it is for the time being. A couple of days after the storm, when the fields are dry enough to get machinery into them, he begins to cut his soybeans instead. The plants haven't lost their tilt from the powerful wind, and according to the combine's onboard computer, the yield when the plants are listing toward the machine is about 25 percent higher than when they are leaning away. Accordingly, Zack decides to cut in only one direction. Since the combine has to deadhead back to the top of each row, the process will be more time-consuming and expensive, but the difference in yield will more than pay for the extra hours and fuel. After the beans, Zack turns his attention to the corn. Driving slowly, the Kansan is able to harvest most of the flattened ears. As for the cotton, the plants look ragged, but the consensus is that they'll be all right, since the bolls were still closed at the time of the storm. The theory sounds reasonable, but no one will know for sure until picking begins.

———•———

The Saturday after Katrina happens to be the opening of the first dove season (there are three in Mississippi, stretching from September into January). Dove hunting is popular, partly because the birds' speed and erratic flight make them a challenging target. Also, unlike deer hunting, it's more of a group activity, since several hunters spreading over a single field help keep the birds in motion. In light of the more social tradition of the sport, Zack usually marks the occasion with a hunt for thirty or forty people, followed by a pig roast. But this year, with the scarcity of gasoline, continuing power outages, and the general upset from the hurricane, he isn't sure he'll hold it. Finally he decides to go ahead, though instead of cooking a whole pig, he plans just to barbecue some slabs of ribs and some chicken halves.

By two in the afternoon, several mud-splashed pickups are pulled under the pecan tree in front of Zack's shop. Doves are most active just after dawn and in late afternoon. So as they wait for the appropriate hour, the camouflage-dressed men oil their guns and sip from cans of Bud Lite, which they extract from plastic coolers in the beds of their trucks. Zack's cotton picker, bright green and two stories tall, is parked squarely in front of the shop where the hunters are gathered. While a young man with a black eye recounts his fistfight and subsequent arrest in Memphis, Willie and Matt continue to prepare the huge machine for the upcoming harvest. In their only acknowledgment of the festivities around them, the two temporarily quit their banter.

As the afternoon lengthens, more pickups turn into the driveway, and the ranks of hunters swell to about thirty men and boys. About three o'clock, we pile into the backs of the trucks and jounce out to take our positions in a field of unpicked soybeans, one of the birds' staple foods. As we climb down from the pickups, we're greeted by gunshots coming from a neighbor's land.

I've already been out hunting early this morning. To get me ready, my wife's cousin Danny, an electrical engineer at the fertilizer plant, took me to the levee outside Yazoo City yesterday afternoon and gave me some practice with a Browning over-and-under. It was the first shotgun I ever fired, and I surprised us both by managing to hit some of the clay pigeons that he flung into the air. So with that experience under my belt and a seven-day dove license in my pocket, I rose before dawn, put on whatever green clothes I could find, and drove with Danny through the still-dark Delta. We met Zack in front of the cotton gin, then followed him to an area that he'd planted with sunflowers to attract the birds. On my one

shot of the morning, I aimed too far behind the target and succeeded only in scattering some tail feathers. Zack and Dan didn't
fare much better, killing just one dove apiece. But at that hour we
were alone in the field. Now, with dozens of hunters positioned at
intervals, I've decided it would be safer for everyone if I remained
a spectator.

The sky is cloudless, betraying no trace of the hurricane just a
few days ago. A breeze is blowing out of the north, stirring the
dried soybeans and taking the sting out of the afternoon sun.
Doves start to fly into range, and there is the startling sound of
gunfire close by. Spent pellets fall softly around us, fired by hunters
up the way. My role is to spot the birds, and several times I catch
myself pointing to huge dragonflies that appear the size of doves.

Under Mississippi law against "wanton waste," a hunter must
retrieve all killed or wounded animals and either clean and cook
them or give them to someone who will. But it soon becomes
clear that finding the fallen birds requires almost as much skill as
shooting them, since distances can be deceiving on the flat, open
ground, and the doves are very nearly the color of the dry soybeans. Dogs are sometimes used to recover the kill, but Duke
has retired from hunting. Several men have brought their dogs,
though none is trained as a retriever; a little black mixed breed
receives more than one death threat when it starts tracking down
dead doves and eating them before the shooters can get there.
During lulls in the hunting, we crack open some soybeans and
snack on the crunchy seeds right out of the pod.

Zack has been detained by his responsibilities as chef, and he
rides out on his camouflaged four-wheeler a little behind the rest

of the group, dressed in his camo shorts and cap. Over the course of the afternoon, he darts back to the shop several times to check on the ribs and chicken. But that doesn't keep him from shooting several birds. In fact, in the time I watch him, he never misses.

By six o'clock, the hunt is over. The hunting has been good, and several hundred birds have been taken. Some of the men have even bagged the daily limit of fifteen. Satisfied, we climb into the pickups and bump back to the shop. A waist-high white plastic bucket has been set up at one corner of the garage, and the hunters now stand over it and clean their catch. There are various methods, I discover. Do you remove the wings first or at the end? Do you cut them off with scissors or twist them off with your hands? Only the dove's breast has enough meat to bother with, and the hunters press their thumbs into the center of the bird's chest and push outward until the skin splits and slips to either side, revealing the cherry-colored flesh. Occasionally one of the men holds up a carcass for another to inspect, commenting on the size of shot found in it or the type of seed in the bird's gut. Once the breast is uncovered, the rest of the carcass is twisted off and thrown into the trash can. The meat, with some fine feathers still clinging, is dropped into a square plastic dish filled with water. As the feathers float to the top, Zack skims them off in his cupped hand.

One boy, about ten, is reluctant to clean his kill, but his father gently insists. "If you shoot it, you got to skin it," he tells him, passing the youngster one of the birds. The son swallows his disgust and manages to twist off the head. But the father is of the antiscissors school, and the boy doesn't have the knack of snapping the wings off. Twisting one uncertainly, he pulls off half the breast along with it, ruining the bird. The man takes another dove and patiently demonstrates, then hands the carcass to the boy to finish. But he can't exert enough pressure with his small thumbs to split the skin, and the father ends up taking over this part of the job too. He seems satisfied that his son has made an honest attempt, and the boy is allowed to slink away, clearly relieved that this part of his hunting education is over for today.

There's so little meat on each bird that even the several hundred doves shot this afternoon would only serve as an appetizer for this group. So Zack puts the game into the refrigerator and feeds us on his chicken and ribs. Presiding at a black cooker the size and shape of a small locomotive, complete with twin smokestacks and four wheels, he removes some slabs of ribs and puts them in a white plastic cooler to keep them hot. Then he takes some raw meat from another container, where it's been marinating in spices and beer, and places it on the cooker's motorized mesh shelves, which rotate up and around like the seats on a Ferris wheel. The chicken halves, already cooked, are sitting in a third cooler. Hungry guests open the top, hack off some meat, and eat out of their hands, without benefit of plate or napkin or side dishes (other than the Bud Lite). It is without question the best barbecue I've ever tasted.

Zack's party is meant to celebrate not just the beginning of dove season but the start of the harvest. This year, though, the festivities seem a little forced. "Are you pickin' yet?" Zack asks another farmer, bringing up the topic on everyone's mind.

"No," comes the answer, "just cuttin' some beans and corn."

Only cotton is "picked"; beans and corn are "cut." Important as the latter two crops are, there's a feeling that they are only preliminaries, that the main event is the cotton harvest. Even in a normal year, the corn and soybean cutting wouldn't go very far to dispel the end-of-season anxiety that hangs over the Delta. But in this storm-crossed year, the apprehension is palpable. As Zack's cotton continues to ripen, his worry only deepens: The more bolls that are open on the plants, the more vulnerable the crop. Waiting for the cotton to mature "is the worst time of the year," Zack says. "It's like carryin' a 150-pound weight on your shoulders, and it only gets heavier as you get closer to pickin'." A prolonged spell of severe weather or another bad storm could ruin all the work and money invested over the course of a year. The cotton won't be safe until it's picked. Zack never talks about bringing in the cotton; it's always "gettin' the cotton out," getting it out of the bolls, getting it out of the field, getting it out of harm's way.

The cotton plants should be green and lush at this time of year. But the leaves blown upside down by the hurricane haven't reverted to their normal attitude, and the undersides have burned in the intense sun, giving the fields a rusty, ratty look. The wind-blown cotton is still listing at an angle of about twenty degrees, obscuring the well-ordered rows and adding to the tattered appearance. No one has ever seen anything quite like it, but common opinion still holds that, while the plants may not be much to look at, the yield should be unaffected. Zack has a bad feeling though. As he inspects his own and his neighbors' emerging cotton in the coming days, the fiber just doesn't seem abundant on the plants.

But you never can tell what kind of crop you have until you start harvesting, Zack says. "Now," before the plants are defoliated and all the bolls are open, "is the worst time in the world to look at your cotton, because it looks awful, any farmer will tell you that. You fuss and kick over how bad the cotton looks, but then you defoliate and the bolls open up, and you can end up pickin' some good cotton." Even so, he can't shake off his bad feeling. The second week of September, a planter across from him starts to pick, and Zack keeps a running tally of the results. After the first day, with three pickers going, they seem to have harvested only fifty bales. "That's some kinda scary," Zack mumbles.

It's been 140 days since Zack planted his cotton and forty days since it first blossomed. The bolls in the center of the plants are still closed, but those at the bottom have already opened, exposing the nearly half million fibers in each boll. Zack finally begins to think about defoliating. The process consists of spraying the plants with a substance that concentrates a particular enzyme in the stem, near the base of the leaves. The enzyme dissolves the cell walls affixing the still-green leaves and causes them to fall to the ground.

Like much of farming, the timing of defoliation is as much art as science. Since the loss of the leaves stops the plants' growth, it also prevents the bolls from maturing any further. Thus if you defoliate too early, you decrease both the quality and the quantity of your cotton. But if you wait too long, you increase the risk from late-season insects and inclement weather. Zack cuts into one of the unopened bolls from the center of a plant and sees that the seeds have formed a thin brown shell, indicating that they and the fiber are mature. The bolls on top still aren't ripe. But cotton, unlike corn and beans, is actively growing until defoliation, so it's never possible to harvest every boll. Zack decides this field is ready.

He doesn't have a RoGator, one of the tall rigs that allow farmers to spray their crops right up until harvest. And even if he did, the plants' posthurricane tilt might make it impossible to use without crushing them under its wheels. So Zack calls Ricky Davidson of Southland Flying Service and arranges for him to apply the defoliant from the air. At the same time, Ricky will put down a hormone that will encourage any mature-but-still-closed bolls to open.

The point of defoliation is to ease picking and reduce the extraneous plant matter mixed in with the fiber. This step is necessary because of the mechanical picker. By the early part of the last century, farmers had machines to plant their cotton and plow their land, but the crop was still harvested by hand. During the picking season, entire families would troop into the fields at dawn. With a long canvas bag looped over one shoulder and trailing on the ground, they would stoop over each plant and pluck the lint from the boll with a quick, practiced motion, trying to avoid pricking their fingers on the burs' brutally sharp tips. At the end of each row, they would dump the fiber from the sack into a tall basket, then step to the next row and continue. Up and down the fields they would work until nightfall, with just a lunch break during the worst of the afternoon heat. At the end of a seven-day, eighty-four-hour week, each picker would have gathered about one bale of cotton.

For more than a hundred years, people searched for a way to harvest cotton by machine. The first mechanical picker was patented in 1850, but it didn't prove effective. Over the next century, various approaches were tested, including pneumatic pickers that used air pressure to suck out or blow off the fiber; threshers that cut the entire stalk then separated the fiber from the stems and leaves; strippers that used metal teeth to yank the cotton from the plants; and spindle pickers that extracted the fiber from the bur by wrapping it around metal rods. Of all these, the last seemed the most promising, but the spindles tended to clog with lint and leaves.

In 1936 two Texans named John and Mack Rust introduced an improved design, and the brothers were hailed in the popular press as the "next Eli Whitney." But it was obvious that a mechanical picker would put an end to sharecropping, and now that such a device finally seemed feasible, the prospect didn't meet with universal enthusiasm. True, planters habitually bemoaned their dependence on tenants. But far more than a business arrangement, sharecropping had been the predominant social organization in the Delta since Emancipation. If tenants were no longer needed on the plantations, what would become of them? The idea of millions of unemployed, homeless African Americans was more than southern whites cared to contemplate. The *Jackson Daily News* expressed the wish of many when it suggested that the new machine "be driven right out of the cotton fields and sunk into the Mississippi River." But the Rusts never perfected their model, and cotton remained one of the least mechanized of American crops.

Then a few years later, International Harvester took the lead in developing a mechanical picker. The wartime labor shortage added urgency to the effort, and by 1942 the company had a working prototype. To solve the problem of clogging, the machine, like today's pickers, used water mixed with detergent, along with wheels called doffers, to remove the fiber from the spindles. Although the technology was finally in place, steel was lacking to manufacture the new design. But on October 2, 1944, nearly 3,000 people eager to get a glimpse of the future attended a public demonstration of the machine on a plantation outside Clarksdale, Mississippi.

It was 1948 before International Harvester finally got the first commercial cotton picker into production. Though it worked only one row at a time, the device was capable of picking half a ton of fiber per hour, doing the work of over fifty people and reducing harvest costs from nearly $40 per bale to a little more than $5 (today the cost of picking is back up to about ten times that amount). Just four years later, more than 20 percent of American cotton was being harvested by machine, and in the decade after that, the figure rose to more than 70 percent.

By then it was apparent what would become of the former sharecroppers—they would move North to feed that region's booming industrial economy, and in numbers even greater than those loosed by the First World War, the boll weevil infestation, or the Great Flood of '27. In 1940, 77 percent of American blacks lived in the South, 49 percent of them in rural areas. Over the next three decades, 5 million African Americans left to find employment in the factories and stockyards of cities like Chicago, Detroit, and St. Louis. In the Delta, the rural population dropped 19 percent in the 1940s and another 50 percent in the 1950s.

Meanwhile, the population of Chicago grew by 77 percent in the '40s, from 278,000 to 492,000; in the following decade, it increased another 65 percent.

There is still some debate over how much the mechanical picker caused this migration and how much it was a response to it. Did planters buy the pickers because their workers were going north in search of a less repressive racial atmosphere and better wages (about seventy-five cents an hour compared to the four dollars a day to be made picking cotton)? Or did sharecroppers flee northward as they were replaced by the new technology? Whatever the precise mix of push and pull factors, there is no doubt that the two trends reinforced each other, and that African Americans would not have left in such huge numbers if both stimuli had not been in place.

Over the next sixty years, the nation would experience an internal ethnic migration greater than any wave of immigration to the United States. Cotton had brought blacks to the Delta, but the mechanical picker made them extraneous there. And whereas southern planters had once taken extraordinary, even illegal measures to guarantee sufficient labor in the fields, they were now just as eager to see their erstwhile tenants vacate. In the words of NAACP officer and Mississippi state legislator Aaron Henry, "They wished we'd go back to Africa, but Chicago was close enough."

Whereas the exodus was greeted with relief in the South, in the North it was received with consternation. As early as 1947, Mississippi writer David Cohn warned that the United States was "on the brink of a process as great as any that has occurred since the Industrial Revolution. . . . If tens of thousands of Southern Negroes descend upon communities totally unprepared for them psychologically and industrially, what will the effect be upon race relations in the United States? Will the Negro problem be transferred from the South to other parts of the [country]. . . ? Will the victims of farm mechanization become the victims of race conflict? [It is] a problem that affects millions of people and the whole structure of the nation."

Not only did the newcomers help expand the northern economy, they enriched mainstream culture in many realms, including language, food, and music. But bearing the sharecropper's baggage of undereducation, violence, and alcohol abuse, many migrants failed to achieve the familial and financial stability they had hoped for in their new homes. Considered a destabilizing influence by their established neighbors, they were met with hostility by whites, who scrutinized them in starkly racial terms. They were often greeted coolly by the settled black middle class as well. As the preeminent black newspaper the *Chicago Defender* commented, "It is evident that some people coming to the city seriously erred in their conduct in public places, much to the humiliation of all respectable classes of our citizens, and by so doing on account of their ignorance of laws and customs necessary for the maintenance of health, sobriety and morality among people in general, have given our enemies grounds for complaint."

Just as Cohn had foreseen, the legacy of ethnic strife was transplanted from the cotton fields of the South to the urban centers of the North, in a pattern that would alter American life for the rest of the century and beyond. By the time the migration had ended, wrote Nicholas Lemann in *The Promised Land*, "the country had acquired a good measure of the tragic sense that had previously been confined to the South. Race relations stood out nearly everywhere as the one thing that was plainly wrong in America, the flawed portion of the great tableau, the chief generator of doubt about how essentially noble the whole national enterprise really was."

———•———

After defoliant is applied to Zack's cotton, there is more waiting. The chemical needs from seven to fourteen days to do its work, but its effects are seen fastest in hot, sunny, humid weather, exactly what the Delta has been experiencing since Katrina. The intervening period is tense, but it's far from empty. Even more than planting, picking requires an imposing collection of specialized machines, and in the coming days, Zack and his crew continue to prepare the equipment for the work ahead. Once the harvest begins, he doesn't want to be held up by breakdowns, so every piece of machinery is overhauled. Oil filters, hydraulic filters, water filters, air filters are changed. Grease is applied. Hoses are refitted. Equipment is swept out and washed down. Some modifications are made to avoid problems experienced last year. So Zack welds a cradle on the back of his tractor to keep the hydraulic pump from working loose and getting wrapped up in its hoses. It's an improvement entirely of his own design. "I hope this works," he says, "'cause I'm gonna patent this damn thing."

One morning I arrive at the shop to see gray smoke billowing from a piece of equipment called a module builder, used to compact the cotton before taking it to the gin. Painted construction yellow, with the proportions of a lap pool, the builder is a metal

box with ten-foot sides and an open top and bottom. Keath is affixing new lights that will allow the men to work at night, and
some sparks from his welder have dropped inside and ignited
scraps of cotton left from last year. All the other hands are working somewhere else, and not wanting to quit what he's doing,
Keath has let the fiber smolder. But now there are real flames, and
he asks me to go through the builder's double doors and stomp
them out, which I do. Later Zack comes by and notices the black-
ened heap. "What happened here?" he wants to know. When
Keath tells him, he shakes his head. "Don't like see no fire on a
cotton farm," he mutters.

Altogether, the men will spend the better part of two weeks
readying their implements for picking. As Zack waits, he hopes to
see the cotton opening thicker on his plants, but his sense of fore-
boding only deepens. The day before picking is to begin, there's a
change in the weather. In place of hazy sunshine, the sky is dotted with clouds, white and puffy on top, leaden on the bottom.
Zack begins the morning at the chemical place, shelling peanuts
and sipping a Diet Coke. The computerized weather map shows
bands of green, yellow, and red descending on Tchula.

Outside, the northern sky has turned the color of a bad bruise.
"Does it look like rain to you?" I ask.

"Not from that direction," Zack says. He points toward the west.
"Our weather comes from over there, but that don't look so bad."

At the shop, he continues to get the machinery ready for tomorrow. But Katrina has made him even more sensitive to the
weather than usual. At one point, he lifts his head from the back
of a tractor he's working on.

"Was that thunder?" he wants to know. But I didn't hear it.

Using his cell phone, he calls a friend in Greenwood and learns that it's already raining up there. By midday, the breeze has died in Tchula, the humidity is intense, and the clouds have begun to swing around to the west. Then the wind suddenly whips up, propelling empty cartons across the shop yard and threatening to sweep the tractor caps off our heads. In minutes, the temperature drops by twenty degrees. The change wakes the dog from his nap, and he pads into the yard, stretches, and looks around expectantly. To the north we can now see sheets of rain falling in the distance.

"Was that thunder?" Zack asks again. This time I say it was.

He examines the worsening sky. One September twenty years before, he tells me, he was picking cotton and the clouds looked exactly like this. It started raining that afternoon, and it poured for the next three weeks. "I'm talkin' flood!" he whistles with another skyward glance. "It's like this. When you have the weather comin', all you can do is hope for the best. You're thinkin', am I goin' to be able to pay the bank or pay my equipment notes? But if a storm hits the cotton, you can't do nothin' about it."

Finally it begins to sprinkle, then abruptly ends without even wetting the ubiquitous dust.

The next morning, heavy clouds are scuttling along on the northerly breeze. Around the shop, the atmosphere is expectant. A lanky older man arrives from John Deere to make last-minute adjustments to the picker. Involving metal shims three-thousandths of an inch thick, it is a painstaking process that will take the better part of the day. Zack knows he has no hope of getting into the fields until late afternoon, but he'd still like to get a little picking in before dark, if only to test the equipment and get it into position for tomorrow. In the meantime, he runs to the Wal-Mart in Greenwood and buys two rakes and two plastic garbage cans for sweeping up cotton scraps.

At four-thirty that afternoon, the picker is ready. Everyone climbs into tractors, trucks, and cars, and rumbles off to the cotton field. As we leave, the open-sided shed where the machines are usually parked stands oddly vacant. This is the moment that Zack has been working toward all year, through planting, spraying, fertilizing, irrigating, worrying. But there's no palpable feeling of accomplishment, no air of celebration. Though augmented by a new sense of purpose, Zack's anxiety hasn't lifted. "Pickin' is like plantin'," he explains. "You're nervous. You're excited, but you're not, because you don't know what the outcome will be. It's only when you get to countin' bales and you're gettin' toward the end and you know that you can pay out, then you get real excited, because it looks like you'll be able to farm again the next year."

In the cotton field, the wide sky is dramatic, even by Delta standards. The clouds' curvaceous tops are luminous with late-afternoon sun, while the earthward sides are gray and level. Shafts of hazy, golden light angle down to earth, lending the wide landscape a devotional look. Jumping out of my car, I see that the ground is dry, hard packed, cracked. In the rows, the leaves are gone from the plants, exposing the white fiber against the reddish stems.

Zack pulls up on the picker, the biggest piece of equipment found on a cotton farm. In front, about ten feet off the ground, is a curved glass cab for the driver, accessed via a metal ladder and catwalk. Below that are six vertical slots, one for each row of cotton to be harvested. Framing each opening are triangular, yellow plastic guides that direct the plants toward the openings. Inside each slot is a vertical cylinder about six feet tall and bristling with hundreds of horizontally mounted spindles. Each spindle is about the size and shape of a spark plug, made of stainless steel and fitted with rows of small, sharp barbs. As the cylinder turns, the spindles rub against pads moistened with water to keep the cotton from getting tangled. When the plant enters, the rotating spindles catch the fiber on their barbs and gently draw it out of the bur, not cutting it but actually picking it, much as human fingers used to do. The stalk, still standing, passes out the back of the machine, while the picked cotton is brushed from the spindles by the doffers, stacks of heavy plastic rounds that resemble gears with flattened teeth. The fiber is then blown through six wide, square black plastic ducts and into the large metal basket that forms the picker's top.

Zack positions the picker over the first six rows and, without pause or ceremony, starts to harvest his cotton. As it rumbles across the field, the picker gives off an assortment of noises—the bassy rumble of the diesel engine, the metallic clattering of the spindles, the high whine of the blower, the chattering of the cotton stalks as they pass through. Traveling at three to four miles an hour, the picker lumbers down the long row like a hermit crab scuttling over a seabed. A mist of cotton dust floats in its wake, scenting the air and making my eyes itch. Behind it, near-white, star-shaped burs dot the plants, along with scraps of fiber that the machine has missed. As the picker increases its distance, the rumble of the diesel becomes less prominent, and the whirring of the fan becomes the principal noise reaching back across the field.

At the far end, nearly half a mile away, Zack turns and starts back. When he reaches this side again, now six rows to the left of where he began, a tractor pulls up beside him, towing a bright yellow boll buggy, essentially a big, hexagonal metal basket on wheels. Using its twin hydraulic lifts, the picker raises its own container over the boll buggy's cage. Metal conveyors are set into motion, and the cotton is transferred. Unlike the combine, the picker has to stop for this operation, but the whole process takes less than thirty seconds. Afterward Zack climbs out of the cab and Willie takes his place at the controls.

The boll buggy trundles to the turn row, where the module builder is waiting. Cotton used to be carried to the gin in a wooden cart. Now it's packed into bricks called modules, thirty-two feet long, seven feet wide, and eight feet high. Pulling alongside the module builder, the boll buggy raises its basket and, using metal conveyors like those on the picker, dumps the cotton inside. Of course, the picker itself could have done this, but the idea is to keep the crucial piece of machinery in the field working while the buggy shuttles back and forth to service it.

Sliding along tracks on top of the module builder is a steel beam called a dolly, mounted perpendicular to the builder's width and powered by an idling tractor. Sitting at the builder's controls located high on the end, Matt directs the dolly from one extreme to the other, compressing the cotton as he goes. He's never operated a module builder before, and Zack climbs up the metal ladder and watches him for a minute. "No, not like that," Zack says, taking the levers from his nephew. "There's an art to everythin'. Roll that cotton back like this, and it'll pack the shit out of it." After four dumps from the boll buggy, the module builder is full. Matt jumps in, sinking to his hips in cotton, and positions a vinyl tarp over the top. Then the builder's wheels are lowered and its tall metal sides lift off the ground. The horizontal bar fastening the back doors is knocked open with several raps from a sledge hammer, and the tractor creeps away, leaving more than a ton of cotton lying in the dust.

As the builder withdraws, the tarp is eased partway down the module's flanks, then cinched with a heavy strap. Taking a numbered tag from the stack distributed by the gin, Matt ties one copy to the strap and places a duplicate in a cigar box to serve as Zack's record. Using black paint specially formulated not to damage the fiber, he sprays one side of the module with KCC, for "Killebrew Cotton Company," along with the number from the gin tag and the numeral 1, indicating that this is Zack's first module of the season. Alone in the turn row, topped by its blue vinyl cover, the module has a monumental quality, with solid sides that yield only slightly to the pressure of a fist. When you lean your back against it, the cotton gives off a clean smell, not quite plant and not quite fabric. The module will sit here for several days, until it is eventually slid onto a flatbed truck for the trip to the gin, less than a mile away. In the meantime, Zack tells me, the cotton will continue to grow inside, fed by the module's internal heat and the nutrients in the seeds to which the fibers still adhere. As a result, he expects to get more cotton out of the module than he put into it.

Standing in the turn row, Zack is calculating and shaking his head. It has taken four loads of the boll buggy, or four round-trips of the picker, or forty-eight rows of cotton, to build the first module. Last year, the picker had to be emptied at the end of every row in this field, not after each round-trip. He wonders whether the tilt of the hurricane-blown cotton is causing the picker to miss an unusually high percentage of the fiber, the way the soybeans' list reduced their yield. But the scraps hanging from the plants don't seem any thicker than usual, and there doesn't appear to be any discrepancy from one direction to the other. The yellow plastic guides are lifting the tilting plants and directing them into the picker as intended. The problem isn't that the machine is missing an unusual amount of cotton, he decides, but that the cotton just isn't there to begin with. "When you get up and over the cotton and you can't see the ground, that's good cotton," Zack says. "But see here, you can see dirt right through the plants." He's trying to reserve judgment, because the amount of fiber always varies from field to field. But so far, he sees nothing to change his feeling that this year's crop is going to be a disappointment.

When cotton was picked by hand, the process went from daylight to sunset, "from can to can't." Cotton is still picked from can to can't, but now that the equipment is fitted with headlights, it isn't sunshine but dew that determines the work schedule. If the fiber is harvested wet, it can suffer in both quantity and quality when it's packed inside the module. Dew results when the air cools enough for water vapor to condense; the temperature at which this happens is called the dew point. A function of air temperature and humidity, dew "falls" at different times from night to night. If the thermometer never dips below the dew point, it doesn't form at all. In the morning, as the sun rises and the air re-heats, the dew evaporates. The hour that this happens also varies, but cotton is usually dry enough to pick by about ten o'clock.

Even with artificial light, maneuvering heavy machinery in the dark requires great care. Still, farmers want to extend their working hours as long as possible to get the vulnerable cotton out of the field. The crew generally likes working at night, because the longer hours mean extra pay and it's more agreeable laboring in seventy degrees than in ninety. But whether dew has fallen or not, Zack generally knocks off around ten, so that everybody can get some rest. Even under ideal circumstances, a picker can cover only about fifty acres per day; that means it will take Zack four seven-day weeks to get his crop out. It's long enough that they all need to pace themselves.

The sun sets on this first evening of picking with the clouds shimmering blood red and incandescent gold. The moon rises full and yellow in the east—a harvest moon. As the picker's halogen lights wink on and it traces its linear path across the earth, cotton dust is suspended in the bluish light and the machine takes on an almost diabolical cast. Sounds seem to carry farther at night across the fields, as over open water. In fact, standing on the cat-walk of the moving picker at this hour feels like being on the bridge of a ship. In the gathering darkness, the illuminated equip-ment could be taken for vessels skimming over the surface of the sea. Tonight the cloud cover keeps the air temperature up, and no dew falls. Still, Zack sends the men home about eight o'clock.

The next morning is cool and breezy, and they take to the field at seven-thirty. But at eight o'clock, there is still no cotton being picked. In the dark last night, Willie drove into a drainage ditch and blew out one of the picker's rear tires. Efforts to fix it back at the shop, without a tire machine, have succeeded only in rupturing the replacement tube, and now Zack has driven to Lexington with the huge wheel in the bed of his truck. While Willie waits, he hitches a water tank to another pickup and tows it into the field to hose scraps of cotton off his stranded machine.

By midmorning, the picker is repaired. But after half an hour of work, the gray skies finally begin doing what they've been threatening for two days. It's only a sprinkle, but it's enough to suspend picking. Zack doesn't want to leave a module partially finished and exposed to the weather, so the crew picks enough cotton to top it off and cover it with its protective tarp. Then they settle into the vehicles' cabs and even the picker's huge wheel hubs to get out of the rain. There's a rumble of thunder and a flash of lightning. Somebody looks up at the sky and says, "It's fixin' to rain like a cat pissin' on a flat rock." But forty-five minutes later, the sun is shining weakly. The scant rainfall evaporates quickly in the building sunshine, until the air seems more liquid than gas. "It's fixin' to get hot, y'all," Willie warns, as though the humidity and heat weren't already unbearable. Then half an hour later the weather turns suddenly gray and cool, and for the rest of the day, as the clouds pass through, it fluctuates between harsh sunshine with soaring humidity and pleasant temperatures with a fresh breeze.

On this first full day of picking, the equipment continues to function as designed, and it seems that Zack's painstaking maintenance is being rewarded. The improvised brackets under the tractor's hydraulic pumps, the ones that Zack threatened to patent, perform perfectly. With their huge diesel tanks, none of the machines even needs to stop for refueling. The crew seems focused, and there's a sense of urgency to the work. In the coming weeks their energy will flag, but at least for today they're happy that the long-anticipated harvest has begun. As Matt says, "I'm so glad we've started doin' this and aren't workin' on stuff" in the shop anymore.

As the picker and boll buggy crawl down the dry rows, they kick up so much brown dust that sometimes it looks like smoke from a grassfire. The machines' tires chew up the silty soil, and where it was once dry and cracked, it's now a fine, loose powder two inches deep. Footprints around the module builder resemble the ones left by astronauts on the moon; though this is some of the most fertile soil on earth, the process of picking has made it appear inhospitable and alien. In the field, undignified white scraps hang from the picked stalks like bits of toilet tissue, and the plants look battered from their passage through the machinery. The naked, reddish-brown stems blend with the color of the ground, camouflaging the rows that once imparted a sense of order, as though the organization imposed on the land all season has finally been abandoned, leaving a desolate, decimated terrain.

The crew stops work at ten o'clock that night. They have picked fifty acres and have eight modules lined up in the turn row, representing about 135 bales, or roughly 65,000 pounds of ginned cotton. It's not a terrible result, but Zack still worries they should have gotten more.

The next day, as the rest of the crew continues to pick, one tractor is attached to an implement called a shredder, which resembles the grass cutters used on golf courses. Passing up and down the rows that were harvested yesterday, the shredder chews up the stalks and cotton scraps, leaving it all on the ground as green fertilizer. Just as

corn, soybean, and cotton fields can be distinguished from the moment the plants emerge, they continue to look different after the
crops have been cut down. Corn leaves a thicker stubble than
beans do, and cotton is differentiated by the white scraps on the
ground, which bear a disturbing resemblance to feathers, as though
a million chickens were slaughtered there. With the removal of the
blowsy cotton stalks, the fields have come full circle, once again
reduced to rows and middles, revealing anew the man-made order
that was impressed on them before planting.

The coming week is hot and sunny, and picking continues
more or less as planned. The men arrive at the shop every morning
at seven-thirty. If the cotton is dry, they head out to the fields and
get to work immediately. If there's been dew, they occupy themselves cleaning and adjusting the machines until the fiber is ready.
There have been no major equipment breakdowns, and only the
module builder proves balky, its hydraulic hoses occasionally rupturing where they drag along the machine's metal edges.

Still, when a neighbor asks how the picking is going, Zack tells
him, "It's all asses and elbows." He's been keeping count of his modules, which have been lining up in the turn row like white boxcars.
But the oblong mounds make an inexact measure, and he won't
know for certain how much cotton he's getting until the fiber is
ginned and weighed. The harvest still seems thin to him, certainly
nothing like last year's three bales to the acre, but he's trying to convince himself that at least the year won't be an outright disaster.

Then, three weeks after the devastation of Katrina, a new hurricane, Rita, passes through the Florida Straits and enters the
Gulf of Mexico. Like its predecessor, the storm builds in size and
power over the warm water, reaching category five as it spins

toward Texas. Just before landfall, it wobbles to the northeast and strikes near the border with Louisiana, now downgraded to category three. Houston and its refineries are spared, and Galveston suffers only flooding instead of the obliteration that was feared. But the storm causes severe damage along the coast, and its new trajectory places it squarely on line for the Mississippi Delta.

Though it's not as violent as Katrina, Rita couldn't be more perilously timed. The first hurricane struck when the bolls were still closed, but the second is bearing down on the Delta when the delicate lint is exposed. As Zack experienced two years ago, heavy rains can discolor the fiber and damage its texture, resulting in a lower grade and a reduced price. And high winds can be even more destructive, stripping the cotton from the plants and leaving nothing to harvest. As he listens to the storm reports, Zack begins to wonder whether the season might be a catastrophe after all.

The day before the remnants of Rita are due to strike, the crew begins to pick about ten o'clock under a heavy sky. As they did when cutting the corn in advance of Katrina, they work feverishly through the morning and afternoon, gulping lunch at the controls of their machines. Darkness falls about seven-thirty, but the overcast keeps temperatures up, and there's no dew to impede them. In the glare of the halogen headlights, they pick through the night. They work into the next morning and afternoon, groggy with fatigue but driven to "get out" as much of the cotton as possible. Finally, at four-thirty, it begins to rain, and they're forced to quit after more than thirty consecutive hours. There's nothing more to do but go home and wait.

EIGHT

The Gin

In the Delta, Rita drops seven inches of rain and produces gusts of fifty miles an hour. It also spawns tornados that take down trees and shear roofs off houses. In Belzoni, twenty miles west of Tchula, a man is killed when his mobile home is overturned.

For local farmers, Rita is at least as punishing as its more notorious precursor. The morning after the storm is still and gray, and Zack drives to Horseshoe to inspect his unpicked cotton. The plants' post-Katrina list hasn't worsened, and this time there were no leaves to twist and batter, since the cotton had already been defoliated. But the bolls were open on the naked stems, and Zack can make out ragged white blotches scattered in the mud between the rows. It will be a while before he can quantify the damage, but cotton, unlike corn, can't be retrieved once it's on the ground. Every smudge is fiber that Zack won't be able to harvest or sell. And he can't even be sure about the cotton left on the plants, because the soaking may have left it matted and discolored, graded loss-makingly low.

It will be several days before the fields are dry enough to work again. Coming after the fevered activity of picking, the abrupt hiatus falls hard, especially since it leaves so much time for thinking. Zack knows there's no such thing as an "average" season, that each one arrives with its own challenges, that the farmer's only constant is uncertainty. Yet even that hard-won appreciation hasn't prepared him for this bizarre year. He's seen seasons with one hurricane, but never two.

After Katrina, the consensus was that damage to the cotton was superficial, that though the leaves had been blown upside down, the fiber would be unaffected because the bolls were still closed. But as picking began, the yield proved anemic, just as Zack had feared. At first some farmers believed the storm had swept saltwater up from the Gulf, burning the plants. But now it seems that, by blowing the chlorophyll-rich top side of the leaves away from the sun, Katrina arrested boll development, like a premature defoliation. Then, just as Zack and his neighbors were taking measure of their stunted crop and steeling themselves for a break-even year at best, came Rita to mock even that modest ambition. This season the cotton "is just not a crop," Zack broods. "It ain't worth a damn. It ain't no good."

It's the first time I've heard Zack sound really discouraged. But he's already done the math, and he knows he won't make up the money on his storm-damaged corn. The one bright spot is his soybeans. He's managed to average sixty bushels to the acre, more than he's ever harvested before. Still, he isn't sure that those profits will offset the losses on the rest, especially his cotton.

"I'm ready to piss on the fire and call in the dogs," he says. "This farmin' just don't look good to me. There ain't no profit out there." Heath and Keath are no better off. "They're takin' it like a farmer's supposed to take it. They just back their ears and get with it, and hope that things will get better down the road. But the storm is goin' to knock a hole in their savin's. We'll lose our ass this year. There's no way we'll make any money, not with the bills we got, from fuel and everythin' else."

Not only have the hurricanes decimated the crops, they've disrupted petroleum supplies and raised Zack's expenses even higher. If he goes too deeply in debt, he may not be able to borrow enough money to plant next spring. Maybe this will be the year he's finally forced out of the game, like so many of his neighbors. Or if he does come back, maybe he'll stop growing cotton and corn and raise nothing but soybeans, which are so much cheaper to grow. Maybe the hurricanes have actually done him a service by helping him realize that the cost of growing cotton has become insupportable. Next season couldn't have been business as usual, he sees now, even without the losses from the storms. He hasn't decided what he'll do, but he knows that if he's going to keep farming, he's going to have to make some kind of change.

But first Zack has to get through this year. He still has half his cotton to harvest, another two weeks of work. In the days following Rita, the weather turns dry again. There's no breeze, and the fine, pale dust grows thick in the middles. As Zack says, "There's nothin' but dirt and cotton." Conditions are perfect for fieldwork, and he resumes picking his storm-damaged crop.

One hot, bright morning in early October, the crew is working across the road from the shop. They've been picking here all week, and as Zack passes in his truck, he pauses to watch. Everything seems routine. Willie is driving the picker, Bill is manning the boll buggy, Matt is packing the cotton in the module builder. Zack glances down the turn row, where the finished modules are strung in a long line, snug under their blue vinyl tarps. He's about to drive on when something attracts his attention. He cranes out the truck window. There it is again, a wisp of white smoke. Zack strains to find the source, but the only flammable objects in view are the modules themselves. Then, with a sudden intake of breath, he realizes: His cotton is on fire.

Zack pulls off the road and steers across the picked field, the bare cotton stalks scraping the sides of the truck. When he reaches the module builder, he stands on the pickup's running board and leans on the horn until he gets Matt's attention. "The damn cotton's on fire!" he yells. "Tell Willie and Bill to stop what they're doin', then get everybody over there! Bring the rakes!"

Nearby is the portable five-hundred-gallon water tank that the men use to hose cotton scraps off the equipment. Zack couples it to the pickup, then jolts down the rows. When he arrives, he sees that not one module is burning but four. The fires must be deep within, because no flames are visible, only the telltale curl of smoke. Bounding out of the truck, he snatches a tire iron from the toolbox in back. By now the others have joined him. Using the tire iron and rake handles, they dig toward the center of the first module, strewing fiber on the ground behind them. As they penetrate deeper, the smoke grows thicker. Then as air reaches the blaze, the flames explode with a *whoosh*, like a match striking gasoline. The others fall back, and Zack trains the hose on the module. There's a hiss, and the men are enveloped in clouds of pale smoke.

They rush to the other modules, open them, and spray them down. By the time the water tank is empty, the cotton is dripping but still smoldering. Zack realizes there's no way to fully extinguish the fire, but at least they've kept it from spreading. In two of the modules, they will be able to salvage half the fiber. In all, the fires have destroyed fifty bales, or 25,000 pounds, or thirty acres, or more than $15,000 worth of cotton.

This is Zack's first fire in three decades of farming, and it seems an appropriate culmination to this strange and disheartening season. But now he has to find the cause, to keep the mishap from repeating itself. Because the blazes started deep inside, building slowly in the tightly packed, oxygen-starved environment, Zack figures a piece of burning fiber or trash must have been introduced when the modules were built. At first he suspects a dropped cigarette butt, then thinks better of it. Although that might account for a fire in a single module, it seems unlikely to explain blazes in all four.

So Zack turns his suspicion to the machines that come in contact with the cotton—the picker, the boll buggy, and the module builder. Before the men resume picking, he scrutinizes each piece of equipment. The picker has the most moving parts and therefore is the most susceptible to overheating. But it also moistens the spindles, the doffers, and the cotton itself. The purpose is to keep the fiber from clogging the mechanism, but it also makes fires less likely. Zack checks the machine's water tank; it's nearly full. Opening the picker's six front panels, he sees water dripping from the dozen little plastic heads, just as intended.

Next he inspects the module builder. The sole moving part is the dolly that rolls along the top, tamping down the cotton, and that slides along polished steel wheels, unlikely to cause a spark. The hydraulic hoses are the only other pieces that come into contact with the container's metal edges, and they're made of rubber. Zack toggles the dolly back and forth, up and down, but notices no shorts or smoke, or anything else suspicious. Matt tells him he hasn't seen anything either.

Moving to the boll buggy, Zack peers inside the hexagonal metal basket. The buggy's principal moving part is the chain-operated conveyor that transfers the cotton into the module builder. He has Bill start the conveyor, but he sees nothing out of the ordinary. He leans against the machine and strokes his beard. The fact that the fires were in four consecutive modules means they weren't a fluke. But why were they the only modules affected? Why not those before or after? Did the problem correct itself, or have the men just been lucky over the past day or so? The rest of the morning and afternoon, Zack paces from machine to machine. He finds nothing.

About six-thirty, the sun sets in a swirl of magenta and apricot. The men switch on the halogen lights and continue working in the cool darkness. Zack makes a tour through the turn row, looking for a glimmer inside the other modules, but all appears normal. As he walks back toward the module builder, the boll buggy happens to be coming alongside with another load of fiber, and Zack stops to watch. Bill tilts the buggy's basket and starts the conveyor, and the cotton tumbles into the builder's tall metal box. In the dusk, Zack can see what he couldn't in the daylight: sparks emanating from the conveyor's chain. As Bill lowers the empty container, Zack climbs up the tractor's steps. Through the cab door, he signals to Bill not to move. Then he clambers inside the huge basket. In the area where he saw the sparks, he touches the chain guard, meant to keep cotton out of the conveyor's mechanism. He jerks his hand away from the hot metal. Under the light from the module builder, he sees that the guard is rubbing against the chain. How did it work its way loose, and why didn't someone notice it before? He knows he was lucky that more modules didn't burn, and he's relieved to have found the cause. It will be an easy fix. But he can only shake his head. Fifteen thousand dollars seems like a steep price for a loose chain guard.

The picking goes on. The weather continues perfect—bright, warm, and dry. But as the days multiply, time seems to slow for Zack's men. They've been harvesting for a month. They can see the stripped landscape where they've already been, and the white-flecked acreage where they have yet to go. They know they're in the closing spell. But the eagerness they felt at the start of the harvest is gone, displaced by the drudgery of fifteen-hour days and seven-day weeks. They're tired, they're numb, they want to finish. "I'll be glad when this sucker of a year's over with," Zack says. With a poor harvest and high debts, he'll celebrate the close of the season like the cessation of a chronic headache.

On October 17, the crew begins at seven-thirty in the morning, takes a short lunch break, and works into the afternoon, same as always. But today there is a sense of anticipation, like that on the first day of picking, though now tinged with weariness and relief. At three o'clock, Willie drives the picker down the last six rows of cotton. He tips his load into the repaired boll buggy, then turns the huge machine out of the field and onto the road leading back to the shop. The buggy dumps the fiber into the module builder and Matt tamps it down. He positions the tarp and spray-paints the side *115*, marking the final module that Zack will harvest this year. With no more ceremony than it be-gan, the picking has closed. Zack has finally gotten his cotton out.

But even after the harvest ends, the weirdness of this singular season continues. Late in October, a tornado touches down south of Tchula, where a farmer has three modules waiting to be carried to the gin. The wind strews the fiber across the road and onto someone else's land. The field has already been picked but the stalks haven't been cut, and now cotton dots the plants as though it had grown there. The owner of the errant fiber gets permission to collect it, then drives his picker through his neighbor's rows. It's the first time he's ever had to pick the same cotton twice, but the effort is worth it. The second harvest nets three bales to the acre, the best yield he's had all fall.

In November, when deer season starts and Zack heads to the woods, he'll discover something he's never seen before: scraps of cotton draped from the tops of trees like white Spanish moss. Whether it was blown there by one of the hurricanes or by a tor-nado, he won't even speculate.

———•———

You can tell when a cotton gin is running, because the building is enveloped in a cloud of dust and fiber, which drifts to the ground like fine, warm snow. The effect is even more striking at night, when the cotton floats in the lamplight like the blizzards I remember from my boyhood in upstate New York.

Holmes Gin Company, where Zack's cotton is trucked after it leaves his fields, is located near Horseshoe Lake, outside Tchula. It's a wide, low building constructed of corrugated metal and surrounded by an expanse of gravel that looks like the parking lot of a shopping mall. But instead of cars, the space is lined with cotton modules waiting in angled, orderly rows. Ginning season stretches from early September to the middle of December, and in a good year Holmes Gin processes nearly 30 million pounds of cleaned cotton, all grown by the nineteen local farmers who are the gin's shareholders. It used to be that every town, and even every large plantation, would have its own gin, but the new facilities are so efficient that they have driven the smaller ones out of business. Now Holmes Gin is one of only perhaps a hundred left in Mississippi.

Zack's cotton makes the mile or so trip to the gin in a specially designed tractor-trailer. The truck backs up to a module and lowers a conveyor that looks like a set of parallel chains with hooks set in them. The conveyor is slipped under the module's leading edge, and the tightly packed cotton rides onto the trailer's bed. When it reaches the gin, the module is lowered into its parking space, then when its turn comes, it is lifted onto a similar truck and driven to the front of the building. A scale records the module's weight, and a conveyor slowly draws it toward a hose, or "sucker pipe," which vacuums up the bolls.

Inside the gin, tangles of ductwork snake across the ceiling and down the metal walls. The noise from the machinery is intense, and the cotton-filled air smells like fresh lumber. A control panel stands in the center of a long, narrow room with a concrete floor. Painted pea green and bristling with rows of colored lights, the console looks like the bridge of Buck Rogers's spaceship.

The cotton first enters a series of rollers that regulate its speed through the gin according to the fiber's moisture content. It's propelled through the ducts by hot air, which dries the lint as it transports it. If the cotton is already on the dry side, the sensors speed up the process; if the cotton is damp, the rollers automatically slow. The ideal moisture level is about 6 percent. Much above this, say 8 or 9 percent, and the extraneous plant matter, or "trash," that is mixed in will adhere too tightly and make the fiber difficult to clean. The cotton will also tend to clog the gin's machinery.

To remove any burs, the woody remnants of bolls, the cotton is transported up a slanted grid and under a series of spiked rollers that shake them free. The fiber then passes through two huge drums, which use centrifugal force to spin out sticks and leaves. Next is the gin saw, a row of flat blades ninety-two inches wide and rotating at 1,200 RPM. As on Eli Whitney's gin, the saw pulls the cotton through metal ribs, leaving the seeds behind. Still wrapped in a thin capsule of fiber, the seeds are transported to a warehouse behind the main building, where they pile up like dirty snow.

Since lint makes up only about a third of each boll's weight, ginning generates a lot of seed, about 60 million pounds at Holmes Gin over the course of the season. This won't be used to plant more cotton, which would be in violation of the farmers' licensing agreement with Monsanto. Instead, it will be sold to a mill, and the money will be used to pay the gin employees' salaries and other overhead, with any left over being distributed as dividends to the nineteen client-owners. At the mill, the seed will be dried, any remaining lint will be removed, and the outer hull will be stripped off. Then the oil, which accounts for 20 percent of the seed's weight, will be extracted and used in products ranging from margarine to cosmetics to cookies to soap. The leftover hulls and meal will be used for high-protein livestock feed.

After the seed has been removed, the cleaned lint tumbles down a chute toward a press that compacts it into bales averaging a little less than five hundred pounds. But the bale (like the module) is a measure of volume—about thirty inches thick by fifty-four long by twenty wide. The farmer is paid for his fiber by the pound. Because dry cotton weighs less than moist cotton, before the lint is baled and weighed, the gin must replace the water that was earlier removed. So as the cotton falls through this final stretch of ductwork, it passes through humid air, which restores its moisture level to 8 percent.

The lint lands in a large metal box where it's compressed by a square, ramrodlike apparatus called a tramper. A device with delicate stainless steel arms fastens six metal wires around the bale. Then it topples onto a scale, and workers pinch out from each side a quarter-pound tuft of cotton, which they place in two barcoded bags. The bale is weighed and wrapped in clear plastic, and a matching barcode is slapped on the front.

The bagged samples are sent to the U.S. Department of Agriculture's local classing office in Dumas, Arkansas, where they are run through machines that grade them. Now used throughout the world, the USDA standards are complex, employing twenty-five grades for color (from "good middling" to "below grade"), twenty-three for fiber length, eight for leaf content, five for uniformity, and five for strength, among other measures. The program is voluntary, but since ungraded fiber is virtually unsalable, 98 percent of American cotton goes through the process, with growers paying for the privilege.

Next door to the gin's scale is a small office, sheltered from the howl of machinery by wood-paneled walls. Inside, two women sit at a counter next to a plate glass window with a slot at the bottom, like the ones that protect bank tellers in bad neighborhoods. Through the slot, the women slide barcodes to the workers operating the scale, at the same time recording the number and weight of each bale on a clipboard. After the bales are wrapped, a compact propane-powered forklift darts into position and seizes four at a time between two vertical stainless steel bars. The bales are driven to a series of low metal buildings nearby, where they will await sale and shipment. In the meantime, they will fall under the supervision of Zack's sister Linda, who oversees the gin's warehouse.

Holmes Gin's full-time, year-round manager is Bart Easley. A slight man in his fifties, Bart has been around cotton gins most of his life. His father built this one, and before that managed another, where Bart started helping out from the time he was fourteen. He doesn't like being called a manager, but Bart's job is to keep the gin running twenty-four hours a day for more than three months straight. His paneled office has two large windows looking out onto the gin floor, and a cot where he sleeps every night during ginning, to be on hand in case there's a problem. The gin runs two twelve-hour shifts, which means that over the course of the season, each employee will clock over a thousand hours. It's not long before the eighty-four-hour workweeks begin to take a toll. Tufts of cotton adhere to the workers' hair and clothing, and by December they're walking with a weariness normally seen in punched-out prizefighters.

———•———

Except for a few white supervisors, one black man operating the central console, and another driving a forklift, every employee I see at Holmes Gin is Mexican. Echoing what I've heard from some of the farmers, Bart Easley tells me they're better workers than the local people, more reliable and with more initiative. Not that the foreign labor hasn't presented its own challenges, involving housing, language, and cultural differences. The Mexican population is growing in Mississippi and in the Delta, as in other parts of the country. In Yazoo City, a town of 12,000, the supermarket produce sections now stock fresh *nopales* and several varieties of *chile*, and one of the two Mexican restaurants advertises a service for wiring money across the border.

Of course, the foreign workers at the gin mean that the overwhelmingly black residents of Tchula don't benefit from those jobs, temporary though they are. But since the introduction of the mechanical picker and weed-killing chemicals, the high jobless rate in the Delta has always fallen most heavily on African Americans. Their ancestors were brought to the Deep South to plant cotton, and for nearly a century after Emancipation, the

black sharecroppers remained bound to those same fields. Then
when their labor was no longer needed, they were expelled from
the land, either to find work in the cities or to languish in the
same towns that their forebears had helped to build.

But this exodus was also a kind of liberation. More than Abraham Lincoln or even the Illinois Central, it could be said that
technology finally freed the slaves, or at least the sharecroppers. In
this new freedom—more urban, more independent, better connected to the outside world—African Americans launched one of
the great social revolutions of the past century. Cotton had been
the instrument of their subjugation, and now freed from the yoke
of cotton, they began to demand their civil rights.

Life had already begun to improve for black Americans after
the Second World War, even though they didn't share equally in
the new prosperity. By 1945, there were 1.25 million black union
members, double the number just five years earlier. In the early
1950s, median black family income reached $2,338, or 57 per-
cent that of whites (up from 41 percent in 1940), and black life
expectancy had improved to 61.7 years (versus 53.1 in 1940).

Black attitudes were also starting to change. First during the
war, then in the cold war that followed, America's enemies exposed the hypocrisy of a nation that claimed to be the world's
bastion of democracy even as it practiced racial oppression at
home. At the same time, nonwhite peoples in Asia and Africa
were beginning to seize their independence from European colo-
nialists. And as black soldiers reentered civilian life, they, like
their Civil War counterparts, returned with a broader view of the
world and the conviction that their sacrifices entitled them to

something better. As one Mississippi veteran recalled, "I went over yonder and done all these things in the South Pacific and everywhere—Midway, the destroyers and everything—and come back home and can't even get a cool drink of water."

Not only were southern blacks still prohibited from using the same drinking fountains as whites, they couldn't attend the same schools, eat in the same restaurants, sleep in the same hotels, or share the same seats on public transportation. Poll taxes and arbitrary tests were still being used to prevent them from exercising their constitutional right to vote, and by 1950 only a quarter of eligible southern blacks had managed to register. In Mississippi, that figure was just over 5 percent, and in some Delta counties less than 2 percent. In Holmes County, where Zack lives, no black person had even tried to register to vote in the twentieth century.

In 1954, in the case of *Brown v. the Board of Education of Topeka, Kansas,* the Supreme Court ruled that the old doctrine of "separate but equal" schools for blacks and whites was an oxymoron. But the Court left it to local school boards to determine how and when desegregation would be achieved. Ten years after *Brown,* just 2 percent of southern black students would be attending integrated institutions.

No state resisted racial change in these years more vehemently than Mississippi, and no part of Mississippi more than the Delta. The nation was shocked in August 1955, when fourteen-year-old Emmett Till was murdered outside the town of Money for flirting with a grocery clerk. I once asked a planter's son, who had been a young man during these years, how people who were otherwise dutiful citizens, caring family members, and devoted churchgoers could have done some of the unspeakable things they did. And how could so many others have gone along with them, until the entire society was corrupted, until even the police and the courts had become instruments of repression rather than protection? "The culture never discussed it," he said, "never examined it. It was a result of seeing the other group as less than human." And in that climate, threatened whites could justify the violence and intimidation as self-defense, as protection of their own people, their patrimony, their "way of life." "We killed two-month-old Indian babies to take this country," one Mississippian marveled to the *New York Times* several years after the Till case, "and now they want us to give it away to the niggers."

Even as raw violence continued, a new group began to take a more insidious approach to racial ascendancy. Founded by prominent citizens of the Delta in 1954 and quickly spreading throughout the South, the White Citizens Council was dedicated to opposing civil rights largely through economic intimidation. In 1955, Yazoo City witnessed the effectiveness of this method when fifty-three middle-class blacks petitioned the local school board to desegregate. Soon afterward the Citizens Council placed an advertisement in the *Yazoo City Herald* listing the signers, who began to lose their jobs or their white clientele; within four months, every one had either withdrawn his name from the petition or left town. Later, the Citizens Council began an investigation into a white family in Yazoo City after the father made the mistake of using the honorific "Mrs." in writing a check to their black maid.

In 1954 in Zack's town of Lexington, Hazel Brannon Smith, the owner of the local newspaper the *Advertiser,* was fined $50, given a fifteen-day suspended jail sentence, and put on two years' probation for interviewing the widow of a black man who had been whipped to death by a gang of five whites. When Smith later published an article castigating the local sheriff for shooting a black man in cold blood, a white jury awarded the lawman $10,000 in libel damages. (Like the first verdict, this was eventually struck down on appeal.)

That same year, a black schoolteacher in Holmes County was shot by a white man after she complained about his driving a car over her lawn. Though the gunman wasn't prosecuted, both the teacher and her husband were fired from their jobs. When Smith reported on this incident, the Citizens Council launched a boycott of the paper and her husband lost his administrative position at the local hospital. Zack's mobile home happens to be on property next to the Smiths' old house, and one day from his back deck he points out the tall white columns and the sloping front lawn where crosses were burned.

Through it all, Smith continued publishing, and in 1964 she was awarded the Pulitzer Prize for Editorial Journalism (following in the tradition of Hodding Carter II, who had received the award in 1946 for his work on Greenville's *Delta Democrat-Times*). Her editorial philosophy, she wrote, "is not to favor Negroes any more than anyone else, but to uphold equal protection of the law for all people, including Negroes. Unfortunately, some of my fellow Mississippians do not look upon Negroes as 'people,' although they would be shocked if you told them that."

Around the same time that Hazel Brannon Smith was being prosecuted, the white operators of a 2,700-acre plantation outside Tchula called Providence Farm were being harassed for their charitable activities benefiting blacks, including a medical clinic, a nonprofit store, a credit union, movies, and a summer camp. After the farm's resident doctor testified on behalf of Smith in her libel suit, the organization's insurance policies were canceled, a deputy sheriff was posted to record the license plates of all visitors, and the operators received death threats. Eventually they left the county.

Throughout the South, the battle for civil rights was fought in bus stations, lunch counters, county clerk's offices, and the streets, as ordinary citizens acted with staggering heroism in places like Montgomery, Birmingham, and Selma. In Mississippi, civil rights workers such as Aaron Henry, Amzie Moore, Fannie Lou Hamer, and Unita Blackwell (all children of sharecroppers) were met with violence as they pressed their campaign for voter registration. In Tchula, a movement organizer was murdered.

Also in Holmes County, the house of a farmer named Hartman Turnbow was burned down after he became the first black since Reconstruction to try to register to vote there; despite overwhelming evidence to the contrary, he and three members of the Student Nonviolent Coordinating Committee, or SNCC, were convicted of staging the incident themselves. When he was attacked a second time, Turnbow shocked the assailants by returning fire with a twelve-gauge shotgun he had purchased. "I don't know where all that there braveness come from," he later said. "I just found myself with it. . . . I had a wife, and I had a daughter, and I loved my wife just like a white man loves his'n, and I loved my baby daughter just like a white man loves his'n, and a white man will die for his'n, and I say I'll die for mine."

In nearby Greenwood, the Leflore County board of supervisors punished civil rights activity by refusing to distribute surplus federal food to eligible families. A movement office was destroyed in the city, half a dozen black businesses and homes were bombed, and seven voting rights workers were shot, including one who was machine-gunned. Despite attacks by police dogs, more than a thousand would-be registrants turned out at the county courthouse in the coming months. Even so, from June 1962 to January 1964, only thirteen new black voters were admitted in Leflore County, bringing their proportion to just over 2 percent.

In Jackson, the state capital, demonstrators at a Woolworth's lunch counter were assaulted and six hundred student marchers were carted to jail in garbage trucks. A restaurant was burned for hiring blacks, and churches and the houses of movement sympathizers were destroyed. And it was in Jackson, on the night of June 11, 1963, after President Kennedy had gone on television to call for national civil rights legislation, that NAACP field secretary Medgar Evers was shot to death in the driveway of his home. The assassination—the first murder of a civil rights worker accorded that term—gave a new focus to growing black rage. On the day he was buried in Arlington National Cemetery, thousands marched through the streets of Jackson chanting, "After Medgar, no more fear!" According to a poll by *U.S. News & World Report*, race relations had become the single most troubling issue for Americans in 1963, ahead of the cold war and its threat of nuclear annihilation.

In July of the following year, President Johnson signed the Civil Rights Act, which prohibited racial discrimination in employment and in public places such as restaurants and theaters and authorized the attorney general to bring suits to end unfair voting practices. That year, buoyed by the new legislation, SNCC declared Mississippi Freedom Summer and invited north-ern college students to the state to help register black voters in advance of the fall presidential election. The volunteers also formed Freedom Schools to teach basic skills and black history, and opened Freedom Clinics to provide no-cost health care. Over the course of the summer, thirty movement houses were burned across the state, thirty-five churches were bombed, a thousand civil rights workers were arrested, at least eighty people were beaten, and six were murdered. Among the victims were black Mississippian James Earl Chaney and white New Yorkers Andrew Goodman and Michael Schwerner, who were killed out-side Philadelphia, Mississippi, after being arrested on a trumped-up traffic charge, then released to a waiting Ku Klux Klan posse. Despite it all, over the course of Mississippi Freedom Summer just 1,200 new black voters were registered.

In March 1965, a week after police brutally assaulted five hun-dred marchers on the Edmund Pettus Bridge outside Selma, Ala-bama, President Johnson called for a new voting rights bill in an emotional televised speech before both houses of Congress. "At times history and fate meet at a single time in a single place to shape a turning point in man's unending search for freedom," he said. "So it was at Lexington and Concord. So it was a century ago at Appomattox. So it was last week in Selma. . . . Their cause must be our cause, too. Because it is not just Negroes, but really it's all of us, who must overcome the crippling legacy of bigotry and injustice." Then he stunned the nation by quoting the hallmark phrase of the civil rights movement. "And we shall overcome."

In August, the Voting Rights Act was passed over the objections of southern lawmakers and signed into law. Suspending literacy tests and employing federal rather than local examiners to enroll voters, the new legislation proved effective where previous measures had failed. In 1964, the year before the Voting Rights Act, 7 percent of Mississippi blacks were registered to vote; four years later, 59 percent were. Throughout the South, the number of black voters more than tripled over the same period.

———•———

Beyond the suburban strip malls, Selma appears not to have changed much over the past forty years. Like many southern downtowns, it seems a little faded, a little too quiet. But Broad Street still has its turn-of-the-century brick storefronts with their wrought iron porches and balconies, and the stolid Brown Chapel AME Church, which served as headquarters of the voting rights movement, still rises above the projects near the intersection of Martin Luther King Jr. Street and Jeff Davis Avenue.

As you enter town on U.S. 80, you come to a modest frame house that has been converted into a tourist center, presided over this day by a thin, animated white man in his seventies who is obviously proud of his city. The shop dispenses information and offers the usual souvenirs—caps, T-shirts, key chains, shot glasses. But the most popular image on this merchandise is not the Brown Chapel or the antebellum mansion called Sturdivant Hall or even the Voting Rights Museum, but the plain metal bridge on the edge of town named for Confederate general and U.S. senator Edmund Pettus. Many of the brochures and maps in the wooden rack also recall this time in Selma's history, which you might have thought it would just as soon forget.

On March 25, 1965, three weeks after the violence on the Pettus Bridge, the voting rights marchers, their ranks now swelled to 12,000 blacks and whites from all over the country, finally reached the Alabama state capitol under the protection of a federal court order and the National Guard. Their fifty-mile route along U.S. 80 is now designated the Selma to Montgomery Historic Trail, and its end point, a city of neoclassical buildings and generous boulevards, has also converted the struggle for racial equality into a tourist attraction, with sites such as Martin Luther King's Dexter Avenue Baptist Church and a new Civil Rights Memorial Center. And if you follow the Alabama Civil Rights Museum Trail northwest to the city of Birmingham, you will find a six-block Civil Rights District, including the Sixteenth Street Baptist Church, the Jazz Hall of Fame, and the Civil Rights Institute, all duly listed on the Greater Birmingham Convention and Visitors Bureau web page.

It may seem strange (if quintessentially American) that the somber venues of the civil rights era are now touted in glossy handouts of "things to see and do." But couldn't the same be said of Civil War battlefields? After all, civil rights monuments have been erected to celebrate, not the violence and intransigence of the losers, but the courage and persistence of the winners. That these events are now considered worthy of memorials is perhaps the most telling indicator of how much things have changed in the South over the past four decades.

As the 1960s progressed, government continued to exert its power on behalf of civil rights. In 1966, LBJ appointed Robert Weaver the first black cabinet member (Housing and Urban Development) and the following year named Thurgood Marshall the first black justice on the U.S. Supreme Court. Also in 1967, a white Mississippi jury returned the first-ever civil rights conviction against white defendants, in the murders of Chaney, Goodman, and Schwerner. In 1968, the year of Martin Luther King's assassination, a new Civil Rights Act barred discrimination in housing. That fall in Holmes County, Robert G. Clark became the first black elected to the Mississippi legislature since Reconstruction. The following year, the U.S. Supreme Court ordered the immediate end of Mississippi's dual school systems, finally forcing the state's districts to desegregate as of the first term of 1970, sixteen years after *Brown*. By 1972, southern schools were actually more integrated than those in the rest of the country, with 44 percent of black students in predominantly white schools, versus only 30 percent in the North.

After his election in 1976 with 94 percent of the black vote, Jimmy Carter appointed more African American officials than any president before him, including judges, ambassadors, and two cabinet secretaries. By 1980, 2,500 southern black officials held elective office, including several members of the U.S. House of Representatives. In Alabama, diehard segregationist George Wallace began to work for racial reconciliation; in 1982, he was elected to his third term as governor with widespread black support. A decade later, more than six hundred blacks had been elected in Mississippi alone, including Congressman Mike Espy of Yazoo City. In 1995, Mississippi finally ratified the Thirteenth Amendment to the U.S. Constitution, the one abolishing slavery, 130 years after every other Confederate state.

The black middle class also expanded. From 1994 to 2000, black family income grew from just under $25,000 to $31,000 (versus $35,126 and $45,904 for whites). But by 2004, 25 percent of black Americans were still living below the federal poverty line, whereas only 9 percent of whites were officially poor. In fact, according to several studies reviewed by the *New York Times*, the plight of young black men is actually deepening. Fifty percent of black males in their twenties are jobless, the *Times* reports. Among high school dropouts (who make up the majority of black males in the inner cities), 72 percent are unemployed. As the article points out, "more black male dropouts in their late twenties are in prison on any given day—34 percent—than are working—30 percent."

Why has social and economic progress stalled so miserably for some blacks, such as Zack's workers Ben and Charlie? It used to be obvious what was holding African Americans back in places like Mississippi—segregationist laws, white violence, economic intimidation, a corrupt legal system. Today the answer is more complex. Some suggest we still haven't done enough to offset the economic dependence, the disruption to family life, and the lack of education wrought by centuries of slavery and sharecropping. Others argue that the playing field has been leveled, that blacks now have the means to advance themselves if they want to. Yet Ben and Charlie and their families, like American blacks in general, are still living in second-rate housing and attending inferior schools, are earning less and are imprisoned more. Clearly, despite the progress of forty years, the racial problem hasn't been "solved" in Tchula any more than in the ghettos of the North.

But even in Tchula this bleak picture doesn't encompass everyone. Willie Waters, Zack's longest-tenured employee, could have left the Delta, as thousands of others have done. Yet he's decided to stay. He has a permanent, year-round job that gives him satisfaction, and his wife is a teacher in a day care center. Still, with three kids, finances are tight. "Sometimes I wish we had more," Willie allows, maybe to buy a second car, so he wouldn't have to rely on lifts back and forth to work. "I wouldn't say we're strugglin', but everythin' is so expensive. It's hard to save." They're living in a two-bedroom mobile home, and they're trying to put aside money for a down payment on a house, so all the kids, two girls and a boy, won't have to share a single room.

Willie has no plans to give up farming, but he's not complacent about his future. One day he'd like to rent some land and work for himself. Maybe he'd start with thirty acres, planting some soybeans in his spare time. Gradually he could build up to sixty acres, then a hundred, and eventually to several hundred, enough to make a living—much the way that Zack got his start. Unlike Zack, though, Willie wouldn't plant any cotton. "Too risky," he says.

What about his three-year-old son? Would Willie like to see him get into farming? "No," he answers immediately. "I want somethin' way better for him, and for the girls, too. I want them to go to college and become lawyers or somethin'." But whatever they choose to do, he's certain that discrimination won't hold back his children, that they'll be free to be whatever they have the will and the ability to become. Does he ever think about how different life will be for them compared to how it was for his father and grandfather? "Absolutely," Willie says. Only in his mid-thirties, he's too young to remember the civil rights movement.

"Sometimes I see programs on TV, and I can hardly believe those things ever happened. It's like ancient history. There are still some people around like that," he admits, meaning racists, "but it just doesn't affect my life."

Willie is right; the struggle for black equality is an old story. For three centuries, relations between the races were dictated by cotton's demand for cheap, abundant labor. Today that need is gone, but cotton continues to haunt our racial landscape just as it still dominates the flat, sultry terrain of the Mississippi Delta.

PART IV
Winter

NINE

The Mill

I have passed through Selma because I'm following the route that Zack's cotton takes after it leaves his field. Continuing east on U.S. 80 for seventy-five miles beyond Montgomery, I arrive at Columbus, Georgia. Founded in 1828 at the fall line of the Chattahoochee River, where rapids prevented ships from navigating farther upstream, Columbus served first as a trading and shipping center for cotton. After the railroad came in the 1850s, the falls were increasingly harnessed to produce cotton cloth. By the start of the Civil War, the city was one of the leading textile centers below the Mason-Dixon Line, "the Lowell of the South." Though the mills were destroyed during the fighting, they were running again by the end of 1865.

Soon northern textile manufacturers began to shift their operations to states such as Georgia and the Carolinas, where employees (including former sharecroppers) were willing to work for wages 30 to 50 percent lower than those in New England, and where laws permitted longer mandatory working hours. The southern states were also less finicky about child labor, and by the early 1900s, 60 percent of their female mill workers were thirteen or younger. By the 1930s, three-quarters of American cotton spinning was located in the South. Columbus benefited from this trend, and new textile plants continued to open there as late as 1950, employing thousands of workers. Today the factories along the Chattahoochee have been converted into condos and offices linked by a scenic river walk, and downtown has been reborn as an entertainment district, the old brick buildings renovated into restaurants and bars.

But cotton textiles are still being manufactured in Columbus. On the east side of the city, in a tidy industrial park surrounded by corporations such as Kodak, Bayer, Weyerhauser, and Cessna, is a warehouse belonging to a company called Swift Spinning. Celebrating its centenary this year (its name commemorates George Parker Swift, one of the industrialists who expanded Columbus's textile trade after the Civil War), Swift is now owned by the huge Japanese trading company Marubeni, and the corporate marriage has produced a twenty-first-century merging of cultures. Swift's chairman is a slender Japanese man named Keigo Inao, who speaks idiomatic English and prefers life in Georgia to that in his native country. The company president is a compact, intense southerner named Trey Hodges, who represents the fourth generation of his family to work in the textile mills. At the monthly award luncheons, fried chicken is served alongside teriyaki.

Most of Swift's 80,000-square-foot warehouse is stacked with plastic-sheathed bales of cotton and shrink-wrapped pallets of thread (or "yarn," as it is known in the business). But one area has been set aside as a classing room, where the fiber that the company uses is examined before purchase. A hundred years ago, when all cotton was graded by hand, classing rooms were built with a northern exposure to avoid the deceiving effects of direct sunlight. To approximate those conditions, this windowless space is painted a particular shade of gray, and fluorescent light fixtures with special bluish bulbs are hung precisely ten feet off the floor. Knowing how easy it is to be misled, David Koon, Swift's vice president of cotton procurement, refuses to judge fiber anywhere but in this room.

Laid out for inspection this morning on a waist-high black wooden table are fifty tufts of fiber four inches wide and twice as long, each sawed from a different bale. And as indicated by the paper barcode tucked inside, each sample originated from Holmes Gin Company in Tchula, where Zack's cotton is processed. The samples arrived here through the efforts of middlemen, who have played a central part in the cotton trade since the nineteenth century, when so-called factors loaned planters money, furnished them with tools and slaves, then bought their crop. Today there aren't many factors left, and instead of the all-encompassing role they once enjoyed, they simply connect a grower with a merchant in exchange for a commission of a couple of dollars a bale. The great majority of planters now either sell their cotton directly to a merchant, who resells it to a mill, or market it through a farmer-owned cooperative, which sells it to a mill on the farmers' behalf.

Swift Spinning maintains this classing room because all bales of cotton, even those from the same field, vary in qualities (such as color, fiber strength, length, thickness, uniformity, and the amount of extraneous material) that matter to those who convert it into fabric. (Cotton grown in different seasons is so dissimilar, in the way it absorbs dye, for instance, that Swift never mixes crop years in a single run of thread.) Although the U.S. Department of Agriculture grades virtually all American cotton, Swift finds that, for its purposes, trained eyes and hands are superior to the government's machines. So, selecting from computer printouts that list each bale's specifications as determined by the USDA, David Koon chooses his candidates and orders his samples.

When the tufts arrive in their tall kraft paper bundles, he pinches the fiber apart to see whether it's as good as the Department of Agriculture says it is. If in doubt, he can open one of the gray cardboard boxes he keeps on the classing table and consult the official standards arrayed inside like six little cotton pillows. When the cotton meets his approval, he tells the merchant or co-op to ship the bale. But he rejects between a quarter and a third of the samples as not living up to their test data. It's not that the government process is inherently flawed, he explains; it's just that the testing machines aren't recalibrated as often as they should be.

The selected cotton arrives at the Swift Spinning warehouse in truckloads of ninety bales each. Then, like a winemaker mixing grapes, David Koon uses a computer program to help him choose the sixty-nine bales that will constitute a laydown, the fiber that will be blended to produce a particular batch of thread. In part, he is guided by what it will be used for—towels, T-shirts, socks, or blue jeans.

The bales for each laydown are trucked to the other side of the industrial park, where Swift's East Columbus plant is located.

Occupying 300,000 square feet, the factory employs 150 workers in two twelve-hour shifts and produces 18 million pounds of thread a year. That makes it a small operation overall but a medium-size player in its specialty, a process called combed ring spinning. Marubeni has invested millions of dollars to transform this mill into one of the most highly automated facilities of its kind in the world. After the forklift operator drops the bales for the laydown in a long, straight line on the plant's concrete floor, the fiber will not be handled again until it emerges a week later as finished thread, wound onto cardboard spools and arrayed on black plastic pallets.

Plant manager Mike O'Brien leads me through a pair of metal doors, and we're greeted by a warm gust. The work area is maintained at 82 degrees and 52 percent humidity. If it were much cooler or drier, the fibers would become brittle during processing; much warmer or moister and the "trash" mixed with it would adhere too tightly. The air has the same lumberlike scent as at the cotton gin, and despite the miles of air filtration ducts, I feel a tickle in the back of my throat.

The spotless, fluorescent-lit space seems devoid of people but is crowded with inscrutable machines. Though the means have become almost unrecognizably high-tech, their purpose is the same as always—to align the fibers, draw them out, and twist them into thread. For millennia, this was accomplished through the simplest of devices, with spinners feeding the lint through their fingers and twisting it onto a bobbin turned by a rotating disk or wheel. Then in the late 1700s the process was mechanized, first by Hargreaves's jenny and later by Arkwright's series of water-powered rollers, each

moving faster than the one before. Despite all the computeriza-
tion, that latter method is essentially unchanged today.

The first device the fiber encounters at Swift Spinning is the
cotton plucker, a metal box that rolls on a narrow track. Project-
ing from the plucker's body is a boom fitted with jagged metal
wheels that ride over the bales of the laydown, digging into the
fiber and teasing off a little at a time. In the process, Mike says,
the plucker occasionally uncovers a surprise, like spools of baling
wire, tractor engine parts, and once a dead cat.

The dislodged cotton is sucked up through a wide hose that
fluffs the fiber and starts to blend it. To minimize the risk of fire,
the hose is equipped with a metal detector. If foreign matter is
sensed, a flap opens and it drops harmlessly into a waste bag. Next
the fiber is transported to a series of closed machines whose in-
sides bristle with wheels and beaters to remove the trash and continue blending the cotton to ensure uniformity in the finished
thread. The devices are known as the Unifloc, Unimix, ERM, and
Mini-Mix, names that bring to mind the earliest computer termi-
nals, whose size and boxy form many of them resemble.

The cotton emerges in a delicate white blanket called a card
mat. Blown along on a cushion of air, the mat enters the card, another metal box, where the process of turning it into thread begins
in earnest. Whereas nineteenth-century carding machines used
cylinders studded with wire bristles to remove any tangles (or
"neps"; like many terms associated with spinning and weaving,
this one is ancient) and align the fibers, today's version guides the
cotton through a series of toothed rollers and drums. By the time
it exits the card, the cotton has been formed into a ropelike sliver

(rhymes with *diver*), a narrow, continuous mat an inch thick, eight miles long, and 130 pounds in weight.

Five slivers pass through a series of rollers that merge them into one. Then the next machine seems to take a backward step, spreading the fiber out again into a broad, flat sheet called a lap, which is wound onto a large roll. But this stage is necessary to prepare the cotton for the comber, a wide metal device with thirty teeth, or "nicks," per inch. As the lap passes through the comber, the fibers are further aligned, and those shorter than half an inch (called noils) are pulled out. Not all cotton goes through this step, but fiber that does is softer to the touch. It's also more expensive, since combing removes about 15 percent of the material, which will be collected and sold to manufacturers of products such as tampons and cosmetic puffs.

At the far end of the comber, the lap encounters more rollers, which blend it with eight others and reshape it once again into a narrow sliver, so it can be drawn into thread. The sliver enters the roving frame, which uses four rollers to give it a slight twist and draw it out to about the width of a piece of string. This roving is collected on a bobbin, a thin plastic spool seventeen and a half inches high. Then it is passed to the huge spinning frame, which occupies a third of the plant's area and fills the space with its metallic chattering.

Ring spinning, which dates back to 1828, produces high-quality thread that is strong and soft and, because it's slightly less uniform, lends greater character to the articles made from it. On the spinning frame, the roving is fed through rollers that draw it out to the desired thickness. The thread's diameter, or count, depends on what it will be used for, and is measured by an antique system in which the higher the number the thinner the thread. (Thread used for blue jeans typically has a count of seven or eight; that for socks might have a count of twelve; for a dress shirt, thirty.) It next passes through C-shaped clips called travelers, which revolve around a metal ring. As they spin, the travelers twist the thread eighteen to twenty turns per inch; too few and it will be weak, too many and it will be kinky. The finished thread is pulled to the center of the ring, where it is collected on a rotating plastic bobbin. Swift's East Columbus plant operates 32,640 of these spindles simultaneously. By comparison, the first Lowell mills, built about 1830, averaged between 3,000 and 4,000 spindles; by 1850, when it was the country's preeminent cotton manufacturer, the entire city had a total of 320,000 spindles, supplying 10,000 looms and employing more than that many people.

At the winding machine, the thread from sixty spindles is combined into one large, flattened cone called a package or, in the old parlance, a "cheese." First the thread is unwound, then the separate lengths are spliced together by jets of air, which produce patches that are invisible even under a microscope. Two centuries ago, the bobbins were changed by children known as doffers, but today the empty spindles are simply released onto a conveyor, where they waddle away like so many marching penguins. Measuring eight inches on top (slightly wider on the bottom) and weighing six pounds regardless of the count, the packages trundle down slanted conveyor belts and through a steamer, which sets the thread's twist. Then they are automatically collected onto pallets, which are loaded onto trucks and carted back across the industrial park to the same warehouse where they arrived as bales of fiber.

Depending on its count, a single pound of cotton can make between 800 and 2,500 yards of thread. A five-hundred-pound bale could eventually become 215 pairs of blue jeans, 249 bedsheets, 409 sport shirts, 690 bath towels, 765 dress shirts, 1,217 T-shirts, 1,256 pillowcases, 2,104 boxer shorts, 2,419 jockey shorts, 4,321 midcalf socks, 6,436 women's briefs, or 21,960 handkerchiefs. Most of these items are now manufactured overseas. But some of Swift's thread ventures no farther than next door, to a weaving plant owned by a company called Denim North America. The location isn't an accident; DNA was also owned by Marubeni until a management buyout several years ago.

Like Swift Spinning, DNA is a medium-size player in its market niche. It's also one of only half a dozen denim mills left in the United States. (The buffalo was selected as the company's logo not just because of its association with the Wild West, but because of its rescue from near extinction.) Jeans are an American icon, but trousers made of heavy blue material were worn by European workingmen centuries ago, and the word *jean*, derived from *Genoa*, dates back to the 1500s. When the cloth arrived in England in the seventeenth century, via France, it was known as *serge de Nimes*, later shortened to *denim*. *Dungaree* was coined about the same time, first referring to cheap calico, then to pants made of the material, and eventually to what we now call blue jeans.

But perhaps the name most closely associated with denim is that of San Francisco dry goods merchant Levi Strauss. After one of Strauss's customers, Jacob Davis, invented a system of riveting pant seams for added strength, the two went into business together. A patent was awarded in 1873, and the improved "waist overalls" (as work pants were known then) were an immediate success. More than a century later, blue jeans are worn around the world, no longer just as work clothes but as leisure wear and even high-fashion status symbols. It's no coincidence that everyone I meet at DNA today, including the company's affable president, Monte Galbraith, is wearing jeans.

Like the Swift plant, this is a state-of-the-art facility. Though it employs only forty workers more than its neighbor, the DNA mill doesn't have the same automated, depopulated feel. Compared to the compact metal boxes that do most of the work at Swift, the machines needed for dyeing and weaving are bigger and messier, requiring more human intervention to keep them running. And instead of producing insubstantial filaments of pure white thread, they disgorge massive sheets of dark, heavy cloth. In the spinning mill's futuristic, antiseptic atmosphere, you feel the plant could almost be producing pharmaceuticals. But here in the Dickensian recesses of the weaving mill, you are continually reminded that this is a very old technology.

Monte Galbraith introduces me to another manager, Toby Sklar, a slight man with a New Jersey accent and the raspy timbre of a longtime smoker. The first step in producing denim, Toby explains, is to take Swift's neat packages of thread and unravel them in a process of controlled chaos known as warping. Some 360 packages are stacked on long stainless steel frames called creels. The separate threads, or "ends," are guided through a series of loops to a central point, where they converge in midair like a maniacal spider web, then magically condense into a rope about an inch and a half wide. The rope is coiled around a spool three feet across and four feet long, called a ball warp, then carted to the dyeing area.

Denim is one of the few fabrics that is dyed before weaving, which is part of the reason for its characteristically uneven color. The variation also has to do with the nature of indigo. Once extracted from plants in the pea family, indigo has been used as a dye for at least 4,000 years. About a century ago, a synthetic form was invented in Germany, and today all commercial indigo is man-made. But the synthetic retains the same characteristic as its natural cousin—it is a particularly poor dye for cotton, whose fibers can't absorb it. In fact, the process resembles painting more than dyeing, explains Tom Butler, who is manufacturing manager at DNA. What would seem to be a drawback has been turned to a marketing advantage, because it is this lack of absorption that allows each pair of jeans to develop its individual character as the indigo leaches out from wash to wash.

Fourteen stainless steel vats and a convoluted assemblage of rollers are required for dyeing, extending half a city block and rising two stories above the plant floor. The rope is first scoured by being drawn through a caustic liquid smelling of photographic chemicals. Then it's passed through the sudsy baths of indigo, which give off a sweet, almost floral aroma. Depending on the depth of color wanted, the thread receives up to nine immersions, emerging at first not blue but pale green. Between dippings the rollers carry it high toward the plant's ceiling, and only when it descends, after a minute's exposure to the air, has the rope assumed its characteristic violet-blue shade.

Following the indigo baths, the ropes are passed through three vats of fresh rinse water and finally a sulfur dye. Unlike the indigo, the sulfur is absorbed by the cotton, and it stains the center of the thread a dull gray to reduce the contrast with the dark exterior. Finally, the ropes are fed through a set of steam-heated rollers. When they exit two minutes later, already dry to the touch, they're coiled into steel tubs six feet wide and four feet high, each containing more than a mile of rope (or 360 miles of individual threads).

The ends have been pulled together to facilitate dyeing, but before they can be woven, they must be spread into a flat sheet through a delicate process called beaming. The dyed rope is first lifted from its can, twirling toward the roof like a slender blue tornado. It passes through a loop in the ceiling that untwists it, then descends to waist height, where it is guided through a series of metal teeth called a hack, which convert it into a six-foot-wide horizontal band of narrowly spaced threads. The strands are next carefully wound side by side onto a roll called a beam, which resembles a giant version of the spool of thread you might buy at the five-and-ten. The process is monitored by the beamer tenders, who are among the most highly trained workers in the plant, having taken a full year to learn their craft. Not only must the tenders keep the thread perfectly straight as it whips onto the spool at 3,000 to 6,000 yards an hour, they have to listen above the whirring machinery for the telltale *snap* that signals a break, then stop the beam and cleanly retie the ends.

At the slasher, twelve beams are fed simultaneously through a milky blue, 204°F concoction of starch and wax called sizing, which gives the thread the necessary strength and slickness to survive its journey through the loom. But if too much of the solution is applied, the thread will become brittle and break under the stress of weaving. As they emerge, stiff and slippery to the touch, six hundred ends are wound onto another wide roll called a loom beam.

The looming area is segregated from the rest of the plant by concrete walls and steel doors. Tom warns me to insert my ear-plugs before we enter, but I'm still astonished by the metallic roar produced by the 110 looms. He screams in my ear that these models are much quieter than the old ones. Still, this is easily the loudest place I have ever been.

A beam is affixed horizontally to one side of the loom, and the hundreds of ends are inserted in a complicated process that takes three hours even with the aid of specialized machines. When the loom is started, the threads slowly unwind, first passing under a set of drop wires. If a strand breaks, that wire will fall and stop the mechanism until it is retied by one of the weavers, who are the most skilled employees in the mill. The resulting knot is generally invisible in the finished fabric. In fact, the process proceeds so smoothly that only one weaver is needed to tend fifteen looms.

Brown denim is being woven today. Toby confides that next fall all the chain stores will be carrying jeans this shade, but looking at the flat, muddy color, I can't help having my doubts. As the brown threads that form the lengthwise strands, or "warp," are drawn into the loom, they pass through a series of harnesses that open and close to allow the crosswise threads (the "weft" or "filler") to be inserted. The harnesses govern how the warp and filler cross, and adjusting the pattern of their motion alters the appearance of the finished fabric—determining, for instance, whether it will have the smooth texture of the so-called plain weave or the subtle diagonal ridges that characterize twills (including denim).

The weft used to be formed by one continuous piece of thread, but passing it from one side of the loom to the other (the process mechanized by the flying shuttle nearly three centuries ago) proved prohibitively slow. So now the filler consists of individual lengths of thread, which are shot from nozzles on blasts of compressed air. White cotton is generally used for this, which is why the wrong side of a pair of blue jeans has a pale color; to make stretch jeans, white Lycra is substituted. At either edge of the fabric, the harnesses reverse their stitch pattern, which locks the loose filler in place and keeps the material from unraveling. Then a metal comb slaps up against the finished stitch, or "pick," pushing it tight. The loom makes seven hundred to eight hundred picks per minute, but even at that rate, one beam of warp thread will last for three 24-hour workdays before needing to be replenished.

At the far end of the loom, the woven cloth is gathered into wide bolts, or "shells," each containing more than a linear mile of fabric. The shells are taken to the finishing area, where they might be given a special wash or additional dyeing. Then they are sanforized, which involves slowly passing the denim through steam-heated rollers. Unlike wool, cotton fibers themselves do not shrink; any reduction is caused by the threads pulling closer together within the fabric. So by performing this step at the mill, manufacturers minimize any shrinkage in the finished product. Sanforizing was invented about seventy-five years ago in my hometown of Troy, New York, by Sanford L. Cluett, of the shirtmakers Cluett, Peabody and Co. Cluett's patented method used a contracting elastic belt to shrink the material, and by the time he died in 1968, the system had been licensed to over four hundred mills in fifty-eight countries.

Finally, the shells are manually inspected and any defects are marked. Then they are wrapped in clear plastic for shipping. It's taken three to four weeks to convert the packages of thread into shells of denim. Whereas Swift Spinning has the advantage of producing a commodity ("Thread is thread," as a Swift manager puts it), a denim mill like DNA is much more dependent on marketing and fashion. Even though the company sews no clothing, it maintains a design staff in New York, offers eighty different styles of cloth, and introduces a new product line each season.

With denim, Monte Galbraith explains, "the look is about getting the dye on, then getting some of it back off." Technology is key, because new methods of treating the fabric are always being developed, such as selective bleaching and hand-sanding. Even though these processes are generally performed after the clothing has been sewn, DNA keeps a showroom in the Columbus plant where sample jeans are displayed to help customers visualize what can be done with its fabrics. On the table, there's a pair of weathered tan jeans that look so soft and comfortable I have to touch them. I'm astonished when Monte says this is the same denim I saw on the loom today. By removing exactly the right amount of color, the designers have given the jeans the perfectly worn look of your favorite weekend pants. But it will be more than a year—after the cloth is sent overseas, cut into patterns, sewn, then shipped back to the United States—before they will appear in retail stores.

———◆———

There's a reason that the Swift Spinning and DNA plants are state of the art—if they were any less efficient, the companies wouldn't be able to survive their foreign competition. Late in the past century, the same economic forces that brought textiles to Columbus and other southern cities began siphoning off those same jobs. As American salaries rose and the industry became increasingly global, spinning, weaving, and sewing began to move to Latin America and the Far East, where wages and working conditions were much more favorable to employers. Between 1990 and 2000, the American textile industry lost some 300,000 jobs; today there are about 700,000 left, roughly 7 percent of all factory positions remaining in this country.

The only way American mills can stay in business is to keep costs as low as possible, and this has meant replacing their relatively high-wage employees with machines. More American textile jobs have been lost to automation than have been exported, and even China, the world's largest producer, is laying off workers as it modernizes its mills. As a result of mechanization, textile production in the United States has held more or less steady over the past fifteen years, even as the number of workers has fallen by 60 percent.

Most of the remaining textile jobs are still located in Georgia and the Carolinas, but Swift is the only spinning mill left in Columbus. A manager at the company says that when he used to attend industry luncheons of his peers from other companies, there would be so many people he couldn't keep all their names straight; if such an affair were held today, he'd be eating by himself. Swift has laid off two-thirds of its employees in recent years, and company president Trey Hodges worries about the loss of manufacturing jobs that have been a traditional path to the middle class for families like his own. Monte Galbraith of DNA followed his father into the mills as a boy. "I just love this industry," he says, repeating an oft-heard sentiment. "Everybody knows each other. It's like a family. We say that's why the company is called DNA: It's in the genes." But today it's doubtful whether Trey's or Monte's children, or those of their workers, will be able to make a career in their parents' business.

Most of the goods produced from Swift thread and DNA denim are sewn in countries such as Mexico, the Dominican Republic, Honduras, Guatemala, and Nicaragua, since that region provides the closest, cheapest labor pool for the United States. Thanks to ever-changing fashion, sewing has frustrated every effort at mechanization, and this labor intensiveness made it the first stage of the process to move abroad. But even Latin American workers have become too expensive, and countries such as Mexico have been losing textile jobs to the Far East, where wages are even lower. China now controls more than 30 percent of the apparel export market, selling a billion garments a year to the United States alone. Much of the cotton in this clothing originates in China, which grows more of the fiber than any other nation, about 5 million tons per year versus 4 million in the United States. But even this is not enough to sustain the country's 40,000 garment factories, so the Chinese also buy up nearly a third of the world's cotton exports, another 2 million tons. It is the drain of weaving and sewing jobs out of the Western Hemisphere, rather than out of the United States, that now poses the greatest risk to companies like Swift Spinning and Denim North America. When the Far East imports cotton, it is generally in the form of fiber, not thread or fabric. So if the Latin American factories close, their U.S. suppliers will be hard-pressed to replace those customers.

To slow the exodus of textile jobs, the federal government levies tariffs on foreign clothing entering the United States. It also pays American makers for using domestic cotton. Textiles are the most heavily protected area of U.S. manufacturing, with payments to mills or exporters averaging more than $250 million a year. But even with the protection, the United States simply can't compete with low-wage countries like China in the long run. American companies moving their spinning, weaving, and sewing operations offshore have been labeled as greedy and unpatriotic, but in many cases the corporations are facing a harsh choice: relocate or close.

As Pietra Rivoli points out in her insightful book *The Travels of a T-Shirt in the Global Economy*, this search for ever-cheaper labor, which has been called "the race to the bottom," is nothing new. For two centuries, from Lancashire and Lowell onward, cotton manufacturing has been an "entry-level" industry, eventually superseded by higher-tech businesses requiring more experienced, better-educated workers. Some cities, like Columbus, have managed to attract insurance and telecommunications companies to fill the gap left by the defunct textile plants, and as a result they have prospered in the age of globalization. Other places haven't been so fortunate or so farsighted. And for displaced employees without the education or skills to make the jump to the new economy, the loss of manufacturing jobs has been anguishing.

Just as textile manufacturing is the most heavily protected sector of American industry, cotton is the most heavily subsidized branch of U.S. agriculture. This is no coincidence, since both ends of the industry are subject to similar international pressures. Just as Swift and DNA can't pass along their higher domestic labor costs to their customers, Zack can't charge for his cotton according to how much he's invested in the crop. To help make up the difference, each year the federal government pays the 25,000 American cotton farmers roughly $4 billion, which acre for acre is five to ten times the supports paid for corn, soybeans, or wheat. In fact, as the subsidies' critics have noted, these amounts surpass the entire gross domestic product of some poor cotton-growing countries in Africa.

Federal payments to agriculture date back to the 1930s, after commodity prices fell during the Great Depression. The Agricultural Adjustment Act of 1933 paid growers to take land out of production, as a way of reducing supply and improving market prices. (Of course, this also had the effect of putting tenant farmers out of business.) To offset the drop in acreage, farmers turned to chemicals and machines to increase their yields. As a result, the harvest did not decrease. Just as automation in the mills has held American textile production steady over the past decade and a half despite a steep reduction in the number of workers, the introduction of more efficient growing practices has kept the cotton harvest virtually unchanged. Today in the United States, only one-third the land is devoted to cotton as in 1929, but the harvest is virtually the same, about 20 million bales a year.

The AAA was not the first time lawmakers had come to the aid of cotton planters. By condoning slavery, Washington allowed antebellum plantation owners to circumvent the free labor market and ensure that they had abundant, cheap workers when

they needed them. After Emancipation, state crop lien laws prevented tenants from negotiating on an even basis with landlords.
Then four years after the AAA, the Agriculture Act of 1937 introduced our modern system of federal supports for cotton and
other crops, in which farmers are guaranteed a specified price regardless of market fluctuations. Adopted by every developed
country, such subsidies have been in place ever since.

Today this government largess is awarded through a byzantine
maze of overlapping programs. Under the current farm bill, Zack
qualifies for a direct payment of $40,000, because he has a mini-
mum of five hundred acres in cotton. In addition, if the market
price falls below the benchmark of 72.4 cents per pound, he is
guaranteed a "countercyclical" payment of up to thirteen cents per
pound for fiber corresponding to 85 percent of his acreage, up to a
maximum of $65,000 per year. Then there is a crop-deficiency pro-
vision, which works like the countercyclical, paying Zack the difference if the market price drops below a stated minimum, up to
$75,000 a year. A crop disaster program reimburses him for losses
due to unusually bad weather. There is also crop insurance, and a
low-interest loan program that forgives part of the principal if the
market price drops. It's all so complicated that Zack himself can't
tell how much he's entitled to until his Farm Service agent gives
him the figures.

When you add up all the various programs, how much help can
Zack count on from the government on an annual basis? In a good
season, when he has a large crop and the market is high, he will
receive only the direct payment of $40,000. But in a bad year, the
programs could yield $350 per acre of cotton, which for Zack

could add up to $350,000. That may not be enough to put him in
the black, but it might let him break even or give him the means
to plant again the following spring. And besides these payments,
Zack benefits indirectly from government supports to American
mills, which make his fiber more affordable in this country, and
from subsidies for cotton exporters, which make it more competitive overseas. It is largely through this government assistance that
cotton is still a viable industry in the United States.

Poor nations that can't afford to support their farmers to this
degree have long cried foul over the agricultural policy of developed countries, especially the European Union and the United
States. American cotton has come in for particular criticism, especially the export payments, which in effect pay producers to dump
fiber on the world market. Supported by the World Bank, Oxfam
International, and other organizations, West African countries
such as Benin, Burkina Faso, Chad, and Mali charge that the subsidies, by ensuring that more cotton is grown, depress the market
price for every grower in every nation.

Brazil, another cotton exporter, appealed to the World Trade
Organization for relief, and in April 2004 the WTO ruled that
American supports for cotton violate international trade rules.
Threatened with severe penalties on its goods abroad, in July of
that year the United States agreed to phase out export subsidies
as well as payments to textile manufacturers for buying domestic
fiber; under the agreement, amounts paid directly to cotton farmers would also drop by 20 percent in the first year. In exchange,
other nations agreed to ease import restrictions on U.S. wheat,
corn, and soybeans.

There is no question that American subsidies give U.S. farmers an edge in the international market (which is their purpose,
after all). By encouraging planters to grow cotton, they have
been found to increase world supply and lower the market price
by anywhere from 3 to 26 percent, depending on the study. Organizations such as Oxfam present the case against U.S. cotton producers in starkly moral terms, charging that "American cotton
subsidies are destroying livelihoods in Africa and other developing regions." But how much would Third World farmers really
benefit from reduced American supports?

The truth is that the success of U.S. cotton farmers is based
only partly on government subsidies. In the nineteenth century, it
wasn't just slavery that allowed American planters to overtake
older cotton-growing areas such as India and China and become
the world's largest exporter of the fiber. From the beginning, U.S.
agriculture prospered under a business-friendly atmosphere and an
entrepreneurial culture that didn't exist in those more traditional
societies, where a variety of government and economic factors
gave growers little incentive to take risks or increase production.
Today in the United States, federal and state governments, universities, and the cotton industry all work together to create a political, financial, technological, and marketing infrastructure that
provides tremendous assistance aside from any direct payments.
Just one example of such public–private cooperation is Mississippi's boll weevil eradication program; another is the extensive
technical assistance offered by Mississippi State University, which
develops more productive, cost-efficient methods of growing
crops, then shows farmers how to use them.

Growers in West Africa don't benefit from such a supportive environment. Living standards in tiny Burkina Faso, which has an astonishing 2 million cotton farmers—eighty times more than the United States—are the third lowest of any country in the world, and life expectancy is less than fifty years. Throughout the region, cotton is grown on small family plots, averaging one to three acres. Per-acre yields are about four hundred pounds, less than half what they are in the U.S., and African farmers can undersell their American competitors only because labor is very cheap and often provided by family members. Technology is extremely limited. African cotton is still handpicked (as it is in other developing countries). Fertilizer and pesticide use is sporadic, and when these products are available, the generally illiterate farmers often don't know how to use them safely or effectively. The government system of grading cotton is rudimentary and unscientific, and gives growers no incentive to improve the quality of their crop.

But not only are West African farmers not abetted by their highly centralized government, they are actively victimized by a web of overregulation and official corruption. Bureaucrats, not the market, determine what the farmers will plant and how much they will be paid. Village leaders are often illiterate and don't know how to multiply, which means they have no way of checking the figures. And even if they aren't swindled, growers receive only half the world export price, with the rest going to the government to pay for seed and other supplies.

Even if the United States eliminated all subsidies and the world price of cotton increased by Oxfam's most optimistic figure of 26 percent, a large West African grower planting three acres would see his income rise from about $300 per year to $378. If we use the more moderate figures of two acres under cultivation and a price increase of 15 percent, farmers' income would rise from about $200 annually to $230. While any increase for these desperately poor people is not to be disparaged, would another $30 or even $78 a year really be enough to lift them out of the cycle of grinding poverty? To significantly change these people's lives, it's clear that fundamental reforms are needed, beginning with how the African governments deal with their own farmers.

Subsidies also receive their share of criticism from domestic opponents. In addition to distorting international trade, they argue, the programs mostly benefit a few big producers. By inflating farm profits, the supports also drive up the cost of buying or renting farmland, which raises planters' expenses and leaves the United States even less competitive. Proponents of cotton subsidies counter that it's only fair that large growers receive the highest payments, since they produce the most commodities. They also point out that the aid reduces clothing prices for U.S. consumers and sustains a traditional way of life and an industry important to the local and national economies.

Even so, there's no question that agricultural subsidies represent a triumph of politics over market, and it's hard to see how they are going to survive in their present form. The current farm bill was particularly generous. But when it was passed in 2002, Congress was looking at projections for continued federal surpluses. Now deep tax cuts for the wealthy and an expensive war in Iraq have driven the federal deficit to historic highs, and funding for a wide array of government programs is being reduced. So the next farm bill will be debated in a very different atmosphere than its predecessor. Given the state of the federal budget and the agreement with the WTO to reduce subsidies, few believe that the new legislation, which will go into effect in 2007, will be so generous.

The question is how bad it will be for farmers like Zack. Some are hoping the government will find the money to compensate growers, while others are planning to shift production out of cotton altogether. Delta planters know it's no easier to predict the workings of government than the path of a thunderstorm. But as Congress gets ready to begin debate, Zack and his neighbors are bracing for a change in a long spell of very favorable weather. Katrina and Rita blew up from the Gulf, but it seems that the next storm to hit the Delta will be rolling down the eastern seaboard.

TEN

The Reckoning

October and November are among the driest months that Zack can remember. The days are soft and fine, and yellow leaves linger on the trees like reluctant party guests. Taking advantage of the weather, Zack hooks first his paratill then his middle buster to the tractor, breaking the land and rowing it up, getting it ready for next year's planting. Usually the Delta's wet autumn delays this chore till springtime, and Zack is glad to be able to take care of it now. For one thing, the winter rains will soak into the broken soil more readily, collecting beneath the surface like money in the bank. Also, it will give him one fewer task to worry about next March. Many of his neighbors have done the same thing. "There's no excuse," Zack says. "If you're not ready this fall, you'll never be." After the New Year, he'll begin overhauling his tractors and planter for the coming season, then he'll apply for his

crop loan. But for the time being he's reached a lull in the schedule dictated, like everything on the farmer's calendar, by the
weather. Happily, Providence has furnished an activity to fill this
hiatus: deer season.

Hunting has been a preoccupation of Delta residents since before the coming of the white man. In his novella *The Bear*, William Faulkner extolled the hunter's skill and courage, virtues he
feared would vanish with the wilderness itself. And it was on a
hunting expedition in the Delta, in 1902, that President Theodore Roosevelt refused to shoot a black bear, inspiring the epony-
mous toy that has shared children's beds ever since. There are still
bears in the Delta. When my wife's cousin Lee was ten years old,
he once became separated from his father during a day's hunting.
"Daddy, Daddy!" he cried as he ran back to him, "I saw a damn
bear!" "Son, watch your language," was the matter-of-fact reply.

When the Delta was still frontier, men killed whatever they
could, whenever they could. But now the what, when, and how
are strictly limited. Bears are no longer hunted in Mississippi, so
deer are the largest game animal. The season starts on October 1
and stretches, in one permutation or another—bow and arrow,
muzzle loader, gun with dogs, gun without dogs—until the end of
January. Gun season, by far the most popular, begins around
Thanksgiving and runs for about a week, then picks up again in
December and goes until late the following month. It's an eagerly
anticipated time, when men greet each other not with "What's
new?" or "How you doin'?" but "Kill anythin'?"

There's no minimum age for hunting in Mississippi, but children under twelve must be accompanied by a licensed adult, and

youths between twelve and sixteen have to complete a safety course. Hunters are restricted to one buck per day, not to exceed three for the season. Spotted fawns may not be killed, though one doe may be taken each day, also to a maximum of three per season. But unless their freezers are empty, many hunters won't shoot does. For one thing, the unadorned heads don't make good trophies; for another, sportsmen have an interest in perpetuating the species, not in culling breeding females. Zack adheres to this code. "I just wasn't brought up to kill a doe," he says.

To be fair game, a buck must have at least four points, which the law defines as "any antler protrusion that would hold any size ring." But Zack generally won't shoot a young male either, preferring to let it mature into a prize worth taking. For the same reason, hunting clubs often prohibit the killing of bucks with fewer than, say, eight points. (The other common way of gauging the trophy value of a buck is to measure the spread of both antlers, known as a "rack.")

One afternoon toward the end of December, Zack offers to take me hunting. I'm eager to go, because I've heard stories about deer camp for decades, but I've never been. Not that that has prevented me, thanks to my reading of books such as *The Bear,* from imagining the intrepid hunter stalking his prey through trackless forests, his rifle crooked over his arm as he bends to examine fresh tracks.

Like doves, deer tend to be most active right after dawn and just before sunset. So Zack and I meet at four o'clock one afternoon at his mobile home outside Lexington. It's warm, and he's wearing blue jeans, a long-sleeve camo shirt, and a big black cowboy hat. We'll be going in his pickup—not the white F–150 but a

black secondhand Toyota that he keeps so he doesn't have to subject his good truck to debris-laden trails. As I cross behind it, I
notice what looks like an internal organ lying in the pickup's
bed. It's a duck heart, Zack tells me. He was out this morning but
managed to shoot just one bird. Afterward he cleaned the carcass
over the truck, but when he scooped up the feathers and innards,
the heart went astray. We climb into the dusty cab, and I notice a
tawny, fuzzy cover stretched over the four-wheel-drive lever.
When I ask Zack what it is, he laughs and tells me it's a deer
scrotum.

We follow the highway toward Tchula, then veer off onto a
dirt road, passing a junkyard and a decrepit trailer. A little farther
on, Zack motions out the left window, where the pine woods
come up to the edge of the road. That's the beginning of his land,
he says, eighty-two acres of hill country that he bought just for
hunting. Mississippi has thirty-eight publicly owned wildlife
management areas, including several right here in the Delta. But
Zack, like many sportsmen, prefers to hunt on private land,
where the legal season is open longer and where there's less competition for the game.

He steers the truck onto a grassy path that runs through the
woods between his property and his neighbor's. When the trail
stops, so do we. As we get out, Zack warns me in a low voice not
to slam the door. But instead of turning into the trees, we continue straight ahead, into a cut made to accommodate a row of
high-tension wires. As we follow the undulating terrain beneath
the power line, Zack grows uncharacteristically quiet, communi-
cating with hand signals and walking quickly, not wanting to ad-
vertise our presence.

After several minutes, we come to a green plywood building standing ten feet off the ground on metal legs. Without speaking, we climb the ladder and enter the blind, which is four feet by eight and barely six feet tall. We take our seats on two low, camouflage-colored stools, and, tugging on a pair of ropes, Zack raises the narrow, flaplike windows. He points to a dark green patch standing out against the brown grass of the cut. It's a combination of rye and oats, he whispers, planted there by the land's previous owner to attract hungry deer. The blind was also on the property when Zack bought it. He tells me he prefers to bushwhack—stalk deer through the woods and take them by surprise. Even if this property doesn't qualify as trackless wilderness, that method sounds closer to my hunter fantasy than sitting in a plywood box waiting for an animal to wander by looking for rye and oats. But we're here, I realize, in deference to my inexperience. Zack says this is only the second time he's used the blind. The first was when he went hunting with his new girlfriend, Cindy, a pretty blond with a big laugh who has a printing business in Greenwood. At least she brought a license and a gun; I've come armed with only a notebook.

We sit quietly, Zack cradling his rifle in his lap. It's a brand-new Remington 7mm08 with a twenty-two-inch barrel and a Leopold 3x9 scope, all of it a Christmas present from Cindy. Zack likes the rifle because it weighs just seven pounds. It's accurate at 400 yards, he says, but he prefers to shoot from about 250. Just then a strong breeze riffles the pine trees on the edge of the cut, and Zack shakes his head. Deer don't like to move when it's windy, he tells me. They also don't stir when it's warm, like this afternoon. I begin to suspect that Zack's stock of hunting wisdom is as prodigious as his weather lore. Still we wait, the only discernible life the buzzards roosting on the high power poles. At five o'clock, as the winter sun is disappearing behind the hills, we hear shots in the distance. A short while afterward, Zack lifts his rifle to his shoulder. I strain to follow his line of sight, but I can see nothing in the dusk. He lowers the gun wordlessly.

We sit in the blind for another half hour, until it's so dark that we couldn't see a deer if one materialized. I can tell Zack feels he's disappointed me, as though the dearth of game were a personal failing. And it does seem ironic that I routinely spot more deer gathering along the highway, threatening to dart out in front of my car, than the only time I've ever gone into the woods in search of them. To make it up, Zack invites me on another hunt the following morning. This should be a good one, he says, because they'll be using dogs.

The next day, I leave Yazoo City in the cold and dark, hugging a cup of coffee from the corner Shell station. There aren't many vehicles on Highway 49, just a few pickups and the ubiquitous log trucks, but there's more traffic than I would have expected at this hour—about as much at six in the morning as I'm used to seeing at six in the evening. By the time I breeze through Thornton, wispy, magenta-tinged clouds have emerged in the east, plastered below the thinnest, whitest sliver of moon. By six-thirty, when I reach Tchula, the horizon is glowing a fiery shade of tangerine, capped by pure robin's-egg blue. There was some rain last week, and fine ribbons of water are standing in the vacant fields. Ten minutes later, I'm parking in a clearing under a cell phone tower between Lexington and Tchula, where Zack and I have arranged to meet.

As I drain my foam cup, he arrives in the black pickup. I get in, and we bump through the woods toward deer camp. It's only forty degrees, but Zack reminds me that cold weather makes the deer more active. Unlike yesterday's expedition, today's won't be conducted on his property. These 2,000 acres belong to a local family that rents them to Zack and two dozen other men, who have formed a hunting club. Now that Zack has his own land, he could cancel his membership here. But deer hunting, unlike dove or duck or rabbit hunting, tends to be a solitary occupation, because the racket of a crowd tramping through the woods, or even their concentrated scent drifting out of a blind, would spook the prey. And if a deer were spotted, how would you decide who took the shot, maybe the only one of the day? So after a few hours alone in the woods, it's nice to have a place to reconvene, share a meal, and hear who saw what and who killed what. Sometimes Zack thaws out his catfish fillets, carts out his cooker, and fries fish and hushpuppies for everybody.

As we drive over the rough dirt roads, we pass several deer stands, some store-bought wooden boxes like Zack's, others homemade open platforms or plastic swivel seats mounted in trees. From the way people talk about deer camp, I have an impression of tents and bonfires. But on first sight, the genuine artifact appears to be a cross between a boys' summer camp and the worst Tobacco Road you've ever seen. As we enter, we pass pens of curious beagles and an open shed with a serious metal hook, which I assume is for hoisting the kill. Then we park in the mud with the other splattered pickups, amid an unsightly collection of trailers and shacks in various stages of disintegration. One building is larger than the others, an oblong, framed affair, and we go inside.

To the left of the door is a commercial kitchen, whose deep stainless steel sink is stacked with dirty dishes from the night before.

Across the way is a counter with simple wooden stools, and beyond that three picnic tables draped with sheets of plastic and dotted with bottles of condiments—Worcestershire sauce, red-hot peppers, Caro syrup. The rest of the open space resembles a teen center rec room, with cast-off couches and recliners, nondescript paneling, and a linoleum floor. In the far corner, mounted high on the wall, a television is broadcasting CNN. Beyond the sitting area are two small bedrooms and, between them, a primitive bathroom.

Three unshaven middle-aged men are sitting at the picnic tables having breakfast. Zack and I help ourselves to some fresh biscuits and homemade wild boar sausage patties that are warming in trays on the oversize oven door. The sun is well up by now, but the hunters are in no hurry. For the next hour, Zack and the others reminisce about practical jokes played long ago and gossip about absent companions, including a man with a preternatural gift for malapropism and another, now deceased, who would drain a pint of whisky every night of deer camp, then fall into bed without supper.

After a while, a burly man gets up and goes to the living room. Bending over one of the vinyl couches, he rips the comforter off a tousled teenager who is sleeping on his stomach, wearing just a pair of blue jeans despite the cold. When this gets no results, the man returns with two pot lids and crashes them together over the prostrate figure. "It's time to get up!" he yells. The boy still doesn't move, not even to retrieve his cover from the floor. The man shrugs and rejoins the conversation, which has continued without any notice of his efforts.

At eight-thirty, other men begin to drift in from the flanking buildings, where they've been sleeping. The boy finally stirs himself, pulls on his camo shirt, and sleepily takes two biscuits. Plans are drawn for the hunt. While the beagles' owner takes the dogs to a nearby ridge and releases them, the other hunters will fan out through the woods, in the hope that a deer will be driven in their direction. Zack knows this land, having hunted it since he was eighteen years old. In his truck we ease down steep, rutted trails to a clearing that he identifies as a deer crossing. He turns off the engine and cocks his head to judge the dogs' position. Scenting prey, they are baying, which sounds more like the squealing of car tires than a noise you'd expect an animal to make.

We sit in the pickup for a while but see no deer. Zack takes a little cigar out of the package and chews on it without lighting up. The sound of the dogs fades. He starts the truck and jounces along the trail, every so often stopping, killing the engine, and listening. Then he creeps forward again, repeating the process. Eventually the baying disappears. The dogs are finished, Zack tells me. Whatever deer they flushed out apparently fled somewhere else. By now it's ten o'clock, and Zack is expected in Lexington to pick up some hay. He says he's sorry that he's taken me out twice and we haven't even seen a deer.

I'm not disappointed that we didn't kill anything. I didn't admit it to Zack, but I wasn't relishing that possibility. And I've seen enough deer along the highway that glimpsing one in the woods didn't promise much of a thrill. Although Zack is sorry on my behalf, I can tell he's not really disappointed for himself. When men go bird hunting, they expect to take something home every time. But deer are big animals, and whatever my unscientific roadside survey might suggest, there just aren't as many of them in the woods as there are smaller game. Naturally skittish, they also seem to sense that people are trying to kill them. So deer hunters don't expect to get one on every outing. The sport is about patience and possibility, in a word, hope.

And at least for Zack, it's not the woods that are the main attraction. When we lived in the Northeast, my wife, Teresa, and I often enjoyed weekend hikes along the Appalachian Trail. In my naïveté, I imagined that hunters, like hikers, are drawn to the forest in search of Nature with a capital N. But Zack says what attracts him is the anticipation of finding a big trophy buck, then the thrill when one appears in his rifle sight. If you ask him how his season is going, he'll tell you how many deer he's killed, of what sex and size. He won't say how nice the weather has been or how many pleasant hours he's passed communing with the environment. For him, hunting isn't about process but results—putting meat in the freezer and, especially, a head over the mantel. "It's like farmin'," Zack says. "Just like you always hope you'll have that big year of three bales an acre, you hope you'll run up on that big buck one of these days. But then you have that year when you don't make a big crop, and the year where you don't see that buck." Hikers go into the woods for the pure experience, but Zack has a purpose in mind. That's why he takes a gun. Zack keeps score.

As a consolation after our unsuccessful outings, Zack gives me two big packages of ground deer meat from his freezer. I use it to make chili, which Teresa and her mother eat a little warily. Even with the heavy seasonings, it has a slightly stronger taste than hamburger, but I suspect their reluctance has more to do with the fact that the meat came from the woods and not from a supermarket. Then a few nights later, Zack invites Teresa and me up to his trailer for dinner. He does all the cooking himself—deer steaks in gravy, biscuits, lima beans, mustard greens, creamed corn, and Bud Lite. Like everything Zack cooks, from catfish to barbecued ribs to sautéed quail, the meat is delicious, very tender with a surprisingly delicate flavor. In Zack's hands, it seems to come from a different animal than what was in my chili. After the dinner, I put away any lingering disillusionment. Although the act of getting it there was not what I had imagined, I can see that even today it is no small comfort to put fresh meat on the table.

———•———

As Zack has sat in the woods this deer season, he's been mulling more than the hunting. In the end, he netted 880 pounds of cotton per acre. That's far below the 1,300 pounds of last year, but more than he thought he might do after the drought and hurricanes. And it's better than most of his neighbors, some of whom are yielding under seven hundred pounds. It also looks as though the fiber will grade acceptably, having withstood Rita's soaking without matting or discoloring. Even so, Zack will get less for the cotton than he spent to grow it. Though he'll make money on his beans, he'll also come out behind on the wind-damaged corn. With his government subsidy, he figures he'll just about break even. Heath and Keath will end up the same. Like their father, they have some savings they can draw from while they hope that next season is better.

Zack never thought he'd be so glad to work all year for nothing. "It was kinda mediocre," he says, "but it could have been a lot worse. I told the boys that at least we get to go home and live in our own houses. People on the Coast don't have a place to eat or lay their heads. We're lucky enough to satisfy the banker and go again. It takes a special person to be a farmer, somebody that's not afraid to fool with a rattlesnake, because you're gonna get bit. The rattlesnake is the crop. It can turn around and bite you. The weather can be the enemy or the best thing ever." He shakes his head. "I guess you have to be a little bit insane to farm."

Zack is making plans for the coming year, but beyond that he's not sure. The new farm bill is scheduled to be passed in 2007, and no one knows what it will mean for small growers like him. Keath tells me that he and Heath have decided to quit if the cotton subsidy is reduced by even 1 percent. "There's no money in it now," he says. "You get a good crop maybe every third year. If they cut the payments to farmers, there won't be anythin' left."

Not only will they stop growing cotton, Keath tells me, they'll get out of farming altogether. Last summer, the brothers bought a piece of equipment called a Gyro-Trac, which resembles a bulldozer but has teeth that can grind a tree into mulch in two minutes. There were only a few of the machines in Mississippi, and the boys were planning to clear land for power lines and highways. But after Katrina, a partner took the Gyro-Trac to the Coast, where he's been busy clearing debris ever since. This past year, Heath and Keath earned more from their investment in the contraption than they did from farming, and they figure they can always make a living that way. What about Zack? I know he's discouraged after this past season, but he hasn't said anything to me about quitting. "Well, I don't know," Keath smiles. "He's been threatenin' to get out ever since we were little boys."

If Heath and Keath do give up farming, Zack will have to make some serious adjustments of his own, because next year he and the twins have decided to work together as never before. To help him cut overhead like loan payments and insurance premiums, he's going to hire the boys to plant and pick his land, paying them a per-acre fee. The arrangement means that Zack will be able to sell all his equipment except for a tractor or two, and he won't have to worry about meeting a payroll every week. Without regular workers to supervise, he'll spend more time in the field himself, which will save him even more on labor. "It's fun drivin' a tractor," he says. "But I'm not too good at it. I get to thinkin' about things and forget what I'm supposed to be doin'. I wouldn't have made too good a pilot, I reckon." To help with chores like spraying and cultivating, Zack will hire a hand for a day here or there. In any event, he'll be farming less land next season: To save on rent, he's letting the twins take over the Yazoo field. Also, the lease has expired on the property outside Tchula, and the owner has decided to take it back and plant it himself. So Zack will have only 650 acres of cotton, 350 of beans, and none of corn.

The new plan is also appealing for the boys. They already have enough equipment and men to work Zack's land in addition to their own, which means they'll be able to spread those costs over more acreage. Ideally they would buy or lease more property, but when no fields are available, farming someone else's land is the next best thing, especially with the ambivalence they're feeling over their future. And Zack's fees will also give them a rare source of cash during the long growing season. For his part, Zack doesn't believe that Heath and Keath will quit. "I hate to see them risk losin' everythin' they've worked for" by continuing to farm, he says. "But they're not gettin' out till they go broke—just like me. I wish I never got my ass into it," he adds, sounding like a sinner too far gone to be redeemed.

If the twins ever do quit, Zack could buy their equipment and hire Willie and Bill, whom he knows to be good workers. But then he would be in a worse position than last year, since he'd have at least the same overhead but fewer acres to plant, and in all probability less help from the government. He could try to lease the land that Heath and Keath have been farming, but that would mean finding additional, untested hands to work the extra acreage, and he knows the problems with that. At his age, he's not looking to assume more responsibility.

So Zack doesn't know what he'll do year after next. He's just taking it season by season, he tells me, but he can't imagine he'll still be farming five years from now. Will he sit in the mobile home watching *Leave It to Beaver* and *Gunsmoke* reruns and turning into the deadbeat he's always feared becoming? He can't see himself re- tiring, he says. Maybe he'll open a little café. Or maybe he'll specu- late in land; he likes that because "you can do some quick addin' and subtractin' and see where your money is. This damn farmin', you don't know how you're goin' to come out." He sighs. "Well, I don't know, I reckon I'll just go out with a sack and a stick and pick cans off the road."

One day Zack points out the fifty acres that his father planted. "It used to be a man could make a livin' on that much land," he says. "Now you got to have thousands of acres to make any money. I'm just disgusted with the whole situation, I swear I am. There're fewer and fewer farmers. One day there'll be only six big farmers left around Tchula. I don't know what's goin' to happen to cotton. I'd be scared to say, 'cause we've got so much foreign competition. It's discouragin' to know you don't have enough land to be able to make any money. Overhead is so high you can't make nothin'. You got to have enough money to pay overhead and your livin' expenses, and I know there aren't enough acres out there to do that with what I'm farmin'."

The new farm bill threatens not just small farmers like the Killebrews but also the large operations that increasingly dominate the Delta. Congress is said to be considering elimination of the three-entity rule, which allows one individual to draw subsidies for three different farm businesses. The provision doubles the payments to big growers (the full amount is paid on the first operation, half on the other two), and if it's eliminated, major players will surely be driven out as well.

Jim Corley, the USDA Farm Services agent for Holmes County, foresees a Delta where only international conglomerates will wield the economies of scale needed to make farming pay. Under this model, already adopted by the pork, poultry, and cattle industries, the corporation would contract with a farmer to grow so many acres of a specified crop. The farmer would be paid a set fee for his services, and the harvest would belong to the company, which would assume all the risk and receive 100 percent of any profit. The planters would become middle managers instead of independent operators, just one level above their hired hands.

But what will these corporate farms grow? Given its long tenure here and its deep connection to all the Delta was and is, cotton won't go easily from the region. But although tradition

may be priceless, it's not legal tender. Congress has already voted
to eliminate export subsidies and payments to U.S. mills for using
American fiber. If it also stops subsidizing cotton farmers, the
Delta may well lose the crop that has long dominated its landscape, its economy, its people's lives.

What would take its place? Catfish production has been dropping, the victim of low prices and rising costs. Wheat isn't well
suited to the Delta's high humidity, and the few farmers who have
tried it haven't been encouraged to plant more. Some growers,
including Heath and Keath, are experimenting with peanuts. But
that crop claims only 15,000 acres in Mississippi, and the state
extension service predicts that over the next five years it will increase to just 50,000 acres, or 5 percent of the land currently occupied by cotton.

There are already 2 million acres of soybeans grown in Mississippi, and the United States is the world's leading exporter. International demand continues to grow, but as Jim Corley points out,
"the world only needs so many soybeans," and expanded planting
could create a surplus that would lower prices. Until recently,
corn was a risky proposition because of its high fertilizer use and
uncertain market. But increasing petroleum prices have spurred
demand for ethanol, made largely from corn, and so the outlook
for that crop is improving as well.

Jim Corley believes that in the future no single plant will assume cotton's dominance in the Delta. Farmers (or their corporate
bosses) will shuffle a more diverse portfolio of crops according to
their reading of the market. However, cotton is a much-higher-
value product than any of these possible replacements, generating
about three times the per-acre income of soybeans, for instance. If

revenues from agriculture drop because of a shift from cotton, and if any profits are deposited in corporate treasuries instead of local bank accounts, what will become of "Mississippi's Mississippi," already the poorest region of the poorest state?

In the 1970s, the historic exodus from Mississippi reversed direction, as blacks returned to the state to escape the North's stagnant economy and troubled inner cities. But the Delta was an exception to this trend, and even today the region continues to lose population. Many of those left behind, largely elderly or unskilled, are struggling. Whereas the national discussion on race centers on ensuring that African Americans have equal access to the opportunities around them, that debate is largely moot in the Delta, where the poor economy now presents a greater impediment to black progress than racism does.

Jo G Prichard, director of development for the Mississippi Center for Nonprofits, likens the task of developing the Delta to rebuilding East Germany after the fall of communism. Just as the Eastern Bloc countries were far behind the rest of Europe, the Delta is trailing most of America in terms of education, industry, and infrastructure. The area desperately needs jobs, but employers are loath to locate here, given the low educational level of the workforce. There's tremendous competition for shrinking non-profit and government funds, and Delta communities generally haven't shown the close white–black cooperation needed to make their strongest case to potential donors. "With the new global economy," Prichard says, "the Delta must compete for jobs with Third World countries like India, and that's an uphill struggle."

Another Mississippian who has given a great deal of thought to the future of the Delta is William Winter, governor of the state from 1980 to 1984 and a longtime champion of education and racial reconciliation. The Delta is still suffering from the legacy of sharecropping, Winter says, which generates low expectations and few role models, while preserving the vestiges of racism. But in the long run Winter is optimistic about the region's prospects. Although it's hard to eliminate the remnants of bigotry, he believes that most Delta residents are people of goodwill, and that the younger generation of white leaders realize that the only way for the Delta to prosper is for blacks to prosper. In fact, given their long history together, Winter suggests that Mississippians have an uncommon chance of creating a truly biracial society. But it is not, he warns, "a task for the short-winded."

As a model of the kind of entrepreneurial activity that the Delta needs, Winter and others point to the Viking Range Corporation of Greenwood. Founded by local resident Fred Carl in 1987 to produce restaurant-quality stoves for the home market, the company has expanded into dishwashers, refrigerators, small appliances, cookware, and cutlery, which are now sold in eighty countries. With three manufacturing plants in Greenwood employing more than a thousand people, Viking has revived the city's economy as well as its downtown, where it has restored a dozen historic buildings on Cotton Row.

But how many Viking Ranges are there? How many local entrepreneurs with the vision and the luck and the dedication to transform their communities? In the long run, Winter believes, tourism is likely to prove a greater source of jobs in the Delta than industry. "There is a mystique about the region, which needs to be cultivated as carefully as cotton," he says. "And there is the stunning uniqueness of the landscape itself; in fact, there is no place in America more memorable for the sheer natural features of the land and the richness of the earth. It's a place that has produced so many stories, writers, books. There is a need to build on the region's cultural strengths to make it a place where people want to visit and live." In addition to the dozen floating casinos on the Mississippi River, there are already a cultural museum in Yazoo City, a B. B. King museum in Indianola, blues museums in Clarksdale and Leland, a cotton museum in Greenwood, and an annual catfish festival in Belzoni. Though tourism jobs tend to fall on the low end of the pay scale, farmwork isn't noted for its generous remuneration either, and dealing blackjack, or even waiting tables, is a more attractive and more feasible option for most people than driving a tractor. Even so, when I tell Zack about the predicted tourism boom, he's skeptical. "What's there for people to look at?" he asks incredulously.

One possible answer is trees, since the Delta may be less heavily farmed in the years ahead. Sixty percent of Mississippi is forested, and lumber is already a major industry. In addition, there's growing demand for duck- and deer-hunting preserves in the Delta. One planter near Yazoo City is converting 3,200 acres back to timber, with the help of a government reforestation program. Will more of the Delta's rich earth revert to woods teeming with wildlife, as it was when the first settlers arrived here? Hunting is a form of tourism, but if farmland begins to disappear and the Delta's vast horizons are obscured by trees, will the region retain the mystique that Governor Winter believes will attract nonsporting visitors? Or won't the tourists notice, as they shuttle among garish casinos and spiffed-up blues cafés, that the Delta's raison d'être has vanished?

Although no one can be sure what will become of the Delta in the years ahead, there's a widespread feeling that the region, which has resisted change so vehemently, is on the verge of a transformation possibly as radical as the introduction of cotton nearly two centuries ago. If the withdrawal of federal subsidies puts an end to cotton here, it will most likely have the same effect in the other nine states where the crop is principally grown. And that would be a loss not just for those areas but for the nation, which has been the world's leading exporter of cotton for two centuries and which still ships some $7 billion of the fiber yearly. But the loss would be measured in more than dollars. Considering the pivotal role the crop has played in American history and culture, all of us—not just the descendants of slaves and sharecroppers— are the children of cotton. And even if the shrubby plant is no longer cultivated here in the Delta's abundant soil, even if the spring thunderstorms rumble over nothing but corn and soybeans and trees, we will all continue to feel cotton's legacy.

Now it is April in the Delta. The last of the wild wisteria is blooming, and the trees still have their new yellow-green leaves. Tractors, planters, spraying rigs are crisscrossing the fields and inching along the highways, leaving muddy tracks on the macadam. This afternoon it's seventy-five degrees, with a threatening overcast.

Zack is plowing some land on the old Hyde Park plantation, getting it ready for cotton. At the end of a row, he pulls his tractor next to my car, shuts off the engine, and climbs down. It's close to suppertime, but I've just now brought him his lunch—a fried chicken breast, some batter-dipped French fries, and a Gatorade. Zack would normally have eaten three hours ago, but he didn't want to take time to drive into Tchula, so he asked me to pick something up on my way back from an appointment in Greenwood. Setting the cardboard box on the tractor's front wheel, he tears off the chicken's breaded skin and tosses it on the ground. Then he pulls the white meat apart with his fingers and puts it in his mouth.

This season marks the start of Zack's new arrangement with the twins. Willie and Bill are still working for the boys, but Harold hasn't come back this year, and his place has been taken by a man named Buster, who worked for Zack a long time ago, when the twins were little. Matt won't be back either; his job with the Department of Wildlife came through, and he's about to start basic training in Jackson. The boys have already planted Zack's early soybeans, and they'll sow his cotton when the time comes. But the smaller tasks, like plowing and spraying, Zack is doing himself, with the help of some day laborers. Early this morning, he hired a local man to plow this field, but when Zack stopped by a couple of hours later, he saw that the hand had missed some rows. "Can you imagine?" he fumes. "The man couldn't drive a damn tractor!" So Zack ran him off and, determined to take advantage of a rare dry spell, got into the machine himself.

He has four tractors for sale, and he's managed to cut his debt and his overhead as planned. He's hired a part-time business manager to help him watch expenses, and he's taking a bookkeeping course so he can tend to his own accounts. But this year he doesn't feel the rush of optimism that he generally gets at planting. For one thing, debate hasn't begun on the new farm bill. "Everybody I know is depressed," Zack says. "It's like waitin' to see how big a rope you're goin' to get to hang yourself."

Matt once told me that a lot of thinking takes place behind the wheel of a tractor, and Zack has something else to consider as he guides the machine from row to row: His divorce from Pam will become final later this month. The two are on friendly terms, he tells me, and they see each other at family gatherings. But a year after their separation, he still misses her.

Zack finishes his lunch. He wipes his hands on a paper napkin. Then he mounts the tractor's steps, settles himself in the driver's seat, and turns the key. The diesel fires up, filling the air with its deep grumble. As I stand on the side of the road and watch, the tractor pulls away across the flat, waiting land, towing its plow, churning the pale Mississippi earth, and preparing it to receive the seed.

Acknowledgments

I owe an enormous debt of thanks to Zack Killebrew. No author could ask for a more engaging or more amenable subject, and I'm profoundly grateful to Zack for sharing his life and work with me. I'm also proud to call him a friend.

My sincerest appreciation to Heath and Keath and the rest of the Killebrew family, whose own story I have glossed over in my effort to tell Zack's. And thank you to Zack's workers, especially Willie Waters, Bill Hood, and Matt Jones, for letting me watch and learn.

I'm obliged to my agent, Deirdre Mullane at the Spieler Agency, who once again proved herself an energetic representative, a fine editor, and a good friend.

At Perseus Books, thanks go to executive editor Amy Scheibe and project editor Brooke Kush, as well as to Ellen Garrison, for her astute suggestions on the manuscript, and David Shoemaker, whose original enthusiasm made this project possible.

Thanks to my brother and sister, Bill Helferich and Marlene Bergendahl, for their love and support. In Mississippi, I'd particularly like to thank my mother-in-law, Florence Nicholas, as well as Lisa Nicholas, Willie Belle Hood, Danny Hood, Lee Hood, John Langston, JoAnne Prichard Morris, and Sam Olden.

Thank you to my dear friend Lindy Hess, director of the Columbia Publishing Course, for the generous interest she's taken in my career over the past three decades. In San Miguel de Allende, thanks to fellow authors Walter and Miriam Schneir and Walter and Wendy Meagher for their unflagging solidarity.

And as always, my deepest gratitude and love to my wife, Teresa Nicholas, who after thirty years continues to be my partner, my inspiration, and my greatest joy.

I'd like to thank the following for generously sharing their time and expertise: Jim Corley, Holmes County executive director, Farm Service Agency of the U.S. Department of Agriculture, Lexington, MS; Ricky Davidson and Bill Crandall, Southland Flying Service, Tchula, MS; at Denim North America, Monte Galbraith, president, Toby Sklar, senior vice president, and Thomas F. Butler, Greige manufacturing manager; Barton Easley, Holmes Gin Company, Tchula, MS; Virgil A. King III, King's Ag Consulting, Lexington, MS; Jo G Prichard, director of development, Mississippi Center for Nonprofits, Jackson, MS; Vernon Sikes, former managing editor, *Yazoo Herald*, Yazoo City, MS; Charles E. Snipes, Ph.D., former research/extension professor, Delta Research and Extension Center, Stoneville, MS; at Staple Cotton Cooperative Association, Eugene A. Stansel Jr., vice president of human resources and corporate secretary, and Meredith Allen, vice president of marketing; at Swift Spinning, Keigo Inao, chairman and CEO/CFO, Trey Hodges, president and COO, James Wilgis, vice president of operations, Mike O'Brien, plant manager, and David Koon, vice president of fiber procurement; and the Honorable William F. Winter, former governor of Mississippi.

Thank you to Gavin Wright, Ph.D., William Robertson Coe Professor of American Economic History at Stanford University, for reviewing the history portions of the manuscript. Special thanks for reading the entire manuscript go to F. Aubrey Harris, Ph.D., former research professor, Delta Research and Extension Center, Stoneville, MS.

Finally, thanks to the dedicated staff at the New York Public Library, H. T. Sampson Library of Jackson State University (Jackson, MS), Ricks Memorial Library (Yazoo City, MS), Tchula (MS) Public Library, Lexington (MS) Public Library, and Biblioteca Publica de San Miguel de Allende, Mexico.

Author's Note

All the events depicted in this book actually happened. For the sake of dramatic effect, I have changed the order of some incidents and have included events from other years. I have also simplified various circumstances, particularly Zack's business relationship with his sons, which altered several times over the course of the story. All persons and places portrayed herein are real, and I have changed the names only of Zack's workers Charlie, Ben, Johnny, and Harold, and of his neighbor's hands Rob, Jim, and Sam.

Throughout the book, I have quoted racial epithets and black vernacular speech. I'd like to assure the reader that my intention is not to condone or perpetuate stereotypes but rather to expose the conditions and attitudes prompting such usage.

Sources

Principal sources are given below; other resources may have been consulted as well. See the Bibliography for complete information on each book. Where there are multiple sources under a subheading, I have tried to list them in order of importance to my research.

PROLOGUE:
"THE MOST SOUTHERN PLACE ON EARTH"

The Most Southern Place on Earth is the title of James Cobb's excellent history of the Mississippi Delta

Only Texas produces more cotton than Mississippi: National Cotton Council of America website (cotton.org)

80 percent of Mississippi cotton grown in Delta: Bruce Reid, "Future of Farming on Shaky Ground," *Jackson Clarion-Ledger*, December 20, 1999

Nearly a million acres of cotton in the Delta, with fiber valued at almost a billion dollars: Mississippi State University Extension Service website (msucares.com)

U.S. largest antebellum cotton exporter: Donald J. Boquet, B. Rogers Leonard, and W. David Caldwell, "Cotton History," Louisiana State University Agriculture Center website (lsuagcenter.com)

United States has 40 percent of world cotton exports: U.S. Department of Agriculture website (usda.gov)

CHAPTER ONE: THE LAND

Geology and hydrology of the Mississippi River and Delta: Bartlett, Barry, Cobb, National Park Service's Mississippi National River and Recreation Area website (nps.gov)

Percy quotation: Percy

Faulkner quotation: "Old Man" in Faulkner

Exploration of the Mississippi: Virtual Museum of New France website, sponsored by the Canadian Museum of Civilization (civilization.ca)

Early history of Mississippi, Louisiana, and Florida: Loewen

Johnstone quotation and 1774 and 1780 black population figures: Piersen

Eden, Holmes County, Tchula, and Lexington statistics: U.S. Census Bureau website (census.gov)

History of Tchula: Peaster

History of Lexington: Members of the Magnolia Garden Club (see Bibliography)

Mississippi tobacco settlement: "Tobacco Industry Settles Mississippi Lawsuit," CNN Interactive website (cnn.com)

Cohn quotation about Delta planters versus farmers: Cobb

$4 billion in federal cotton supports: Rivoli

Botany and early history of cotton: Wayne C. Smith, Munro, Hobhouse, website of the National Cotton Council of America (cotton.org), Mirsky, Lakwete, Jennifer Harris, Jenkins, Schery, Yafa

World cotton production figures: U.S. Department of Agriculture, cited on Cotton Incorporated website (cottoninc.com)

Dollar bill 75 percent cotton: U.S. Treasury Department website (ustreas.gov)

Pliny quotation: Dodge

Quotation on ancient Indian cotton: Mirsky

Soil must be 65 degrees to plant cotton: website of the Texas Cooperative Extension of the Texas A&M University System (http://lubbock.tamu.ed)

CHAPTER TWO: THE MACHINES

History of the tractor, including statistics on adoption: Gray

Advantages of tractors versus draft animals: Munro

5 million tractors on fewer than 2 million American farms: U.S. Department of Agriculture (usda.gov)

Development of the cotton-weaving industry: Mirsky, Green

British efforts to ban cotton: Rivoli

English cotton-spinning figures, 1765 versus 1785: Hobhouse

Quarter million operatives employed in Lancashire: spartacus. schoolnet.co.uk

English cotton import figures, 1783: Hobhouse

Slave productivity for hand picking and hand ginning cotton: Meltzer

Whitney and the cotton gin: Green, Lakwete, Mirsky

Relative efficiency of Whitney gin and barrel gin: Lakete

English cotton imports, 1825: Mirsky

American cotton production, 1790 versus 1830: U.S. Department of
     Agriculture, *Atlas of American Agriculture*, cited on Economic
     History Association website (eh.net)

Johnson quotation: Green

Coxe quotation: Lakete

Preeminent role of the Industrial Revolution in the rise of cotton:
     Wright

Roller gins were more common and effective: Lakete

Marx quotation: Yafa

Whitney and machine parts: Green, Mirsky

Whitney quotation on milling machine: *Yale Alumni Magazine*
     (yalealumnimagazine.com)

Chapter Three: The Seed

First four-row, tractor-pulled planter marketed in 1945: Agriculture
     in the Classroom website, sponsored by the United States De-
     partment of Agriculture (agclassroom.org)

Germination of cotton seed: Munro

History of American slavery: Kolchin, Berlin, Stamp

Every third colonist a slave: Kolchin

Johnson quotation: Kolchin

Jefferson quotation: Kolchin

Washington quotation: Berlin

Postrevolution decline in slavery: Garraty

Price of field hand fell by half: Hobhouse

Only U.S. crop to double each decade: McPherson, *Battle Cry of
     Freedom*

Cotton production statistics, 1800 versus 1860: *Historical Statistics of
     the United States*, U.S. Census Bureau (census.gov)

U.S. cotton was three-quarters of world's harvest: Donald J. Boquet, B. Rogers Leonard, and W. David Caldwell, "Cotton History," Louisiana State University Agricultural Center website (lsuagcenter.com)

Cotton constituted over half of U.S. exports and 60 percent of imports: Garraty

Hammond "King Cotton" quotation: University of the South website (Sewanee.edu)

One million African Americans shipped South, 1790–1860: Kolchin

Majority of slaves worked on cotton plantations: McPherson, *Ordeal by Fire*

Change in percentage of slaves between Delaware and Savannah Rivers: Berlin

1860 slave population: Kolchin

Delta history, land use statistics, cost of establishing a plantation ca. 1855: Cobb

Mississippi slave population statistics: Loewen

Delta slave population statistics: Cobb

Planter quotation on working slaves: Cobb

1839 and 1860 Mississippi cotton production figures: Loewen

Mississippi producing nearly 25 percent of U.S. cotton: Loewen

Southern economy larger than France's or Germany's: Kolchin

Antebellum southern economic development: Kolchin; McPherson, *Battle Cry of Freedom*

Southern per capita income versus northern, 1860: Kolchin

Slaves represented bulk of owners' wealth: Cobb

South's population and industrial capacity, 1850: Kolchin

Two-thirds of South's food and manufactured goods imported from North: McPherson, *Ordeal by Fire*

Lion's share of southern cotton exported for milling: Kolchin

Change in northern production of cotton cloth, 1817–1837: McPherson, *Battle Cry of Freedom*

More cotton produced in Lowell, MA, than in South: McPherson, *Battle Cry of Freedom*

Importance of slavery to northern economy: SlaveNorth.com; Kolchin; McPherson, *Battle Cry of Freedom*; David Davis

Quotation from Alabama businessman: McPherson, *Ordeal by Fire*

History of Abolitionism: Kolchin; McPherson, *Ordeal by Fire*; Stamp

Planter quotation on superiority of slavery: Stamp

Two-thirds to three-quarters of white southerners didn't own slaves: McPherson, *Battle Cry of Freedom*; Kolchin

Events leading to Civil War: McPherson, *Battle Cry of Freedom*

New York Evening Post quotation: McPherson, *Battle Cry of Freedom*

Quotation from Savannah planter: McPherson, *Battle Cry of Freedom*

Civil War cotton diplomacy: McPherson, *Battle Cry of Freedom*; William Davis; Foote

Cotton manufacturing England's largest industry: McPherson, *Battle Cry of Freedom*

Three-quarters of British cotton from U.S. South: McPherson, *Battle Cry of Freedom*

Hammond quotation on England toppling: McPherson, *Battle Cry of Freedom*

Civil War: McPherson, *Battle Cry of Freedom*; William Davis

Effects of cotton scarcity in England: McPherson, *Battle Cry of Freedom* (including statistics); William Davis

Union blockade, including statistics: McPherson, *Battle Cry of Freedom*

Drop in Confederate cotton production during Civil War: *Historical Statistics of the United States*, U.S. Census Bureau (census.gov)

Cotton manufacturing largest U.S. industry: Faust

Effects of cotton shortage on the North: Faust; Mary Blewett, "Textile Workers in the American Northeast and South: Shifting Landscapes of Class, Culture, Gender, Race, and Protest." Paper delivered at the Textile Conference of the International Institute of Social History, November 2004 (iisg.nl)

Shoes and leather goods North's second largest industry: Faust

Northern industry grew by 13 percent: Faust

Cotton smuggling between the lines: McPherson, *Battle Cry of Freedom*; Cobb

Dana quotation: McPherson, *Battle Cry of Freedom*

Alcorn cotton dealings: Cobb

500 bales of cotton passing through Vicksburg daily: Cobb

Alcorn quotation: Cobb

Civil War in the Delta: Cobb

CHAPTER FOUR: THE HANDS

Goodman case: Jimmie E. Gates, "Man Gets 5 Years for Bilking U.S.," *Jackson Clarion-Ledger*, November 10, 2004; Vernon Sikes, "Guilty Pleas End Subsidy Fraud Trial," *Yazoo Herald*, June 26, 2004; Vernon Sikes, "Yazooan Gets Five Years for Subsidy Fraud," *Yazoo Herald*, November 17, 2004

Weeds: Interview with Charles E. Snipes, Ph.D., Delta Research and Extension Center, Stoneville, MS; National Cotton Council of America website (www.cotton.org)

Agee quote on Johnson grass: Agee

200 weeds affecting cotton: Wayne C. Smith

Agee quotation on chopping: Agee

Roundup herbicide: Interview with Charles E. Snipes, Ph.D. (see above); Monsanto website (monsanto.com); John P. Giesy, Stuart Dobson, and Keith R. Solomon, "Ecotoxicological Risk Assessment for Roundup Herbicide," *Reviews of Environmental Contamination and Toxicology* 167 (2000): 35–120, reproduced on Monsanto website; Environmental Protection Agency website (epa.gov.); Sustainable Cotton Project website (sustainablecotton.org); Andrew Pollack, "Widely Used Crop

Herbicide Is Losing Weed Resistance," *New York Times*, January 14, 2003; Greenpeace website (greenpeace.org); website of Rick Relyea, Ph.D., University of Pittsburgh Department of Biological Sciences (pitt.edu); Yafa.

More than 90 percent of cotton grown in the Delta is Roundup resistant: Interview with Charles E. Snipes, Ph.D. (see above)

History of crop dusters: National Agricultural Aviation Association website (agaviation.org)

Huff Daland history: Delta Air Transport Heritage Museum website (www.deltamuseum.org)

2,200 professional crop dusters: National Agricultural Aviation Association website (agaviation.org)

Mechanics of crop dusting: Interview with Ricky Davidson and Bill Crandall, Southland Flying Service, Tchula, MS

Crop dusters put down as much as a quarter of agricultural chemicals: National Agricultural Aviation Association website (agaviation.org)

Growth habit of cotton: Munro

Civil War aftermath, Reconstruction: Foner, *Reconstruction* and *Nothing but Freedom*; Page Smith; Cobb; McPherson, *Ordeal by Fire*; Meier; Willis; Meltzer

Freedman's wages: McPherson, *Ordeal by Fire*

Black Codes: Cobb; text of laws at about.com website

Alabama resident quotation: William Harris

Freedmen's reduced working hours: Ransom

Vicksburg Times quotation: Morris

Freedmen's officeholding statistics: Cobb, Page Smith

Holmes quotation: Page Smith

Ku Klux Klan, including figure of 20,000 deaths and decline in Republican votes cast, 1873 vs. 1875: Page Smith

Panic of 1873: Foner, *Reconstruction*; Cobb

Post-Reconstruction history: Cobb

Tenant farming and sharecropping: Cobb, Ransom, Loewen, Royce

1890–1930 sharecropping statistics: Cobb

8.5 million tenant farmers in the principal cotton states: Lemann

Georgian's quotation regarding sharecroppers: Foner, *Nothing but Freedom*

One-third of southern black farm families living in one-room cabins: William Harris

Vardaman quotation: Walton

Size of average Delta sharecropper's plot: Cobb

Shaw quote on loss of control: Rosengarten

Interest rates of up to 35 percent: Cobb

Agee quotation on meaning of cotton: Agee

Faulkner quotation on sharecropping: "The Bear," in Faulkner

William Alexander Percy quotation on sharecropping: Percy

The blues: Wilson, Palmer

Big Bill Broonzy lyrics: Lomax

History of Delta sharecropping: Lemann, Cobb

Figures on Delta population and racial composition: Cobb

Leflore County Massacre of 1889: Cobb

Change in black voter turnout, 1888–1895: Cobb

Shaw quotation on disenfranchisement: Rosengarten

Two lynchings per year in the Delta between 1900 and 1930: Cobb

Quotation from U.S. Agricultural Census: Cobb

Quotation from Illinois Central Railroad: Cobb

CHAPTER FIVE: THE WATER

Four inches of water necessary per month: Hobhouse

Roots three times as deep as plant is tall: Wayne C. Smith

Spindly stems, dropped leaves, fewer bolls: Munro

Soil science: Harpstead

Mississippi hunting statistics: Mississippi Department of Wildlife, Fisheries, and Parks (mdwfp.com)

Garcilaso Inca de la Vega quotation: Cited in Barry

Mark Twain quotation: Twain

4,000 miles of levees: Mississippi History Now website, an online publication of the Mississippi Historical Society (mshistory. k12.ms.us)

A dozen floods in late nineteenth and early twentieth centuries, with details: Cobb

Flood of 1927 and its aftermath, including quotations and statistics: Barry, except as noted

$400 million in property damage: Greg O'Brien, "Making the Mississippi Over Again: The Development of River Control in Mississippi," Mississippi History Now website, sponsored by the Mississippi Historical Society (mshistory.k12.ms.us)

World War I and post–1927 black exodus figures: Barry

Illinois Central freed the slaves: Walton

Mississippi politician's quotation on importance of labor: Cobb

CHAPTER SIX: THE PREDATORS

Botany of cotton: Munro, Wayne C. Smith

60 percent of healthy bolls may drop: Wayne C. Smith

Insect overview: O'Toole

Insect pests of cotton: Interview with F. Aubrey Harris, Ph.D., Delta Research and Extension Center, Stoneville, MS; interview with Virgil King, King's Ag Consulting, Lexington, MS; Wayne C. Smith; Mississippi State University Extension Service website (msucares.com)

Pesticides: Mississippi State University Extension Service website (msucares.com); Environmental Protection Agency website (epa.gov)

Bt cotton: University of Tennessee College of Agricultural Sciences and Natural Resources website (utextension.utk.edu); Union of Concerned Scientists website (ucsusa.org); interview with F. Aubrey Harris, Ph.D. (see above); interview with Virgil King (see above); Sustainable Cotton Project (sustainablecotton.org); Pesticide Action Network (pan.uk.org); Wayne C. Smith, Yafa

Organic cotton production, sales figures: Organic Trade Association (ota.com)

Estimated annual costs of insect control: Interview with F. Aubrey Harris, Ph.D. (see above)

95 percent of Mississippi cotton genetically modified: Mississippi State University Extension Service website (msucares.com)

National Agricultural Health Study: National Cancer Institute website (cancer.gov)

Boll weevils: Wayne C. Smith; Noel D. Vietmeyer, "Our 90-Year War with the Boll Weevil Isn't Over," Smithsonian, August 1982; website of the Texas Boll Weevil Eradication Foundation (txbollweevil.org); U.S. Department of Agriculture Agricultural Research Service website (ars.usda.gov); interview with F. Aubrey Harris, Ph.D. (see above); Yafa

Spread of weevil and damage to yields: Noel D. Vietmeyer, "Our 90-Year War with the Boll Weevil Isn't Over," Smithsonian, August 1982

$22 billion in losses from weevil: U.S. Department of Agriculture Agricultural Research Service (ars.usda.gov)

Lyrics to "Boll Weevil": Lomax

Toxicity of arsenic dusts: New Jersey Department of Health and Senior Services website (state.nj.us/health), National Institutes of Health Haz-Map website (http://hazmap.nlm.nih.gov)

DDT: Environmental Protection Agency website (epa.gov); interview with F. Aubrey Harris, Ph.D. (see above); Yafa

World Health Organization statistics on number of lives saved by DDT: Quoted in Reasononline (Reason.com)

American cotton formerly dusted with up to two pounds of chemicals weekly: Interview with Charles E. Snipes, Ph.D., Delta Research and Extension Center, Stoneville, MS

American cotton formerly dusted with 60 to 70 million tons of insecticide per year: Wayne C. Smith; Noel D. Vietmeyer, "Our 90-Year War with the Boll Weevil Isn't Over," *Smithsonian*, August 1982

Carson may have exaggerated some of her claims: Reasononline (Reason.com); Junkscience.com (junkscience.com)

Malaria death toll and benefits of DDT against malaria: Nicholas D. Kristoff, "It's Time to Spray DDT," *New York Times*, January 8, 2005

Malathion health threats: Chem-tox.com

Malathion safety and level of use in the U.S.: Environmental Protection Agency website (epa.gov)

Annual organophosphate use in U.S.: Environmental Protection Agency website (epa.gov)

James Tumlinson and development of Grandlure: USDA Agriculture Research Service paper, "We Don't Cotton to Boll Weevil 'Round Here Anymore," USDA website (ars.usda.gov); interview with F. Aubrey Harris, Ph.D. (see above)

Cost and workings of weevil control program: Interview with F. Aubrey Harris, Ph.D. (see above)

Mississippi's losses from the boll weevil are virtually zero: Mississippi State University Extension Service website (msucares.com)

Half a million African Americans left the South partly as a result of the boll weevil: Hurt

How weevil changed cotton farming: Noel D. Vietmeyer, "Our 90-Year War with the Boll Weevil Isn't Over," *Smithsonian*, August 1982

Enterprise, Alabama, quotation: City of Enterprise website (cityofenterprise.net)

Agee quotation: Agee

Plant growth regulators: Mississippi State University Extension Service website (msucares.com); New Mexico State University College of Agriculture and Home Economics website (cahe.nmsu.edu); University of Missouri Extension website (muextension.missouri.edu); U.S. Department of Agriculture Agricultural Research Service website (ars.usda.gov)

Catfish hand grabbing season: Mississippi Department of Wildlife, Fisheries, and Parks (mdwfp.com)

Chapter Seven: The Picking

Dove hunting: Mississippi State University Extension Service website (msucares.com)

Defoliation: Mississippi State University Extension Service website (msucares.com)

Traditional method of picking cotton: Meltzer

Daily average for handpicked cotton: Hurt

Development of the mechanical cotton picker: Donald Holley, "Mechanical Cotton Picker," Economic History Services website, sponsored by the Economic History Association and other organizations (EH.net); Lemann; Case International Harvester website (caseih.com)

Jackson Daily News quotation: Holley (see above)

Efficiency statistics of first mechanical picker: Lemann

Today's cost of harvesting a bale: Interview with F. Aubrey Harris,
     Ph.D., Delta Research and Extension Center, Stoneville, MS
Rate of adoption of mechanical picker: Holley (see above)
The Great Black Migration, including population and migration
     statistics, growth of Chicago population, and northern wages:
     Lemann
Henry quotation: Cobb
Cohn quotation: Cited in Lemann
Chicago Defender quotation: William Harris
Lemann quotation: Lemann
"From can to can't": Agee

CHAPTER EIGHT: THE GIN

Mechanics of cotton ginning: Interview with Barton Easley, Holmes
     Gin Company, Tchula, MS
Perhaps 100 cotton gins left in Mississippi: Mississippi State Univer-
     sity Extension Service website (msucares.com)
Uses of cottonseed: Wayne C. Smith
Grades of cotton: United Nations Conference on Trade and Devel-
     opment website (untad.org), USDA website (ams.usda.org),
     Cotton, Inc. website (cottoninc.com)
Population of Yazoo City: U.S. Census Bureau (census.gov)
Civil rights movement: Branch, *Parting the Waters, Pillar of Fire, At
     Canaan's Edge*; Sitkoff
Civil rights movement in Mississippi: Cobb; Branch, *Parting the Wa-
     ters, Pillar of Fire, At Canaan's Edge*; Sitkoff
Black progress after World War II, including statistics: Sitkoff
Quotation from Mississippi veteran: "The Legacy of Medgar Evers:
     Forty Years After Civil Rights Leader's Death, a Changed Mis-

sissippi," National Public Radio broadcast, June 23, 2003 (npr.org)

One-quarter of eligible blacks in the South were registered to vote in 1950: Sitkoff

5 percent of eligible blacks registered in Mississippi in 1950: Sitkoff

Less than 2 percent black registration in some Delta counties: Cobb

No black person had tried to register in Holmes County: Cobb

2 percent of black students in the South attending integrated schools in 1964: Sitkoff

Quotation re Indian babies: Cited in Branch, *Pillar of Fire*

Citizens Council investigation of white family: Personal interview

Hazel Brannon Smith story and quotation: Cobb

Providence Farm story: Cobb

Hartman Turnbow story and quotation: Cobb

Mississippi violence during 1963: Sitkoff

Leflore County black voter increase, 1962 versus 1964: Cobb

Medgar Evers killing as "assassination": Branch, *Pillar of Fire*

U.S. News & World Report poll: Quoted in Branch, *Pillar of Fire*

Mississippi Freedom Summer violence: Sitkoff

1,200 new voters registered in Mississippi Freedom Summer: Sitkoff

LBJ quotation: Branch, *At Canaan's Edge*

Increase in black voter registration in Mississippi and throughout the South, 1964 versus 1968: Sitkoff

1972 school integration figures, North versus South: *Columbia Encyclopedia* (Bartleby.com)

Jimmy Carter received 94 percent of black vote: Sitkoff

Number of black elected southern officials in 1980: Sitkoff

Number of black elected officials in Mississippi in 1990: Morris

Growth in black family income, 1994–2000: Nadirah Sabir, "Earnings Gain, Wealth Loss," *Black Enterprise*, January 2005

Poverty rates for blacks versus whites: U.S. Census Bureau (census.gov)

Reports on worsening circumstances of young black men: Erik Eck-
holm, "Plight Deepens for Black Men, Studies Warn," *New
York Times*, March 20, 2006

CHAPTER NINE: THE MILL

History of Columbus, Georgia: New Georgia Encyclopedia, a project
of the Georgia Humanities Council (georgiaencyclopedia.org)

Move of cotton mills from New England to the South, including statistics: Rivoli

Mechanics and the business challenges of cotton spinning and denim
weaving: Personal interviews at Swift Spinning and Denim
North America (see Acknowledgments)

3,000–4,000 spindles per Lowell factory, ca. 1830: Gies

1850 Lowell statistics: about.com

800 to 2,500 yards of thread from a pound of cotton: Rivoli

What can be made from a bale of cotton: Cotton Counts website, sponsored by the National Cotton Council of America (cotton.org)

History of blue jeans and Levi Strauss: The Great Idea Finder website (ideafinder.com); about.com

Origin of *denim, dungarees, jeans: Oxford English Dictionary*

History of indigo: Anne Matson, "Indigo in the Early Modern
World" (bell.lib.umn)

History of sanforizing: The Costumer's Manifesto website
(costumes.org)

Globalization of the cotton industry, government subsidies, cotton
industry in West Africa: Rivoli

Loss of U.S textile jobs, 1990–2000: Rivoli

700,000 remaining textile jobs, or 7 percent of total: U.S. Bureau of
Labor Statistics of the U.S. Department of Labor (bls.gov)

More jobs lost to automation than offshoring, and China is laying off
    textile workers: Rivoli

Production held steady while employment fell 60 percent: Rivoli

China largest textile producer, with 30 percent of export market,
    selling a billion garments annually to the U.S.: Rivoli

Chinese and U.S. cotton production, export, and import figures:
    USDA (fas.usda.gov)

China's 40,000 garment factories: Rivoli

Textile plants the most heavily protected, with over $250 million in
    aid: Rivoli

"The race to the bottom" is the title of a book by economist Alan
    Tonelson, *The Race to the Bottom: Why a Worldwide Worker
    Surplus and Uncontrolled Free Trade Are Sinking American Living
    Standards*, Westview Press, 2002

Cotton most heavily subsidized branch of U.S. agriculture, with $4
    billion in annual subsidies, five to ten times that paid for other
    crops: Rivoli

25,000 American cotton farmers: Rivoli

Farmers turned to chemicals and machines to offset loss of acreage:
    Rhodes

U.S. cotton production unchanged from 1929, at about 20 million
    bales a year: Wayne C. Smith

Mechanics of federal cotton programs: Interview with Jim Corley,
    Holmes County executive director, Farm Service Agency of the
    U.S. Department of Agriculture, Lexington, MS; Rivoli; Yafa

WTO dispute: Rivoli; Elizabeth Becker, "Looming Battle Over Cot-
    ton Subsidies," *New York Times*, January 24, 2004; Elizabeth
    Becker, "Trade Group to Cut Farm Subsidies for Rich Na-
    tions," *New York Times*, August 1, 2004; Elizabeth Becker,
    "Interim Trade Triumph Short on Hard Details," *New York
    Times*, August 2, 2004; Associated Press, "U.S. Predicts Export

Gains Under WTO Deal," *New York Times*, August 2, 2004; "Breakthrough on Trade," *New York Times*, August 3, 2004; Randy Schnepf, "U.S. Agricultural Response to WTO Cotton Decision," Congressional Research Service (order number 22187), 2006 (nationalaglawcenter.org)

Decrease of 3 to 26 percent in price of cotton: Rivoli; Oxfam International, "Cultivating Poverty: The Impact of U.S. Cotton Subsidies on Africa," Oxfam Briefing Paper 30, 2002 (Oxfam.org)

Collaboration between U.S. government, universities, and cotton industry: Rivoli

Problems of African cotton farmers, average size and productivity of their farms: Rivoli

Life expectancy, living standard, number of cotton farmers in Burkina Faso: "The Long Reach of King Cotton," *New York Times*, August 5, 2003

2007 farm bill: Jasper Womach, "Previewing a 2007 Farm Bill," Congressional Research Service, order number 33037, 2005 (cnie.org); blog of Washington attorney Phillip L. Fraas (farmbill2007.com)

CHAPTER TEN: THE RECKONING

Mississippi hunting seasons and regulations: Mississippi Department of Wildlife, Fisheries, and Parks (mdwfp.com)

Catfish, peanut, soy production figures: Mississippi State University Extension Service website (msucares.com)

Jim Corley material: Personal interviews (see Acknowledgments)

"Mississippi's Mississippi": Willis

Black migration from North to South and out of the Delta in the
       1970s: Cobb

Jo G Prichard material: Personal interviews (see Acknowledgments)

William Winter material: Personal interview (see Acknowledgments)

Viking Range Corporation: Company website (vikingrange.com)

60 percent of Mississippi is forested: Mississippi State University
       Extension Service website (msucares.com)

U.S. exports $7 billion of cotton annually: U.S. Department of Agri-
       culture (fas.usda.gov)

Bibliography

Agee, James, and Walker Evans. *Let Us Now Praise Famous Men*. Boston: Houghton Mifflin, 1988.

Barry, John M. *Rising Tide: The Great Mississippi Flood of 1927 and How It Changed America*. New York: Touchstone/Simon & Schuster, 1998.

Bartlett, Richard A. *Rolling Rivers: An Encyclopedia of American Rivers*. New York: McGraw-Hill, 1984.

Berlin, Ira. *Generations of Captivity: A History of African-American Slaves*. Cambridge, MA: Bellknap, 2003.

Branch, Taylor. *Parting the Waters: America in the King Years, 1954–1963*. New York: Simon & Schuster, 1988.

_____. *Pillar of Fire: America in the King Years, 1963–1965*. New York: Simon & Schuster, 1998.

_____. *At Canaan's Edge: America in the King Years, 1965–1968*. New York: Simon & Schuster, 2006.

Cobb, James C. *The Most Southern Place on Earth: The Mississippi Delta and the Roots of Regional Identity.* New York: Oxford University Press, 1992.

Davis, David Brion. *The Problem of Slavery in Western Culture.* Ithaca, NY: Cornell University Press, 1966.

Davis, William C. *Look Away!: A History of the Confederate States of America.* New York: Free Press, 2002.

Dodge, Bertha S. *Cotton: The Plant That Would Be King.* Austin: University of Texas Press, 1984.

Faulkner, William. *The Portable Faulkner.* New York: Viking, 1967.

Faust, Patricia L., ed. *Historical Times Illustrated Encyclopedia of the Civil War.* New York: HarperCollins, 1991.

Foner, Eric. *Nothing but Freedom: Emancipation and Its Legacy.* Baton Rouge: Louisiana State University Press, 1983.

——. *Reconstruction: America's Unfinished Revolution, 1863–1877.* New York: Harper Perennial Library, 2002.

Foote, Shelby. *The Civil War: A Narrative.* Vol. 3, *Red River to Appomattox.* New York: Random House, 1974.

Garraty, John A., and Eric Foner, eds. *The Reader's Companion to American History.* New York: Houghton Mifflin, 1991.

Gies, Joseph, and Frances Gies. *The Ingenious Yankees: The Men, Ideas, and Machines That Transformed a Nation, 1776–1876.* New York: Crowell, 1976.

Gray, R. B., comp. *The Agricultural Tractor: 1855–1950.* Saint Joseph, MI: American Society of Agricultural Engineers, 1975.

Green, Constance McL. *Eli Whitney and the Birth of American Technology.* New York: Little, Brown, 1956.

Harpstead, Milo I., and Francis D. Hole. *Soil Science Simplified.* Ames: Iowa State University Press, 1980.

Harris, Jennifer, ed. *5000 Years of Textiles.* London: British Museum Press, 1993.

Harris, William H. *The Harder We Run: Black Workers Since the Civil War.* New York: Oxford University Press, 1982.

Hobhouse, Henry. *Seeds of Change.* New York: Harper & Row, 1985.

Hurt, R. Douglas, ed. *African American Life in the Rural South: 1900–1950.* Columbia: University of Missouri Press, 2003.

Jenkins, David, ed. *The Cambridge History of Western Textiles.* New York: Cambridge University Press, 2003.

Kolchin, Peter. *American Slavery: 1619–1877.* Rev. ed. New York: Hill & Wang, 2003.

Lakwete, Angela. *Inventing the Cotton Gin: Machine and Myth in Antebellum America.* Baltimore: Johns Hopkins University Press, 2003.

Lemann, Nicholas. *The Promised Land: The Great Black Migration and How It Changed America.* New York: Knopf, 1991.

Loewen, James W., and Charles Sallis, eds. *Mississippi: Conflict and Change.* New York: Pantheon, 1974.

Lomax, Alan. *The Land Where the Blues Began.* New York: Pantheon, 1993.

McPherson, James A. *Ordeal by Fire: The Civil War and Reconstruction.* New York: Knopf, 1982.

_____. *Battle Cry of Freedom: The Civil War Era.* New York: Oxford University Press, 1988.

Meier, August, and Elliott M. Rudwick. *From Plantation to Ghetto: An Interpretive History of American Negroes.* New York: Hill & Wang, 1966.

Meltzer, Milton. *The Black Americans: A History in Their Own Words.* New York: Crowell, 1984.

Members of the Magnolia Garden Club. *Lexington, Mississippi, Holmes County, 1833–1976.* Florence, MS: Messenger, 1976.

Mirsky, Jeannette, and Allan Nevins. *The World of Eli Whitney.* New York: Macmillan, 1952.

Morris, Willie. *My Mississippi*. Jackson: University Press of Mississippi, 2000.

Munro, John M. *Cotton*. 2nd ed. New York: Longman Scientific & Technical/Wiley, 1987.

O'Toole, Christopher. *The Encyclopedia of Insects*. New York: Facts On File, 1993.

Palmer, Robert. *Deep Blues: A Musical and Cultural History, from the Mississippi Delta to Chicago's South Side to the World*. New York: Penguin, 1981.

Peaster, Margaret Grafton. *The History of Tchula, 1830–1954*. Tchula, MS: Tchula Business and Professional Women's Club, 1954.

Percy, William Alexander. *Lanterns on the Levee*. New York: Knopf, 1941.

Piersen, William D. *From Africa to America*. New York: Twayne/Simon & Schuster, 1996.

Ransom, Roger L., and Richard Sutch. *One Kind of Freedom*. New York: Cambridge University Press, 1977.

Rhodes, Richard. *Farm: A Year in the Life of an American Farmer*. New York: Simon & Schuster, 1989.

Rivoli, Pietra. *The Travels of a T-Shirt in the Global Economy: An Economist Examines the Markets, Power, and Politics of World Trade*. Hoboken, NJ: Wiley, 2005.

Rosengarten, Theodore. *All God's Dangers: The Life of Nate Shaw*. New York: Knopf, 1974.

Royce, Edward. *The Origins of Southern Sharecropping*. Philadelphia: Temple University Press, 1993.

Schery, Robert. *Plants for Man*. 2nd ed. Englewood Cliffs, NJ: Prentice-Hall, 1972.

Sitkoff, Harvard. *The Struggle for Black Equality, 1954–1980*. New York: Hill & Wang, 1981.

Smith, Page. *Trial by Fire: A People's History of the Civil War and Reconstruction*. New York: McGraw-Hill, 1982.

Smith, Wayne C., and J. Tom Cothren, eds. *Cotton: Origin, History, Technology, and Production*. New York: Wiley, 1999.

Stamp, Kenneth. *The Peculiar Institution: Slavery in the Antebellum South*. New York: Knopf, 1965.

Twain, Mark. *Life on the Mississippi*. New York: Bantam Classics, 1983.

U.S. Bureau of the Census. *Historical Statistics of the United States, Colonial Times to 1970*. Washington: U.S. Department of Commerce, Bureau of the Census, 1975.

Walton, Anthony. *Mississippi: An American Journey*. New York: Knopf, 1996.

Willis, John C. *Forgotten Time: The Yazoo-Mississippi Delta After the Civil War*. Charlottesville: University Press of Virginia, 2000.

Wilson, Charles Reagan, and William Ferris, eds. *Encyclopedia of Southern Culture*. Chapel Hill: University of North Carolina Press, 1989.

Wright, Gavin. *The Political Economy of the Cotton South: Households, Markets, and Wealth in the Nineteenth Century*. New York: Norton, 1978.

Yafa, Stephen. *Big Cotton: How a Humble Fiber Created Fortunes, Wrecked Civilizations, and Put America on the Map*. New York: Viking/Penguin, 2005.

Index

mey

204 - 210